T0330788

# Learning and Performance

Changing work roles, greater emphasis on individual autonomy, the growing importance of relationships, the complexity of many businesses; all these things call into question the prevailing approach to training needs analysis and evaluation, which still tends to be based on a simple gap analysis between job requirements and an employee's knowledge and skills.

Bryan Hopkins's *Learning and Performance* takes a systemic approach to workplace performance, training needs and the basis on which we can analyse them and evaluate the subsequent training.

The author's approach offers a model for HR and training departments that is relevant and sufficiently sophisticated for today's workplaces. As with all his books, Bryan Hopkins combines a complete understanding of learning and organisational theory with pragmatic examples, ensuring a book that will be read and applied in equal measure.

**Bryan Hopkins** is a learning and development consultant, working primarily with international organisations in the humanitarian and development sectors. For more than 30 years he has specialised in developing learning strategies and designing and evaluating training programmes for large public and private sector organisations.

# Learning and Performance

A systemic model for analysing needs and evaluating training

**Bryan Hopkins**

Routledge
Taylor & Francis Group

LONDON AND NEW YORK

First published 2017
by Routledge
2 Park Square, Milton Park, Abingdon, Oxon OX14 4RN

and by Routledge
711 Third Avenue, New York, NY 10017

*Routledge is an imprint of the Taylor & Francis Group, an informa business*

© 2017 Bryan Hopkins

*British Library Cataloguing in Publication Data*
A catalogue record for this book is available from the British Library

*Library of Congress Cataloging-in-Publication Data*
Names: Hopkins, Bryan, 1954– author.
Title: Learning and performance: a systemic model for analysing needs and
    evaluating training / Bryan Hopkins.
Description: Abingdon, Oxon; New York, NY: Routledge, 2017. |
    Includes bibliographical references.
Identifiers: LCCN 2016022792 | ISBN 9781138220690 (hardback) |
    ISBN 9781315412252 (ebook)
Subjects: LCSH: Employees—Training of. | Performance. | Needs
    assessment. | Organizational learning. | Personnel management.
Classification: LCC HF5549.5.T7 H625 2017 | DDC 658.3/124—dc23
LC record available at https://lccn.loc.gov/2016022792

ISBN: 978-1-138-22069-0 (hbk)
ISBN: 978-131-5412-25-2 (ebk)

Typeset in Bembo
by Apex CoVantage, LLC

To my wife, Helen, whose patience and support during the long hours researching and writing this book made it possible.

# Contents

# Figures

# Tables

# Cover illustration

The cover illustration is a bhavacakra, often referred to as a 'wheel of life', painted in the thangka tradition of Tibetan Buddhism. Such paintings are commonly found in Tibetan Buddhist temples throughout south-east Asia and are designed to remind visitors of the cycle of existence.

The graphical composition is highly symbolic, and different parts of it along with their physical relationship within the painting represent aspects of Buddhist belief such as karma, the law of cause and effect, which means that everything we do has an impact on the world around us, and the impermanence of life: nothing stays the same and everything constantly changes.

Understanding the wheel of life contributes to an understanding about enlightenment. In its most humble way, this book hopes to offer some enlightenment to the world of training.

# Preface

One summer's day in 1976 I walked out of the gates of University College London clutching a degree in mechanical engineering and headed up to the north of England to my first job, working in a quality control team for a company building the containment vessel for what would become Hartlepool nuclear power station. I spent that long, hot summer inside the concrete-and-steel dome, screwing in and screwing out go/no-go gauges to check that screw threads were within specification. Hartlepool nuclear power station is still operational, so I guess that I did my work well enough, but it was not what I wanted to do with my life.

So I decided to take my chances with Voluntary Services Overseas and in 1977 found myself working as an instructor in a technical college in a small town in northern Sudan. I spent two years there and, when I had the chance, tried to travel around the country. It was not easy, as there were no metalled roads and the railway system was unreliable, so any journey took several days and often relied on *suq* (market) lorries, old Bedford trucks loaded high with sacks of groundnuts if they were going north and imported goods if going south. Roads were terrible, in many places just indistinct tracks through sandy or rocky desert, and every now and then the driver would have to slow down to negotiate a *wadi*, a dried-out riverbed.

This put an incredible strain on vehicles, and breakdowns were common. But what always surprised me was how, even in the remotest parts of the country, 'bush mechanics' would suddenly appear, pulling ancient tools out of goat-hair bags and somehow patching up leaking head gaskets or freeing recalcitrant clutches. How did these people learn how to do what they did? Sitting at their father's (and it would have been their father, in a society with clearly defined gender roles) knee? Making hibiscus tea at a roadside truck stop and watching what happened?

As the years went by I saw this phenomenon repeated in many different African countries and eventually decided I would like to learn more. So I submitted a proposal to Leeds University to do a Ph.D., researching the informal training of bush mechanics in West Africa, and was on the point of starting my research when my girlfriend became pregnant.

Feelings of paternal responsibility took over, and I abandoned my plans to spend some years wandering the West African bush interviewing mechanics and found a job with British Steel in Sheffield, designing computer-based training programmes and learning how to be a father.

My professional life evolved into consultancy, and for many years I have worked on the design and delivery of training programmes. As time went by I started to become interested in systems thinking and slowly tried to integrate it into the various training needs analysis and evaluation projects which I worked on. But this was a slow and difficult process, so eventually I decided to enrol for the Open University's M.Sc. programme Systems Thinking in Practice (as an extremely mature student). The various modules that I studied gave me the tools to think more carefully about how people learn to do their jobs and, most significantly, how I could use systems thinking approaches to develop a new paradigm for analysing training needs and evaluating training programmes.

I have come to realise how powerful systems thinking is when trying to make sense of the complexity I see in people's working lives and how it can really help design more effective training solutions. What is particularly exciting for me is how it makes it possible to integrate formal training programmes with informal learning, which actually represents the main way in which people learn how to do what they do.

Which brings me back to those bush mechanics. Are they still popping out of the desert or the forest, coaxing life out of diesel engines? Just how do they learn to do what they do? Maybe it is finally time to do that Ph.D. . . . .

Bryan Hopkins

# Acknowledgements

My first thanks are to a senior management team at an organisation where I was working, whose strong, negative reaction to a presentation I delivered about systems thinking made me realise that it really had something to say. Without their hostility, I would never have enrolled for my Master's programme.

Second thanks are to the academic team and fellow students involved with the Open University's M.Sc. programme Systems Thinking in Practice. The knowledge I have gained, the wisdom I have observed and the hard work it has made me do have helped me along the road from being a confirmed reductionist to an aspiring systems *bricoleur*.

Final thanks are to the people who have spent hours of their precious time looking through draft versions of the book, pointing out my inconsistencies and inaccuracies, straightening my tangled sentences and logic, and helping to shape the book into something that I hope will help fellow training professionals. So thanks are due to:

- Ray Ison, Professor of Systems at the Open University, who reassured me that there is sense in my application of systems thinking to training.
- Barbara Schmidt-Abbey and Joan O'Donnell, fellow students on my Master's programme, who reviewed the drafts and have provided me with moral support during the long time it took to write the book.
- Dr Janet Curran and Christina Schmalenbach, experienced training professionals, who helped me make it more practical and relevant to the people who I hope will use it.
- Helen Clay, my wife, who several times read through the whole manuscript in order to make sure that it was fit to let other people look at it.

# Abbreviations

| Abbreviation | Meaning |
| --- | --- |
| ADDIE | Analysis–Design–Develop–Implement–Evaluate |
| ASTD | American Society for Training and Development |
| ATPA | Advanced Technology Procurement Agency |
| BEM | Behaviour Engineering Model |
| B–P–R | Boundaries–Perspectives–Relationships |
| CATWOE | Customers–Actors–Transformation–*Weltanschauung*–Owner–Environment |
| CSH | Critical Systems Heuristics |
| KSA | knowledge, skills and attitudes |
| LTSI | Learning Transfer System Inventory® |
| PQR | Do P by Q in order to R |
| ROI | return on investment |
| SCM | Success Case Method |
| SCO | Supply Chain Officer |
| SD | System Dynamics |
| SMT | senior management team |
| SNA | Social Network Analysis |
| SSCO | Senior Supply Chain Officer |
| SSM | Soft Systems Methodology |
| TNA | training needs analysis |
| VSM | Viable System Model |

# 1  What is this book about?

As its title suggests, this book looks at learning and performance and how we can evaluate how learning happens and what its effects are. In this context, 'performance' refers to performance in the workplace, how well people are doing what they are supposed to be doing. Generally, we become more interested in people's performance when we get a sense that it could be improved, that things are not being done as well as they could be or changes are being implemented which mean that people need new skills. When this happens we carry out some form of research in order to decide what can be done to help improve current performance or prepare people for change.

'Learning', in the sense of facilitating the learning of new knowledge and skill, may or may not be a way to achieve this. If a strategy to enable this learning is implemented, we then need to see how effective these improvement strategies have been, and this is where the 'evaluation' part of the book becomes relevant.

Responsibility for thinking about how to improve performance is often the responsibility of a training department and its professionals. As such, training becomes a key strategy to be deployed in order to improve performance. The aim of this book is to be a guide to training professionals that they can use to identify what strategies will be helpful in achieving this and subsequently to see how effective these strategies have been.

So although our starting point here seems to be training, as will be elaborated on in subsequent chapters, the scope of this book is somewhat wider. Rather than just being a guide to help training professionals carry out a 'training needs analysis', with its implied restriction to training, it provides a methodology for understanding other factors which may be having an impact on performance so that strategies for dealing with these can be integrated with training responses. Later in the book we will return to discuss the semantics of the phrase 'training needs analysis', but for now we will keep with it as something familiar and comforting.

The design of a training programme provides a good starting point for an explanation as to what this book is about. Figure 1.1 is a representation of a well-known model for designing training, the ADDIE model: Analysis–Design–Develop–Implement–Evaluate.

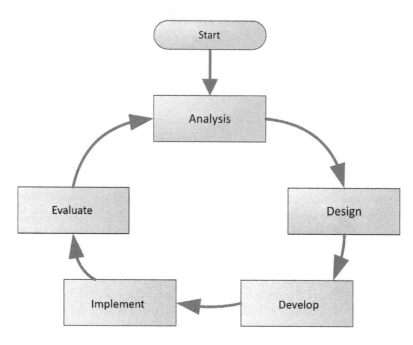

*Figure 1.1* The ADDIE model of instructional design

ADDIE is not the only model used for training development and is not necessarily the best, but it does provide a structure for this initial discussion. Each stage in the process of design has an impact on the overall quality of the training, and a discussion about the relative importance of each is not relevant here. However, within this model analysis and evaluation are arguably the most problematic stages, because they are often carried out in a limited manner, and methodologies for doing them are less well defined. By way of contrast, there is an extensive literature looking at the design, development and implementation of the many different forms of training.

The importance of the needs analysis stage is based on the fact that it is the starting point, so decisions made here will, like a row of falling dominoes, tumble across from stage to stage. Unfortunately, reference literature on training and the academic research available suggests that this stage is often not really done in any systematic or comprehensive way: for example, some research reports that fewer than 10% of training design projects start with a thorough needs assessment process.[1] The design stage may therefore start with a fairly clear description of what the training should be but with a somewhat hazy understanding of why it is needed and who it is for. Decisions about design may often be based on what has been done in the past and what the capacities of the people involved in the design process are rather than on a fully assessed operational need.

In the design stage the technical content for the learning is gathered and organised in a way to make it effective from a pedagogical perspective. Learning activities are developed, and the materials are assembled in formats appropriate for the delivery modality, for example, facilitator's notes for a workshop, storyboards or similar for e-learning and so on. Design often focuses on how to deliver training to make sure that the learning activity is as effective as possible, but if the analysis was weak there may be little attention paid to issues of *learning transfer*, how likely it is that the implementation stage will help learners apply new knowledge and skills delivered within the training in their workplace.

Evaluation follows implementation: what did people learn, are they behaving differently as a result and what impact is this having? Evaluating training programmes can be a fraught subject, with the standard reference framework for training evaluation often being described as being useful as a framework but not as a methodology. And again, without an effective needs analysis, it can be difficult to come to any conclusions about the effectiveness of a learning intervention. How much have people learnt? What changes in performance can really be attributed to the training?

So the initial needs analysis and final evaluation are actually intimately connected. Without the reliable starting point provided by a strong analysis it can be very difficult to carry out a meaningful evaluation. The aim of this book is to look at some ways in which training needs analyses can be carried out using methodologies which take workplace realities into consideration, so that the design, development and implementation stages are undertaken with a much firmer set of foundations and evaluation activities can provide a much more meaningful and useful description of what successes training has had.

Training needs analysis and evaluation are, in essence, the same activities. In a needs analysis we look carefully at a current situation and come to some conclusions about what we can do to make things better; in an evaluation we look carefully at what we have done within a situation and come to some conclusions about how well what we have done has affected the situation. The focus of the two activities may be somewhat different, but the processes we follow are essentially the same.

## Why is the approach within this book different?

The methodologies described within this book are somewhat different to those usually covered within the training literature. They are based on an approach known as systems thinking, an area of knowledge which is often not well understood or clearly articulated.

After many years of working in the training field, carrying out training needs analyses, designing training programmes and evaluating their success, I started to realise that the techniques that I was finding most useful for thinking through the analysis and evaluation parts of what I did came from this systems thinking world. The ideas gave me a way to develop a deeper understanding of why people are not performing as well as they could be and how this could be resolved. As I moved slowly from conscious incompetence to conscious competence in using systems thinking, partly through practice and partly through formal academic study, I tried to write down what I was doing as a process of reflective practice, as a way of learning more about what I was doing. This book is therefore something of a formal record of this process.

The aim of the book is, therefore, to share with training professionals who are trying to develop their skills in training needs analysis and evaluation a practical set of tools that they can use in their everyday work. As such, I have tried to use practical training-related examples whenever discussing systems concepts and have included a number of case studies based on real-life examples to show how systems approaches have helped me. But bringing a different discipline into the field of training presents some challenges to the structure of the book. As systems thinking may be completely new to many readers, the book includes several chapters on theory about systems thinking. This may be somewhat unavoidable if applying the approach is to make some sort of sense, but the reader should find that the systems concepts utilised in the practical case studies are explained as they are used, so if these chapters on theoretical concepts seem too daunting they can be avoided or left until later.

While I was doing research for this book, I came across a sobering statistic (sobering particularly to someone who has spent their entire working life designing and delivering training programmes): less than 10% of what people learn is actually transferred to the workplace.[2] Has 90% of what I and my fellow training professionals have done really been to no avail?

Why might this be the case? Systems thinking provides some perspectives which may help offer some explanation. As is discussed in more detail in Chapter 2, a core principle of systems thinking is that it provides a radically different way of approaching problem solving, such as we do in a training needs analysis. One definition of the word 'analysis' is "the process of separating something into its constituent elements".[3] This is something which comes from the scientific method of understanding: if we are trying to develop an understanding of a complex issue, we often try to break it down into 'constituent elements' which are at a level of complexity that we can understand. For example, in Chapter 3, looking at existing models used in training needs analysis activities, we discuss Tom Gilbert's Behaviour Engineering Model. This identifies six factors which affect performance: provision of information, understanding of information, suitability of the working environment, capacity of people to perform, incentives to perform and motivational needs. These are all relevant factors, but the model treats each as a separate contributor and does not consider the possibility that they may interact with each other. For example, if the working environment does not allow high levels of performance, providing more information to help people perform may actually cause frustration and hence reduce motivation.

Breaking down a complex problem into its apparent constituent parts is a process known as *reductionism*. Reductionist thinking affects the design and delivery of formal learning in a number of different ways:

- Organisational structures are reductionist, breaking down the complexity of the overall organisation into a number of simpler departmental structures, of which the training department is one. How well it is connected to, and how clearly it understands the operation of other departments can vary hugely from one organisation to another.
- Reductionism means that we separate the work that people do from the context within which they perform that work when designing training activities. This means that we do not necessarily think about how the knowledge and skills implicit within a performance relate to the operational context.
- Reductionist approaches to designing learning activities means that we break down the complexity of what people do in the workplace into discrete, simple steps (by task analysis) and then assume that adding these all up in a linear fashion will recreate our original level of performance, when in reality the subtlety of mastery has been lost.

It is important to think more carefully about how reductionism separates performance from where it is performed. In his book *How Music Works*, the musician David Byrne discusses how music has evolved in different times and places in response to where it is performed and how it is listened to. African music, performed in outdoor locations, is based around rhythm and percussion, which travels well through open air; western European classical music, performed in churches and concert halls, is melodic, as the acoustics of solid walls would create reverberations in percussive rhythms which would turn everything to "sonic mush".[4] Modern developments in recording technology and associated changes in how people listen to music (whether in sports stadia for a major concert, in a nightclub, in their living room or through earphones sitting in a commuter train) have also led to different musical forms which are best listened to in a particular context.

Here we have the important word: *context*. Music is not something which exists on its own, separate from reality: it is something which is deeply affected by where it exists. Apparently, back in 1996 Bill Gates said, "Content is king"; well, when you take a systems perspective on the world, the king is context. C. West Churchman, one of the most influential writers on systems thinking, discussed "the fallacy of ignoring the environment"[5] when seeking to find solutions to problems without considering how they are interrelated with their context. So when we look at why systems thinking approaches can provide better solutions for improving learning and performance we find ourselves looking closely at context, deciding what the context is for the situation we are looking at, and understanding it better so that we can work in it and with it.

## How can a systems approach lead to better training?

Using systems thinking approaches in training needs analysis and evaluation helps us avoid the dangers of reductionism and lets us think about the importance of relationships between different components of a situation. Let us consider a few benefits that can come from adopting a systems approach, and we shall see how context is a core principle within each of them.

### *Places more emphasis on informal learning*

It has been estimated that perhaps 80% of what people learn at work comes through informal means,[6] but for various reasons, discussed later, promoting and supporting informal learning is often seen by training departments as 'somebody else's problem'. Of course, if everyone sees it as somebody else's problem, little will be done to try and strengthen processes for strengthening informal learning.

Because systems approaches make us think more about relationships and the need for networks of people to exchange information with each other to maintain learning, it is inevitable that solutions to performance problems must think about informal learning as well as formal training solutions.

### *Focuses more attention to the operational context*

Systems thinking places a great deal of importance on managing the relationship between the situation we are thinking about and its context. Systems-based needs analyses will therefore suggest that learners need to develop their abilities to monitor how their operational context is changing and what impact they may be having on that context so that they can adapt accordingly.

### *Stresses the dynamic nature of the operational context*

Traditional approaches to needs analysis have a tendency to identify at a particular point in time (usually at the time of the needs analysis or the initial perception of the problem), a static set of skills which are needed for responding to the operational context. By the time the training is delivered these conditions may be different, and the value of the training may be diminished. Unless training includes some strategies for improving situational awareness it may be out of date by the time it is implemented.

A systems approach to analysing training should help us identify what people need to learn so that they are better able to deal with changing operational conditions – for example, through improving their abilities to analyse the operational context or solve problems as they appear.

### *Increases the importance of social learning activities*

Social learning describes learning which takes place when people come together, discuss a situation of mutual interest, explore different perspectives and use this to refine their respective understandings.

Reflecting on different perspectives is a key aspect of systems thinking. In the world of human behaviour there can be no definitive definitions of what is happening, and each individual's perception of a situation has validity. So when we are trying to understand what a workplace problem means and how we may be able to improve things, it is important to develop a shared understanding of the situation.

Learning solutions based on a systems thinking–based analysis are therefore more likely to involve a learning process in which people collaborate and talk to each other in order to develop a shared understanding, through activity-based face-to-face learning and truly interactive technology-based learning solutions, as well as the encouragement of informal learning networks.

### Increases the likelihood of learning transfer

As described previously, only a small percentage of what people learn in a formal learning event is usually transferred to the workplace, despite the best efforts of trainers and instructional designers.

One of the reasons this may happen is if, within the process of designing a formal learning intervention, insufficient attention is paid to thinking about *how* that learning will be transferred into the workplace. Even if a formal event is well designed and effectively delivered, when people return to their workplace, local expectations and standards may constrain their ability to do anything differently.

A systems approach to needs analysis means that the context of the workplace has to be taken into consideration, and this will have an impact on both the overall structure of a learning programme and the detail of how the learning is delivered.

### But isn't this all too complicated?

Systems thinking can appear rather complex, time consuming and difficult to apply. But this is a criticism which applies to learning any new skill. The reality is that using a systems thinking approach need not take any longer than existing methods being used to carry out training needs analyses and evaluations and can, with increasing familiarity, help us develop ideas more quickly.

This is because systems thinking is used to plan how to carry out these activities and then to make sense of the data. Using systems thinking approaches does not mean a completely different approach to data collection: we still review available reports, we still interview stakeholders, we still send out surveys. What is different is that systems thinking *provides a way of thinking about data* to help us make more sense of it. It provides a well-structured process for identifying actions which we can take to improve performance in the workplace.

For me, one of the most exciting things about using systems thinking approaches is the way that they can suddenly shine a clearer light on the most confusing of situations. But, like all skills, this needs perseverance and practice. And, while you are reading this book, some patience!

## How is this book organised?

Bridging two different disciplines in a single book always presents challenges. As the primary audience for the book will be training professionals, writing about training is relatively straightforward, but how much explanation should be presented about systems thinking? Too little and its application to training may not make any sense; too much and it may become overwhelming.

So I hope that I have managed to strike the right balance, but I have also tried to organise chapters in the book in such a way that it is easier to avoid the density of the systems thinking theory if readers want to avoid this. Figure 1.2 shows how the chapters are arranged in a way which should make it easier for readers to decide on the most appropriate way to navigate through its content.

As overviews, Chapters 2, 3 and 4 provide introductions to the main topics within the book, systems thinking, training needs analysis and evaluation. Chapters 5 and 6 contain the heart of the systems thinking theory, and then Chapters 7, 8 and 9 cover how systems thinking can be applied to the needs analysis process. Finally, Chapter 10 looks at systems thinking approaches to training evaluation.

Next, let us look at what each chapter contains in a little more detail.

Chapter 2 introduces what is meant by the term 'systems thinking' by reflecting on the history of systemic thought and discussing why our patterns of thinking shifted to become centred around more reductionist principles. It then goes on to look at the three key elements within systems thinking, the importance of interrelationships, the need to consider multiple perspectives and how to define boundaries around a situation of interest. This introduces the B–P–R model (Boundaries–Perspectives–Relationships) which is used as a starting point for systemic approaches to needs analysis and evaluation.

In Chapter 3 we take a look at existing ideas about training needs analysis. It is first important to clarify some terminology, because the ethos of systems thinking does not sit altogether comfortably with the limitations implied by the phrase 'training needs analysis'. The chapter continues by looking at some existing models which have been used for analysing performance, such as Gilbert's Behaviour Engineering Model and the Mager and Pipe performance flowchart.

Chapter 4 starts the discussion about evaluation by looking at the challenges associated with evaluating formal learning interventions and provides a critique of standard models of training evaluation, such as the Kirkpatrick framework and the return-on-investment model.

Chapters 5 and 6 are where the deepest part of systems including theory lies. Reading these chapters will give you a very good foundation for understanding the application of systems thinking in the later chapters, but you may prefer to read through the practical chapters first and come back to this theory later.

Systems thinking involves a large number of different concepts, and the aim of Chapter 5 is to summarise the most important and to explain how they will become important as we start to look at strategies for improving performance

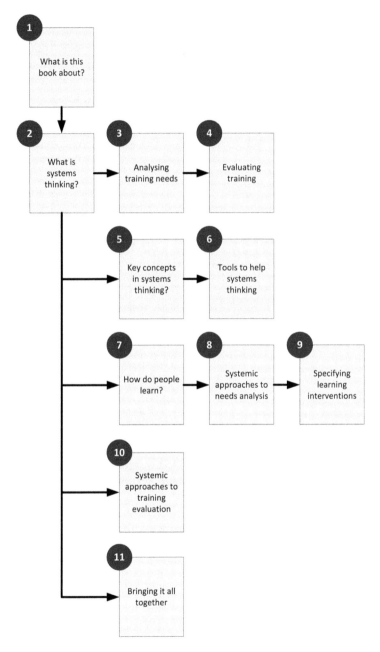

*Figure 1.2* Map of the book's chapters

and evaluating their effectiveness. This covers some relatively familiar ideas such as feedback and causality but also examines the significance of such concepts as emergence, the unexpected and unintended consequences of doing something, non-linearity, the way small changes can have big impacts and complexity, the phenomenon whereby interrelationships create stable yet dynamic systems.

Building on this explanation of concepts, Chapter 6 looks at some specific tools which have been developed in order to harness the power of systems thinking. The chapter starts off with a discussion about drawing diagrams, which is a technique commonly used in a number of systems thinking approaches, and then looks at System Dynamics, a tool which entered mainstream management thinking as what systems thinking was with the publication of Peter Senge's *The Fifth Discipline.*[7] But there is much more to systems thinking than just this, and the chapter goes on to look at other tools such as the Viable System Model, Social Network Analysis, Soft Systems Methodology and Critical Systems Heuristics. These are quite different tools but each has a particular strength: by choosing the right tool or tools we can develop a much deeper understanding of a situation.

Chapter 7 introduces the needs analysis section of the book by looking in some detail at the process of learning. Because a systems approach challenges the narrow boundaries of 'training', the chapter considers both formal and informal learning and explains how integrating the two is important.

Systems thinking is integrated into needs analysis in Chapter 8. Using a number of case studies, the chapter looks at how to use diagramming techniques to develop an initial understanding of the perceived performance issue and then how to gather and analyse data using systems thinking tools in order to arrive at a set of solutions. These solutions are expressed in the form of a theory of change, which will be an important part of the evaluation process, discussed in Chapter 10.

Assuming that the needs analysis process identifies the need to provide some form of learning intervention, Chapter 9 explores the issue of learning transfer in some detail, looking at how the needs analysis process should take this into consideration when developing the specifications for learning interventions of different types. This covers both designing formal interventions, such as classroom events and e-learning, and informal learning, such as supporting communities of practice.

Chapter 10 outlines a process for evaluating a formal learning intervention using systems thinking tools, such as theory-based evaluation and contribution analysis. This refers to the Kirkpatrick levels of evaluation because they are so well known but provides a quite different way of utilising them.

The book concludes with Chapter 11, which is a reflection on what systems thinking can mean for the whole process of training. A key suggestion is that we should shift the focus from designing and delivering training courses towards looking at how we can encourage the development of learning systems, which include both formal and informal learning activities and which can become dynamic and self-sustaining entities.

## Notes

1 Arthur Jr., W., Bennett Jr., W., Edens, P.S. & Bell, S.T., 2003. Effectiveness of Training in Organizations: A Meta-Analysis of Design and Evaluation Features. *Journal of Applied Psychology*, 88(2), p. 242.

2 Baldwin, T.T. & Ford, J.K., 1988. Transfer of Training: A Review and Directions for Future Research. *Personnel Psychology*, 41(1), pp. 63–105.

3 Definition taken from the *Concise Oxford English Dictionary (10th Edition)*.

4 Byrne, D., 2013. *How Music Works*, Canongate, Edinburgh, p. 18.

5 West Churchman, C., 1979. *The Systems Approach and Its Enemies*, Basic Books, New York, p. 5.

6 Frazis, H., Gittleman, M. & Joyce, M., 1998. Determinants of Training: An Analysis Using Both Employer and Employee Characteristics, in *Key Bridge Marriott Hotel, Arlington VA, US Department of Commerce*, Citeseer, Washington, DC; Tough, A., 1999. Reflections on the Study of Adult Learning, in *New Approaches to Lifelong Learning Conference, Ontario Institute for Studies in Education*, Toronto.

7 Senge, P.M., 1990. *The Fifth Discipline: The Art and Practice of the Learning Organization*, Century Business, London.

# 2  What is systems thinking?

In this chapter we shall look at:

- how systems thinking is what we do naturally
- the Enlightenment, a new way of thinking
- Cartesian thinking in management
- traps in Cartesian thinking
- what systems thinking is.

## Systems thinking – just what we do

One of the things which distinguishes human beings from other animals is our sentience, our awareness of our existence in the world. One outcome of this is that we constantly seek to understand why we are here and how what we are doing interacts with everything else in the world. We are sense-seeking creatures; we try to understand how the world around us works and how we can best deal with this.

In a modern, technology-driven society it is rather easy to lose sight of the fact that everything is connected, but in more traditional societies this sense of interconnectedness can be seen much more clearly.

For example, every morning women in Bali take a small tray woven out of banana leaves, carefully fill it with small pieces of fruit, vegetables, biscuits, sweets and flowers and place it outside their house as an offering to the spirits who permeate the world around them. In this way the forces which dictate how the world works will be kept satisfied.

The staple food crop in Bali is rice, grown across the entire island in a patchwork of paddy fields, connected by a complex network of irrigation channels stretching from the volcanic peaks which run the length of the island all the way down to the tropical beaches. Managing the flow of water so that every individual farmer receives what they need is a complex matter negotiated within the *subak* system, in which community representatives and religious leaders discuss who needs water, where and when and then jointly agree on how irrigation channels will be opened and closed. Decisions are made, ceremonies are followed and offerings are made. Through this method, paddy fields are flooded when needed then emptied and left to lie fallow when appropriate in order to maintain fertility and reduce pest infestations.

Although probably few Balinese would articulate it thus, they are systems thinkers. They see the world as a network of influences which needs to be managed carefully in order to achieve a balance which provides well-being.

To some degree this describes most people in the world, having some kind of 'faith' which provides a way of understanding how the world works and how we should behave. Practical decisions about how the world works, how a country works and how a family works are based on these articles of faith.

Mystical beliefs in how the world worked dominated thinking everywhere until the 17th century, when a number of European thinkers started to find this reliance on hidden forces linking everything together deeply troubling. One of the key thinkers of this time was René Descartes (1596–1650), who suggested that, rather than the world being some form of organism governed by spiritual forces, it was more "an inert universe composed of purposeless particles each pursuing its course mindless of others".[1] If the components of the universe floated around independently, therefore, we could increase our understanding of any individual particle by studying it independently of other particles. Descartes decided that if he wanted to understand the world he could "divide each of the difficulties that I was examining into as many parts as might be possible and necessary in order best to solve it".[2] We call this process of breaking a complex structure down into smaller parts which we can study more easily *reductionism*.

Descartes also proposed that we should consider matter and the mind as separate entities: matter could be understood in mechanistic terms, but the workings of the mind were closed to human understanding, a distinction now known as 'Cartesian dualism'. Living creatures were in reality just complicated machines, and this thinking inspired such creations as the mechanical duck automaton developed by the French engineer Jacques de Vaucanson, which is often known as 'Descartes's duck'.

This concept of viewing the material world as essentially composed of mechanical objects proved to be extremely powerful. Descartes's ideas came to play a central role in the development of what we now call the Enlightenment, the period where thinkers started to propose that humanity was composed of individual, rational agents rather than being pawns in some cosmic game being played by spiritual forces. Science was a key beneficiary of Cartesian thinking. In seeking to develop a scientific basis for explaining how the world worked scientists started to examine phenomena in ever greater detail, breaking everything down into its constituent parts.

Reductionism relies on an assumption that the whole is the sum of its constituent parts. It shapes the modern world: through the education system we are divided into 'artists' or 'scientists', and the education one group receives ignores its connections with the other area of knowledge. Within each area of knowledge there is further reductionism, as scientists become chemists, biologists or physicists. In working life people take on further professional specialisms, losing contact with other disciplines. In reality it is difficult to avoid this narrowing down and 'siloisation': the modern, technical world means that professional areas require hard and time-consuming study of specialist topics, and it is hard to conceive of modern equivalents of Leonardo da Vinci, whose talents spanned both arts and sciences.

## Cartesian thinking in management

Descartes's proposal that matter and mind could be separated has been heavily criticised by philosophers over the years, but it has indisputably been a powerful tool to use in the inanimate matter–centred world of the physical sciences. However, there are problems when we start to think that human behaviour systems can be treated as mechanical systems. Humans may be composed of matter, but when their minds interact, the results are unpredictable to say the least.

Nevertheless, Cartesian principles have made their way into all aspects of modern life, including management. Adam Smith's *An Enquiry into the Nature and Causes of the Wealth of Nations* (published in 1776), referring to the manufacture of pins, advocated the division of tasks to allow specialisation (although he also observed that this could lead to people becoming "as stupid and ignorant as it is possible for a human creature to become").[3] One of the earliest books to look at management as a specific subject in its own right was Frederick Taylor's 1911 *The Principles of Scientific Management*. Taylor's proposals were to deconstruct workplace performance and identify the separate activities that are needed in order to achieve the desired outputs. Adding together all of these separate activities would give us the overall output of the organisation. Simple causal linkages connecting different aspects of organisational life were assumed. Workers were machines which could be programmed to carry out specific activities, and little consideration was given to the reality that they might hate what they were doing, they might disagree with how other organisational units operated, they might compete with each other. Problem solving became a matter of breaking down the problem into separate root causes and then, one by one, resolving these so that by a process of linear addition the problem was solved.

Organisations follow this principle by subdividing themselves into functional divisions, each specialising in one particular task. For example, the typical enterprise divides itself up into production and service functions: production covers such things as research and development, sales, design, manufacturing and so on, whereas service functions include human resources where training normally sits. People in the training department may be training experts (with a limited understanding of the production context) or former production staff (with a limited understanding of adult learning issues). Organisational structures can then make it hard for training staff to fully understand very much about how structures, processes, cultures, systems and the like all contribute to workplace performance. Organisations may have a unit devoted to organisational development (OD), which is where the greatest cross-sectoral experience may lie, but the OD team in many organisations sees itself as having a limited role in training development.

Cartesian thinking therefore lies at the roots of the silo mentality in organisations. This creates isolated pockets of expertise, separate from and suspicious of outsiders and protecting domains of influence and expertise. A training department is often one of the weaker silos, cut off from central operational functions as a sub-department within human resources. This often gives it little real political strength which might enable it to be proactive in identifying real learning needs or reacting to demands for training where knowledge and skills issues are not actually the real problem.

Cartesian thinking also creates a top-down dynamic, in which demands flow downwards from the organisation to the individual. Hence learning activities are seen as 'training', something which is 'done to people'.[4] The problem here is that training staff often define themselves as people who transfer knowledge and skills to the workforce and so confine what they do to activities which live in this silo and do not necessarily see themselves as people whose role is to facilitate learning,[5] which opens up a whole range of other possibilities for supporting organisational effectiveness.

## The trap of Cartesian thinking

We can therefore start to see how reductionist thinking can create a trap. But apart from these practical problems, there are some deeper philosophical issues that it creates for us. First, reductionist thinking is so pervasive in modern life that we probably do not think at all about there being any alternative. The educational and professional development processes that we follow lead us to specialise more and more narrowly, cutting off our opportunities to see things from a different perspective.

Second, a reductionist way of thinking means that we tend to see the world as being composed of 'machines' which are simply matter and have a fixed functionality. Hannah Arendt, the American social theorist, saw this as providing reassurance to us as humans: "the things of the world have the function of stabilising human life, and their objectivity lies in the fact that. . . men, their ever-changing nature notwithstanding, can retrieve their sameness, that is, their identity, by being related to the same chair and the same table".[6] We therefore assume that what is in the world appears the same to everyone. This means that we can 'detach' ourselves from the world and ascribe a fixed meaning to everything around us. Seeing the man-made world around us as fixed is known as *reification*:

> [R]eification is the apprehension of the products of human activity as if they were something other than human products – such as facts of nature, results of cosmic laws, or manifestations of divine will. Reification implies that man is capable of forgetting his own authorship of the human world, and, further, that the dialectic between man, the producer, and his products is lost to consciousness.[7]

But actually our reality is socially constructed; the interpretation we give of the world around us being based on our experience of the world, right from the moment we are born through to the moment of perception. If the meaning of the man-made world around us depends on our relationship with it, then we are of necessity connected to the world, and our presence has an impact. We see this in scientific exploration, where the 'observer effect' implies that any time we look at what is happening, we change what is happening and so cannot measure it reliably.

Reductionism also leads to the assumption that what works one way will also work the other way around. This is true with a mechanical device: when I take my bicycle apart and examine each individual component so as to better understand what it is and how it works and then put it all back together, I have my bicycle again. However, this would not be the case if I decided to dismantle my cat.

A similar phenomenon occurs with how people behave in the workplace. Reductionism at the macro level means that when we are looking for ways to improve performance and identify training as a requirement, we fail to consider how training interacts with other aspects of behaviour. For example, training is generally aimed at and designed for individuals, whereas most operational behaviour relies on team interactions. So when an individual returns to the workplace after completing training, their new skills may help improve overall performance ... or may trigger resistance at a perceived attempt to change the existing dynamics. This possibility is discussed in more detail when we later look at the concept of complex adaptive systems (Chapter 5).

At the micro level a key activity in systematic approaches to training design is the task analysis, in which we break down an overall performance system to identify the components that make up the performance; for example, following a reductionist approach we may decide that an overall work outcome is achieved by carrying out task A, task B and then task C.

This is done on the assumption that by adding together all of the individual tasks needed to complete a performance we will end up with the overall performance outcome.

However, by simply identifying separate skill-based activities and areas of knowledge that are needed to carry out a task we may fail to understand how they interact with each other and how one person's performance is related to another's. These interactions may lead to unexpected and unintended consequences, which may be quite subtle or intangible and may counteract the positive influence of the training to a greater or lesser extent. For example, training people increases their attractiveness in the employment marketplace, and such individuals may leave to join competitors; training some members of a team and not others may lead to resentment and resistance to change. Unintended consequences of a set of connected activities is an example of, in systems terms, emergence, and this is also discussed in more detail in Chapter 5.

## Modern ideas of systems thinking

It is beyond the scope of this book to discuss in any detail how modern concepts in systems thinking have developed. However, it is useful to understand in general terms how this has happened, as this helps set the tools used in systems thinking that are used in this book in context.

Although systems thinking may be seen as a 'modern idea' arising as a reaction to Cartesian thinking, it has ancient roots. Aristotle, for example, believed that every object had a natural place and purpose, and every change in the world was a result of something returning to its natural place or fulfilling its purpose. This meant that we could only understand an object in relation to this purpose or function. C. West Churchman describes the *I Ching*, written somewhere around 2000 BC, as a systems-based approach to decision making.[8] However, the Enlightenment came along and changed how we perceived the world around us. The power of reductionism as a tool for understanding the material world lead to it becoming the overwhelming paradigm for understanding, and systems ideas fell into disuse.

The first renaissance in systems thinking seems to have come from the writings of the Russian philosopher and physician Alexander Bogdanov, who between 1912 and 1917 published a three-volume work titled *Tektology: Universal Organization Science*, which discussed the importance of relationships in social and physical sciences.[9] However, this work disappeared from view, and systems thinking lay dormant until the 1950s, when the Austrian biologist Ludwig von Bertalanffy published various articles and books relating to what he called "general systems theory". Drawing on thermodynamics, he proposed that living organisms work in open systems, exchanging information and materials with their environments in order to establish a dynamic equilibrium, in which, while they are in balance with their environment they continue to develop. He contrasted this with much scientific work which treated organisms as closed systems, operating in isolation from their environments.

Although Bertalanffy's work focused on the systemic principles of life, his work acted as a major stimulus to many other people, who started to look at how these principles could be applied to human activity in general. The field of systems thinking therefore exploded into myriad disciplines and sub-disciplines, and there are too many of these to discuss in any detail here. This multiplicity of systems approaches has meant that it has become something of a challenge to explain just what 'systems thinking' is, and it is a frequent topic of discussion amongst 'systemicists' as to how to better communicate what it means and how it can be used effectively. The aim of this book is to look at how aspects of training can utilise principles of systems thinking and so provide a practical guide for using them.

## What is a 'system'?

Before going further it is important to clarify what we mean by 'system', as it is a word which has a number of somewhat different meanings. The *Concise Oxford English Dictionary* offers a number of definitions:

- a complex whole; a set of things working together as a mechanism or interconnected network
- an organised scheme or method
- the prevailing political or social order.

The word 'system' is often used in a pejorative sense: "I couldn't help it. It's the way the system works", "The system is slow today" and so on.

Then we have *systematic*: "done or acting according to a fixed plan or system; methodical". For example, a systematic approach to training design is to analyse training needs, write training objectives, design the training then implement and evaluate it. While systematic approaches are not of themselves undesirable, they are not necessarily *systemic*, our final derivative, which is defined as "of or relating to a system as a whole". So while something done systematically may not be systemic, where an issue is systemic, consequences may follow each other systematically as a result of the system's logic. In general, this book will talk about doing things in a systemic way but will often not define a fixed 'systematic method' for problem solving (which may be frustrating for some readers, but that is the nature of this particular beast).

### Training as a system

Thinking about the first definition of 'system', we can imagine a training intervention as 'a set of things working together' (Figure 2.1). We take inputs (learners, content and perhaps a trainer), put them through a training intervention, and this transforms the learners into trained people. As an enhancement, we check by some sort of evaluation that the people are indeed trained and, if necessary, adjust the training so that the next set of inputs (learners) are even better trained.

This is a very simple view of training, but it is a reasonable description of conventional approaches to training as a system. Let us consider the limitations of this system a little more closely. First, we have separated the system from the world of work: as we have drawn it we are not considering how the trained people interact with the workplace, nor are we taking any further input (such as information) from the workplace over and above what we are starting with. In systems terms this is therefore a 'closed system'. Clearly this is not what real life

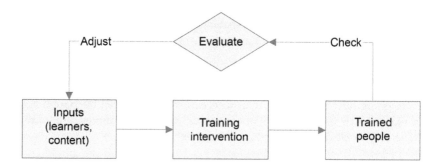

*Figure 2.1* Training as a system

is about. Real life is all about 'open systems', where the change we are interested in (application of new skills and knowledge) interacts with its environment, constantly pulling in new inputs and generating outputs which have an impact on the environment. For example, as our trained people change what is happening in the workplace, the content needed in the training or the nature of the learners may change.

## The key characteristics of a system

Now let us deconstruct our simple system somewhat. To do this we will consider three fundamental aspects of a system:

- *boundary* decisions about what is inside and outside the system
- multiple *perspectives* on the system
- *relationships* between entities within and outside the system

These aspects can be represented by Figure 2.2, which introduces the Boundaries–Perspectives–Relationships (or B–P–R) model, which forms the basis for a systemic approach to needs analysis and evaluation.

### Boundaries

First, let us consider the significance of boundaries. This simple view of training as a system just looks at the training intervention and does not consider the workplace in which the new skills will be practised or the people who will be affected in some way by the learners' new skills. So we have actually drawn a line around what we consider as important within the training and what we leave out: the system has a *boundary* even though we have not drawn it in the diagram.

Boundaries may be physical, virtual or temporal; for example, who or what is considered as having an impact on performance, types of solution which we

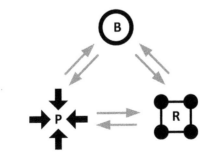

*Figure 2.2* The Boundaries–Perspectives–Relationships model

may or may not consider, if we look at a situation at a point in time or as part of a trend, who we decide to train and who we exclude from training and so on.

Boundaries contain but also exclude. To illustrate some important points arising from this implication, consider Figure 2.3.

This type of diagram is called a system map; it provides a way of showing what entities are involved in a system of interest. In this case our situation of interest includes actors involved in delivering a humanitarian aid programme; for example, we may be interested in evaluating the effectiveness of a training programme aimed at providing shelter in the aftermath of a civil conflict.

The system map provides a way of capturing thoughts about who may or may not be relevant to the evaluation process. We have the humanitarian organisations who are implementing the shelter programme, the persons of concern (the people needing shelter) and the host government. We may consider these to be the key actors involved and that the humanitarian organisations are delivering this programme within an environment comprising non-state actors (rebel groups, paramilitary organisations etc.), the military-industrial complex (official armies and arms vendors), governments providing financial support to the humanitarian aid and finally the media. So on our system map we draw Boundary 1, which defines our system of interest and the environment within which it operates (its context).

As we shall see later, making decisions about where to draw boundaries can have a significant effect on how we analyse or evaluate a situation. For

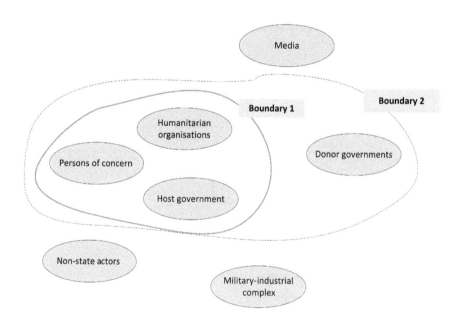

*Figure 2.3* System map of actors in a situation of interest

example, by placing donor governments in the environment, how are we going to change the way in which we involve them in analysis or evaluation? Should we redraw Boundary 1 as Boundary 2 and consider them as a core part of the system? What effect will this have on what we do, who we talk to, our measures of success and so on?

Boundary decisions that we make have an influence on the degree to which we can consider our thinking as 'holistic'. Systems thinking is sometimes described as being holistic, but this is not necessarily a helpful way of thinking about the subject. The *Oxford English Dictionary* defines 'holistic' as being "characterized by the tendency to perceive or produce wholes", but the problem with this is that it is in practical terms impossible to think about a 'whole' situation: we always have to make boundary decisions about what to consider. So while it is true to say that systems thinking can help us to take a *more holistic* look at a situation, it certainly does not look at the whole situation, as we always have to make boundary decisions.

One final consequence of making a boundary decision is how it can confer value on whatever we are considering. For example, when we look at a particular situation and describe it as a 'problem' we are effectively creating a boundary around it, separating good stuff outside from not-so-good stuff inside. This can then lead us to analyse just what we see inside the boundary, our 'problem'. To avoid this linguistic trap, throughout this book we will refer to issues we are looking at as 'situations of interest'.

### Perspectives

Next, there will be different opinions as to how this system actually works. At this point systems thinking literature sometimes refers to a story told in Eastern cultures (versions of the story appear in Sufism, Jainism, Buddhism and Hinduism) about six blind wise men walking in the forest. One day these men were walking through the forest when they came across an elephant. The first wise man bumped into the elephant's side and, reaching his hand out, declared that they had come across a wall. The second wise man reached out and took hold of one of the elephant's tusks: "This is a spear", he cried. The third wise man bumped into the trunk: "Look out, good friends, there is a snake here!" he warned. And so it went on. Another mistook the elephant's knee for a tree, another its tail for a rope and the sixth wise man thought the ear was a fan.

The lesson the story tells is that we all see but a part of the totality and, based on what we see, construct a reality and make judgements. And because our perspectives are limited our judgements are necessarily flawed. As discussed previously, what is happening in an organisation and why it is being done is a socially constructed reality, so each person with an interest will have a different perspective on improvement solutions: the trainer will have an idea about what needs to be included in the training, and the learners will have their own opinions. So our system must be considered from *multiple perspectives*.

### Relationships

The third aspect to consider is that the system consists of entities which are connected in various ways: the trainer is connected to the content and the learners, for example. There are, therefore, *multiple relationships*. In considering performance improvement and training there are, amongst others, relationships between individuals in the workplace, between an organisation's employees and its customers, between departments, between the organisation and political, social, environmental and technological forces and so on.

### Using the B–P–R model

While the B–P–R model provides a convenient way to start thinking about a performance problem as a system, it should be noted that this does not represent a systematic step-by-step process. In practice it is useful to start off any kind of systemic analysis by considering boundary issues, what is in or out, important or not important and so on. However, in doing this we have to simultaneously remember that different people will have different perspectives about where boundaries should be drawn.

Once we have developed a working boundary definition, we may then explore perspectives and relationships, revising boundary decisions as we increase our understanding of the situation. Rather than being a linear model, B–P–R therefore represents a framework within which we can conduct our analysis, using boundary definitions as an entry point.

Systems thinking approaches are designed to help us take these three aspects into consideration and to reflect on how they all interact. In the context of a training intervention this therefore helps us to think about such things as:

- how learners with new knowledge and skills will interact with their workplace and what implications this may have
- how different people may view the value of training differently; the learner may see it as important professional development, their supervisor as a way of helping the team to meet operational targets, the divisional director as an investment for the future
- what implications there might be for the content of the training if we drew our boundaries about who was involved in the design process differently.

There are, of course, many ways in which these three factors all have a bearing on training.

### Summary

This chapter has looked at how a distinction has emerged during the last 300 years between systemic thought and Cartesian reductionism. Reductionism emerged as a way of helping us understand the complexities of our existence but arguably has led us into something of a trap when we are trying to consider human behaviour.

Systems thinking has emerged as a discipline which helps us deal with the complexity of life. It is based around three key concepts: those of boundary definitions, multiple perspectives and relationships.

The aim of this chapter was to provide a basic understanding of what systems thinking means, and the next two chapters look at the key principles of the two main subjects of the book, training needs analysis and evaluation. If you would like to dig more deeply into systems thinking now, then you may wish to move on to Chapters 5 and 6 first. Otherwise, Chapter 3 will help you understand more about the core principles of training needs analysis.

## Notes

1 Malik, K., 2014. *The Quest for a Moral Compass*, Atlantic Books, London, p. 180.
2 Jackson, M.C., 2000. *Systems Approaches to Management*, Kluwer Academic/Plenum Publishers, New York, p. 1.
3 For more information, see: https://en.wikipedia.org/wiki/Division_of_labour, accessed 04 January 2015.
4 Manuti, A., Pastore, S., Scardigno, A.F., Giancaspro, M.L. & Morciano, D., 2015. Formal and Informal Learning in the Workplace: A Research Review. *International Journal of Training and Development*, 19(1), pp. 1–17.
5 Clement-Okooboh, K.M. & Olivier, B., 2014. Applying Cybernetic Thinking to Becoming a Learning Organization. *Kybernetes*, 43(9/10), pp. 1319–1329.
6 Arendt, H., 1958. *The Human Condition*, University of Chicago Press, Chicago, p. 137.
7 Berger, P. & Luckmann, T., 1971. *The Social Construction of Reality*, Penguin, London, p. 106.
8 West Churchman, C., 1979. *The Systems Approach and Its Enemies*, Basic Books, New York, pp. 32–34.
9 For more information, see: https://en.wikipedia.org/wiki/Tektology, accessed 15 April 2016.

# 3 Analysing training needs

This chapter looks at the important principles for the first of the book's primary aims, analysing training needs. It looks at:

- what a training needs analysis should achieve
- challenges in carrying out a training needs analysis
- models for analysing performance
- the potential benefits of a systems-based approach for training needs analysis.

## What is a training needs analysis?

A training needs analysis (or TNA) is a process carried out to identify training which will help improve performance in a situation where this is perceived to be necessary.

Or is it? It can be if we want it to be, but we need to look deeper into what assumptions lie behind this basic definition. The fundamental problem with the definition is the implicit assumption that the performance can be improved by training. This is dependent on the problem being caused by a lack of knowledge or skill, in which case training can help . . . but then only if we let it. So the danger is that if we embark on a training needs analysis and find that training is not needed, then we may return empty-handed. If, on the other hand, we reframe the boundaries within which we carry out the analysis, then we may return with some suggestions for non-training actions which could improve performance. This would be an improvement but then means that arguably we have not conducted a training needs analysis.

So there is a terminology problem. Various alternatives to 'training needs analysis' have been used. It is sometimes called an 'assessment'. Some writers have also suggested that it should be called a 'training requirements analysis', while there is also the more radical 'performance analysis' or 'performance improvement analysis'.[1] The argument for this is (rightly) that strategies for improving performance may include non-training actions, and that training may not be appropriate at all. This is a particularly relevant argument when looking at performance from a systems perspective, where the context of performance is an essential element to consider.

However, while these are valid and meaningful terms, they do not necessarily trip easily off a learning professional's tongue, so in this book we shall compromise somewhat and use the generalised but more familiar term 'needs analysis' to describe the process of investigating a situation in the workplace in order to identify potential training and non-training strategies.

Systems thinking introduces various dilemmas regarding terminology, and these will be discussed where appropriate throughout this book. At this point it is important to think about what word we will use to describe a strategy identified by the needs assessment process. In training jargon this is often referred to as a 'solution', but from a systems thinking perspective this presents a problem. In Chapter 5 we introduce the idea that workplace difficulties are examples of what have been called 'wicked problems', which are essentially problems which can never effectively be eliminated, merely ameliorated. This means that the rather mathematical word 'solution', which suggests right or wrong, is inappropriate. So we will refrain from using the familiar terms 'training and non-training solutions' and instead use alternatives such as 'training intervention', which describes the action and not the result.

## Why do a needs analysis?

A good needs analysis brings many benefits:

- It identifies gaps between current and desired levels of performance, making it possible to prioritise investments in time, money and human resources.[2]
- It provides an opportunity for the organisation to reflect on and learn something about its operation so that it can make appropriate changes.
- It can provide good evidence which can be used in individual performance appraisal activities.[3]
- It increases the likelihood that the training done will be effective.[4] This can have various positive effects in addition to increasing performance, such as improving employee motivation and making people more interested in undertaking further training.[5]
- It identifies issues which will influence the transfer of learning, so that attention can be paid to factors which may prevent the transfer from happening.
- It can identify existing informal learning channels, which can be taken into consideration in the design of training so that it becomes more effective.

## Challenges to the needs analysis process

As discussed in Chapter 1, it seems that in practice needs analyses are often not carried out, at least not with rigour. It is hard to imagine many parts of organisational life in which an investment is made without really considering what it needs to achieve, how its success can be measured or if it is really needed. There are three possible reasons accounting for this.

A fundamental reason may be a tendency in organisations to assume that any problem can be fixed by training. This is based on a belief that as a lack of knowledge and skill is a cause of a problem (in itself a questionable assumption), providing training will mitigate the problem at the very least.

A second problem may be the time needed to carry out a thorough needs analysis: the scope of the perceived problem needs to be assessed, stakeholders must be consulted, specifications must be prepared and consultations about implementation held. It is quite easy for some time to go by while this happens, and of course, if the prevailing belief is that as training *is* the necessary response, this may be seen as a waste of time.

Third, there is often a lack of clarity about what a 'training needs analysis' is or how it should be done. What are its terms of reference? Should it consider training and non-training interventions? How do you carry out a training needs analysis? What skills are needed? Do internal training staff have the necessary understanding of adult learning and organisational development issues needed in order to specify and design a training programme which really will make a difference to performance?

It is also possible that senior-level managers in an organisation may not in reality welcome any meaningful analysis of factors affecting performance. This might lead to uncomfortable change processes, so they see training as a way of being 'seen to be doing something' while not in practice doing anything meaningful at all.

Finally, organisations are often unable to articulate clearly what their actual goals are, making it hard for analysts to identify any discrepancy between desired and actual behaviour.[6]

Given these challenges to carrying out a proper needs analysis, what may actually happen when a needs analysis is done? Sometimes the needs analysis process becomes a 'shopping list' exercise. Instead of considering organisational goals and mismatches between desired and actual levels of performance, the analyst simply asks people what training they think they need. This usually results in people stating what they 'want' rather than what they need, and the end result often has minimal success.[7] There are various reasons for this:

- Training staff feel overwhelmed by the difficulty of analysing the causes of performance problems, or the scale of the analysis process is seen as too great.
- Training staff do not have the necessary skills for investigating the nature of a performance problem and identifying possible responses.
- There is an assumption that individual workers will know what is best for them.

The needs analysis may just be done at the personal level, looking at individuals carrying out their task and focusing on a narrow range of factors affecting performance.

Finally, needs analyses often fail to adequately consider how learning will be transferred into the workplace. Although a profile of the target group may be developed, inadequate consideration may be given to the dynamics of how the workplace operates and the degree to which new knowledge and skills can be generalised into what people do and maintained over a period of time.

As a result of all these limitations in the needs analysis process, the training interventions identified as necessary may be inappropriate or poorly defined, obstacles to people implementing new skills may be overlooked and success criteria may not be adequately defined. The whole design process starts off on the wrong footing, and subsequent evaluations become problematic.

## Levels of analysis

There are two aspects to consider when carrying out a training needs analysis: the level of analysis and the process to follow. We will first look at the levels of analysis.

Systematic approaches to needs analysis recommend that the analysis should be carried out at three separate levels: organisational, operational and personal.[8] However, for many training professionals this must seem daunting. Training managers may be somewhat isolated from centres of political influence and find it difficult to arrange time with senior management to discuss broader organisational issues; consultants may be presented with terms of reference which seem to make such broader investigations impossible.

Pragmatically, the easiest solution is to confine any analysis to the lower levels, but it is important to appreciate that even small-scale or low-budget training interventions may well be affected by and affect higher levels within the organisation. Systems thinking methodologies do provide various tools which can help deal with such tricky issues: for example, drawing a 'rich picture' (discussed in Chapter 6) can quickly draw attention to broader issues which need to be addressed in the analysis process, making it easier to claim time in a director's appointments calendar.

The nature of the situation of interest is also relevant: introduction of new policies and processes will clearly have knowledge and skill implications, while solving chronic problems of poor performance may not. These may require more engagement within the analysis by senior management to reflect meaningfully on structural issues.

The degree to which analysis is needed at each level is therefore dependent on boundary considerations; what is in the environment or within the situation of interest itself? Later chapters look at some tools which can be used to help decide where these boundaries are (or should be).

### The organisational level

This is analysis at the highest level of the organisation. Key issues to explore here are:

- What are the organisation's strategic priorities?
- How do the organisation's goals align with the (possibly hidden or not articulated) goals of operational departments or individuals?[9]

- In what areas are the potential for improvement the greatest?
- What are the norms, resources and support available for training activities?
- What needs to be done at an organisational level to make the implementation of any training more effective?[10]
- How is training seen in the organisation? Is it an occasional, one-off distraction or an integral part of promoting organisational change and development?[11]
- How can the analyst establish the levels of trust necessary in order to be confident of support from senior management in order to carry out the necessary analysis and then design and implement the necessary interventions?[12]

### The operational (or task) level

This is analysis carried out at departmental level, for example, operations, production, research and development and so on. Strategic decisions made at the organisational level help inform which operational parts of the organisation need to be examined in more detail.

Typically analysis at this level covers such things as:

- What is the perspective of operational departments on the priority issue?
- What is the relevant operational context?
- What are the linkages with other parts of the organisation?

### The personal level

At the third level we have analysis of the individuals who actually carry out the necessary interactions with their environment. Here we find answers to questions such as:

- Who are the individuals responsible for the performance?
- What levels of knowledge and skill do they have?
- What are the knowledge, skill and attitudinal (KSA) requirements for working at the required level?
- What are the learning transfer issues? What issues will make it more or less likely that any new knowledge or skill will be transferred to the workplace?

This is the level at which most needs analyses are generally carried out, with the result that there is very much a focus on task-specific knowledge and skill topics and less attention paid to how the performance of interest relates to operational or organisational issues.

## Processes for carrying out a needs analysis

Another possible reason suggested for the infrequency of carrying out a needs analysis may be the capacity of training departments to carry out a needs analysis. It would therefore be useful at this stage to look at some existing models which have been developed for carrying out different types of needs analysis to see how well they support this activity.

Conventional approaches to carrying out a training needs analysis follow systematic principles. For example, Goldstein and Ford recommend a five-step process (an essentially sequential process of gaining organisational support, organisational analysis, requirements analysis, task and KSA analysis and person analysis).[13] Kraiger and Culbertson advocate a four-step process of needs identification (which uses existing information to decide whether a full TNA process is needed), needs specification (which defines performance gaps and proposes responses), the full TNA process (which in practice really covers Goldstein and Ford's conception of the process) and completed by the evaluation stage.[14]

### Gilbert's Behaviour Engineering Model

Tom Gilbert's Behaviour Engineering Model (BEM) provides a rounded picture of factors affecting individual performance.[15] Figure 3.1 is a slightly adapted version of the BEM.

It proposes that there are two dimensions affecting performance, one which comes from the person themselves (the repertory of behaviour) and the other from the actual workplace (the supporting environment). Within each of these there are three separate areas that we need to consider: information, equipment and desire. To explain more fully what each of these factors are:

- Provision of information is about making sure that people have adequate instructions about what they are supposed to do and how well they need to do it and that they receive appropriate feedback on their levels of performance (so that they know if they are underperforming).
- Suitability of equipment is about making sure that people have the right tools for the job.
- Incentive is making sure that there are rewards for good performance and implications for underperformance.
- Comprehension is making sure that people understand the information that they have, and this is where training comes in.
- Capacity is the physical ability to use the tools (for example, through issues such as ergonomics and scheduling).

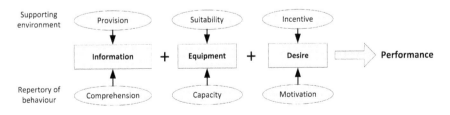

*Figure 3.1* Gilbert's Behaviour Engineering Model

- Motivation is each individual's desire to do the work to the level required (but notice that this will be different for different people (according to culture, age, gender etc.) and that only a matching combination of motivation and incentive creates desire.

Gilbert's recommendation for analysis is to work through the supporting environment factors first, from left to right, and then consider the repertory of behaviours, again left to right. His reasoning for this is that by doing it in this way you can make the easiest changes first, saving time and money. This has been described as a matter of 'behavioural economics' and that while it makes some sense from an implementation perspective, it may actually an effective strategy in practice.[16] For example, an analyst could identify a weakness in the provision of information to individuals and suggest an improvement and then wait for some weeks to see if this has an effect. If this does not happen, they could move onto the next potential response (improving the suitability of equipment) and so on. This would mean that the whole process could take a considerable amount of time before each possible intervention is tried and tested.

The reductionist assumptions behind the model also mean that it fails to examine the systemic relationship among any of these factors: for example, how providing information on performance (such as a supervisor's feedback) influences levels of motivation or how equipment design has a bearing on incentives. So while the Behaviour Engineering Model may encourage a *systematic* approach to training needs analysis, it is not systemic. It is also very much focused at the person level of analysis and fails to consider at all organisational or operational factors unless the analyst makes a conscious effort to include them when considering individual boxes.

### Mager and Pipe's performance analysis flowchart

The flowchart developed by Robert Mager and Peter Pipe[17] represents a step forward from the BEM in terms of usability and provides a highly systematic approach for thinking through the factors influencing individual performance (Figure 3.2).

This follows a very similar approach to Gilbert's model, taking the analyst through a sequence of questions starting with organisational issues, working through to training, potentially the most expensive and time-consuming response in terms of organisational resources which may be needed.

One particular strength of the flowchart is the way that it encourages people to reflect on how performance may be affected by other workplace requirements, which reminds us of the characteristics of a wicked problem, in particular that each problem is the symptom of another problem.

As with the BEM, the flowchart does not consider interconnections between the various factors, and while the flowchart approach makes it an easy technique

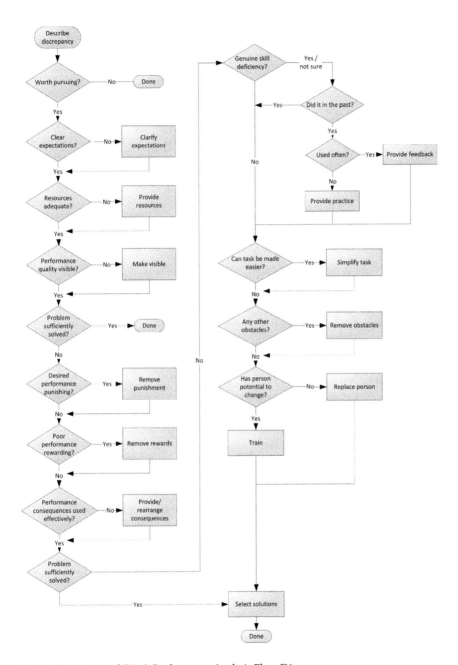

*Figure 3.2* Mager and Pipe's Performance Analysis Flow Diagram

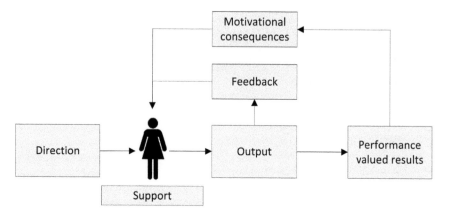

*Figure 3.3* The Performance Systems Model

to use, it can lead to a checkbox approach to analysis. Like the BEM, it is systematic rather than systemic.

### The Performance Systems Model

The Performance Systems Model[18] (Figure 3.3) was developed over a number of years by Donald Tosti, building on Tom Gilbert's BEM and Dale Brethower's Total Performance System.

Here we have a simple input-output model with feedback and motivational consequences added, drawing on the Behaviour Engineering Model. For each element of the model there are key questions for the analyst to ask:

- Support: do people get support that contributes to effective performance?
- Direction: do people get effective direction?
- Performers: are people able to perform well?
- Consequences: are there appropriate consequences for good performance?
- Feedback: do people get helpful feedback about their performance?

There are clear similarities between these questions and those that the Mager and Pipe flowchart suggest, albeit set within a systems model. Nevertheless, the focus remains very much on the individual performer and does not consider issues at a higher level within the organisation.

### Rummler and Brache's three-level model

In the 1980s Geary Rummler and Alan Brache developed a three-level model of an organisation as an adaptive system.[19] Figure 3.4 shows their view of the highest, organisational level of the system. From this 'super-system map', you

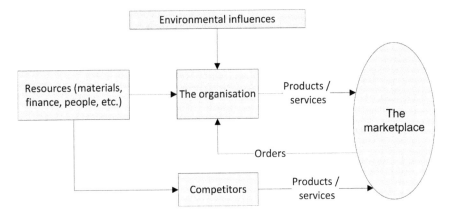

*Figure 3.4* Rummler and Brache's organisation as an adaptive system

can see that it takes the basic structure of input-transformation-output with feedback mechanisms and incorporates influences from the environment, although it does distinguish between 'general' influences and competitors.

Their second level is that of process, what happens in an organisation in order to produce products and services. The emphasis in Rummler and Brache's approach at this level is to analyse process flows through mapping exercises. Effectiveness should be measured against relevant goals, such as organisational goals and customer requirements. Attention needs to be paid particularly to the interfaces between departments, as it is at these, which they call 'the white space on the organisation chart', where there is the greatest scope for things to go wrong. It is at this process level that Rummler and Brache's model is least systemic.

The third level is that of the job/performer. Here they have defined their Human Performance System, which as you can see from Figure 3.5, is similar to Tosti's Performance System Model, discussed earlier.

The questions that should be asked when exploring issues relating to performance at the job level are broadly similar to those articulated by both Gilbert and Mager and Pipe, albeit here expressed within a systemic framework. For example, questions should be asked about the performance specifications:

- Do performance standards exist?
- Do performers know the desired output and performance standards?
- Do performers consider the standards attainable?

Rummler and Brache's three-level model of performance is therefore the most sophisticated of the systemic models of performance and behaviour. Nevertheless, the different approaches at each level affect the elegance of the model and make it somewhat harder to utilise easily.

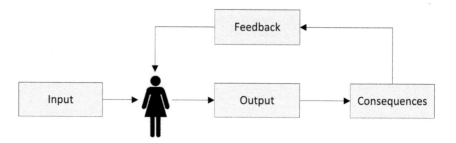

*Figure 3.5* Rummler and Brache's Human Performance System

## Summary

Although it is generally accepted that a needs analysis is an essential first step in the process of designing any formal learning interventions, it has been noted that this is a process which has been somewhat neglected by researchers,[20] and there is consequently a lack of easy-to-use models to support the process.

As noted in this chapter, the emphasis in most needs assessment–focused models has been on performance at the individual, task level. Systems thinking offers a number of tools which can help us transcend this limitation. These are discussed in detail in Chapter 6, and in Chapter 8 they are used in actual case studies.

## Notes

1  Iqbal, M.Z. & Khan, R.A., 2011. The Growing Concept and Uses of Training Needs Assessment: A Review with Proposed Model. *Journal of European Industrial Training*, 35(5), pp. 439–466.

2  Holton, E.F., Bates, R.A. & Naquin, S., 2000. Large-Scale Performance-Driven Training Needs Assessment: A Case Study. *Public Personnel Management*, 29(2), pp. 249–268.

3  Iqbal & Khan, 2011, op. cit.

4  Gould, D., Kelly, D., White, I. & Chidgey, J., 2004. Training Needs Analysis: A Literature Review and Reappraisal. *International Journal of Nursing Studies*, 41(5), pp. 471–486.

5  Kraiger, K. & Culbertson, S.S., 2013. Understanding and Facilitating Learning: Advancements in Training and Development. *Handbook of Psychology*, 12, pp. 244–261.

6  Holton, Bates & Naquin, 2000, op. cit.

7  Holton, Bates & Naquin, 2000, op. cit.

8  Goldstein, I.L. & Ford, J.K., 2001. *Training in Organizations (4th Edition)*, Cengage Learning, Boston, MA; Holton, Bates & Naquin, 2000, op. cit.

9  Goldstein & Ford, 2001, op. cit.

10  Salas, E., Tannenbaum, S.I., Kraiger, K. & Smith-Jentsch, K.A., 2012. The Science of Training and Development in Organizations: What Matters in Practice. *Psychological Science in the Public Interest*, 13(2), pp. 74–101.

11  Hurtz, G.M. & Williams, K.J., 2009. Attitudinal and Motivational Antecedents of Participation in Voluntary Employee Development Activities. *Journal of Applied Psychology*, 94(3), p. 635.

12  Goldstein & Ford, 2001, op. cit.

13  Goldstein & Ford, 2001, op. cit., p. 35.
14  Kraiger & Culbertson, 2013, op. cit., p. 246.
15  Gilbert, T.F., 2007. *Human Competence: Engineering Worthy Performance*, Pfeiffer, San Francisco.
16  Sasson, J.R. & Austin, J., 2003. Performer-level Systems Analysis: How Systemic Are Behavioral Interventions? A Ten-Year Review of the *Journal of Organizational Behavior Management. Journal of Organizational Behavior Management*, 22(4), pp. 27–58.
17  Mager, R.F. & Pipe, P., 1997. *Analysing Performance Problems*, Center for Effective Performance, Atlanta.
18  Tosti, D.T., 2005. The Big Five: The Evolution of the Performance Systems Model. *Performance Improvement*, 44(9), pp. 9–13.
19  Rummler, G. & Brache, A., 1990. *Improving Performance: How to Manage the White Space on the Organisation Chart*, Jossey Bass, San Francisco.
20  Kraiger & Culbertson, 2013, op. cit., p. 246.

# 4   Evaluating training

This chapter looks at:

- the importance of evaluating learning interventions
- why evaluating learning is often so challenging
- the strengths and weaknesses of existing learning evaluation methodologies.

## Why evaluate?

Having invested a considerable amount of time and other resources in carrying out a needs analysis and identifying potential ways to improve performance, it is only natural that we would want to find out how effective, valuable or useful our ideas have been. This is the purpose of evaluation. But, like a needs analysis, evaluation is a potentially time-consuming activity, and we need to be clear about what the potential benefits are of doing it. Some of these benefits are relevant to any sort of evaluation, so in this brief summary (which builds on the work of a number of authorities on the subject[1]) we shall look at how evaluation can improve performance improvement initiatives such as training.

### *To improve the quality of a solution*

A core reason to evaluate anything is to see if its quality can be improved in any way. Designing and delivering training programmes represents a significant investment, so it is clearly important to see if there is any way in which the return on the investment can be improved.

### *To decide whether to continue with the solution*

Sometimes a solution may prove not to be efficacious or cost-effective, and so it may be best to discontinue it. Alternatively, depending on the point at which an evaluation is carried out it may indicate that the solution, while initially effective, is no longer so.

### To make sure performance complies with regulation or legislation

Regulation and compliance with legal requirements is increasingly important for many organisations, and the delivery of (in particular) formal learning solutions is an important way for an organisation to show that it is compliant. Evaluation can therefore play a role to confirm this is happening.

### To make sure performance is aligned with organisational strategies

Organisations have a vision of how they want to be in their particular world and develop strategies that will help them to achieve these visions. Formal and informal learning activities are one way of following through with these strategies, so it is important to make sure that whatever learning is happening supports the overall strategy of the organisation.

### To help market the learning solutions

Evaluation can provide data which shows how effective a learning solution has been at improving performance, raising morale, strengthening opportunities for promotion and so on. This data can then be incorporated into internal (or external) marketing materials in order to attract more participants.

It may also be the case that when members of staff see a training programme being evaluated, they assume that this is because this particular programme is important or valuable in some way, and this makes it more attractive. This can also have an impact on how effective the programme is in transferring learning, so the act of evaluation creates a positive feedback loop.[2]

### To show the value of the training department

Pragmatically, evaluation needs to show the value to the organisation of the investment made in both formal and informal learning solutions, and this ultimately shows the value of the training department.

### To show the ethical contribution of human resources

To follow on from this perhaps somewhat cynical reason, there is also the moral point that human resources practitioners have a responsibility for advancing the welfare of individuals within an organisation and so have a duty of beneficence, of doing good for others.[3]

## How often is training evaluation done?

The previous section has highlighted some very significant benefits of evaluation, so an important question to ask is: how often do we evaluate training? The answer to this question depends very much on what we actually do as part of an evaluation process. Looking at data collected by the American Society for Training and Development (ASTD)[4], we find that:

- a little over 90% of training courses are evaluated for reaction (what the participants thought about the course)
- somewhere between 50% and 80% of evaluations check that participants have actually learnt something from attending the course
- somewhere between 23% and 55% of organisations look to see if participants transfer their learning back to the workplace
- somewhere between 8% and 37% try to find out if the training has had a positive impact on the organisation.

It is therefore clear that the amount of evaluation carried out declines significantly as we move away from the delivery of the training itself and start looking at impact. Paradoxically these same surveys have shown that the value attached to evaluations is the inverse of this: that while 36% of organisations attach some value to a reaction evaluation, 75% think that evaluating the transfer of learning and impact is important.

So if these higher levels of evaluation are so important from the organisation's perspective, why do they not happen? This needs to be examined in more detail, as it points to limitations in existing tools used for evaluating learning interventions.

## What are the barriers to evaluating training?

A number of different reasons have been offered to explain why more comprehensive evaluations are not carried out.

### Lack of organisational support

Some research[5] has pointed to the fact that most organisations do not provide training departments with the support or resources they need in order to carry out an effective evaluation at higher levels. It is relatively easy to conduct an assessment when learners are still in the (actual or virtual) classroom but quite another matter when they have returned to their workplaces. Such evaluations are costly, particularly in terms of time of training staff needed to gather and analyse data and of the lost production time of training participants. Supervisors are often reluctant to allow their staff to 'take time off' to take part in any evaluation activities and, in the absence of directives from senior management, are likely to place obstacles in the way of doing this.

Senior managers may also have had previous experience of training evaluations which have not produced any meaningful results and so be reluctant to invest more time and resources into new evaluations.[6] This leads to the next problem, a shortage of evaluation expertise, and a compounding of the problem.

### Shortage of evaluation expertise

A statistically significant evaluation requires a set of skills (such as research design, statistical analysis etc.) which training staff may not have. The way the scope of the training department has been defined may make such skills appear unnecessary. Evaluation at higher levels may also appear to fall into the domain of other organisational functions (such as an organisational development department), who may be less interested in supporting a training evaluation because they see it as somebody else's problem.

The issue of expertise is compounded by the lack of robust tools for evaluating training, a topic which is discussed later in this chapter.

There may also be a reluctance to carry out an evaluation which shows that formal learning interventions have not been effective, as this may reflect badly on the competence of the training staff themselves.

The issue of evaluation expertise may be resolved by engaging an external expert, and this also resolves issues about a conflict of interest. However, external consultants will not have access to the tacit knowledge held by insiders which explains internal dynamics of the organisation which could be having an important effect on the effectiveness of a learning intervention.[7]

### Weaknesses in the learning design process

It has also been suggested that the professional group responsible for the design of much formal learning, the instructional design community, draws boundaries around their professional practice which leads to them not seeing evaluation as part of their concern.[8] They may design evaluation activities which provide data about learning but fail to design activities which can facilitate evaluations at a higher level or to consider evaluation of emergent qualities which are not captured within traditional evaluation frameworks, such as increased networking amongst learners.

### Connecting learning with performance

At a more fundamental level, a major barrier to carrying out meaningful evaluations of formal learning interventions is the problem of establishing causality between attending a learning event and improving the performance of the organisation.

The most commonly used models for the evaluation of formal learning (such as Kirkpatrick's four-level model, which is discussed in more detail in what follows) tend to assume some implicit or explicit causality linking reaction to learning to behavioural change to performance, which if we look at performance from complex adaptive system or wicked problem perspectives is highly questionable.

We must not confuse causality with correlation. Just because someone attends a training course and their subsequent performance improves, we cannot immediately draw the conclusion that the attendance has directly led to the performance improvement. There is a correlation, but the reason may be due to other changes within the workplace which have happened at the same time. It is also possible that they may have learnt very little but still have improved their performance because the mere fact of attending improved their motivation.

### Failing to consider the learning transfer climate

The chain of causality linking learning with performance is closely related to the likelihood of learning transfer (which is discussed in detail in Chapter 9). The likelihood that learning will be transferred to the workplace depends on three factors:

- the design of the training
- the characteristics of the individual trainees
- the transfer climate, how receptive the workplace is to accepting and using new knowledge and skills.

Training evaluations often focus on the design of training and attempt to link this to behavioural changes, but as discussed earlier, if the other two factors have not been taken into consideration even the best-designed training in the world will fail. For example, a training course designed for a British audience may be ineffectual when delivered to people from another culture, or if the climate for implementing new ideas in the workplace is hostile there may be little change in behaviour. In the absence of a thorough needs analysis, which (as discussed in Chapter 3) is more the norm than an exception, these factors may not be fully understood. A reliable evaluation of the effectiveness of a formal learning intervention may be doomed from the very start if a proper needs analysis has not been carried out.

### In summary

We have seen that the amount of actual, significant training evaluation which is done is limited, so we should now take a closer look at the tools which are available for carrying out such activities and consider their strengths and weaknesses from a systems thinking perspective.

## The Kirkpatrick framework

Any discussion about the evaluation of formal learning interventions has to start with a review of Kirkpatrick's four-level framework. First articulated in the 1950s, the framework became better known through the 1980s as a result of his writing on evaluation for the American Society for Training and Development (ASTD), and eventually with the publication of his 1994 book *Evaluating Training Programs*.[9] As 'training evaluation' and 'Kirkpatrick' have become somewhat synonymous in the training world it is important that we start off by considering what his framework is all about.

Kirkpatrick identified four levels of evaluation criteria:

- *Reaction* of the trainees to the learning event
- *Learning* of new knowledge and skills or attitudes
- *Behaviour:* how are the new knowledge, skills and attitudes transferred to the workplace?
- *Results:* have there been changes in organisational performance, such as improvements in productivity or quality, reduction in costs or time taken etc.?

The framework has proved useful in a number of different ways. It provides a simple but systematic approach to evaluation,[10] focuses the evaluation on outcomes and business needs, and has encouraged the use of multiple criteria for evaluation at a number of different levels.[11] According to Theodore Lewis,[12] Kirkpatrick hoped that his proposed framework would lead to more discussion about and development of evaluation methodologies, but this has not really happened. A relatively small number of other evaluation approaches have been developed, but most of these are developments of Kirkpatrick's original ideas.

Despite its ubiquity, the Kirkpatrick framework attracts a lot of criticism, summarised as in this list:

- The four categories essentially represent a taxonomy, a way of classifying aspects to evaluate, rather than a methodology.
- There is an implied causal linkage among the four criteria which may not exist.
- It is not based on a model of performance and so ignores environmental factors affecting performance.
- It simplifies the valuable outcomes of training to those identified by objectives.

### Taxonomy or methodology?

A common criticism of Kirkpatrick's framework is that while it works well as a taxonomy, or classification of ways in which training can create value, it does not provide a sound methodology for evaluating training.

There is some truth in this criticism, but over the years Kirkpatrick did continue to develop the framework by suggesting many practical ways in which evaluation could be carried out. However, when viewed from a systemic perspective not all of these suggestions are practical. For example, in considering how to evaluate the results of a training programme, he suggests that, in order to identify factors other than the implementation of training which may be influencing performance, a control group method should be employed.[13] This is Cartesian dualism in operation, as it assumes that the control group will be kept in ignorance that they are being deprived of training and that the group receiving training will not be influenced by self-perceptions that they are 'chosen people'. In other words, psychological factors may well influence how well the training is received. Training programmes cannot be disguised as white tablets, as they are in clinical randomised control trials. Paradoxically, Kirkpatrick himself comments that using a control group may be impossible![14]

He also acknowledges that it can take time for the results of a training programme to manifest themselves and that how long this will be can vary considerably. This should be taken into consideration, but he provides no clear guidance on how to do this.

One reason offered for the lack of clarity within Kirkpatrick's framework is that it is not actually based on any theoretical model,[15] which makes it impossible to use as a diagnostic tool, as the failure to consider other issues which may affect behaviour and performance means that changes in learning, behaviour and results can only be correlated with and not attributed to the training.

### Do causal linkages exist?

Kirkpatrick's writing is not always clear about how strong these causal linkages are, but there is an implicit assumption which may be expressed within a theory of change model much like that shown in Figure 4.1.

Information is provided for learners, and if they react positively to the training experience they will learn. Learning then leads to a change in behaviour which leads to an improvement in organisational performance. This is a very neat and plausible chain of causality and has an obvious logic associated with it, which is a key reason why the framework has retained its popularity.

Unfortunately research has shown that there are few actual causal relationships among the four levels. For example, in a major review of training evaluation literature, George Alliger and Elizabeth Janak reported one previous review being unable to locate any studies showing inter-level correlation, and they themselves claimed that the "vast majority of articles reviewed did not report inter-level correlations".[16] They suggested that, "the hierarchical model is simply assumed to be correct",[17] that it is an assumption not based on any data.

Exploring reaction, it seems self-evident that people will only learn if they enjoy the training experience: enjoyment leads to paying attention leads to learning. As Kirkpatrick himself claimed, "If they [participants] don't like a program, there is little chance that they'll put forth an effort to learn".[18] There may be some degree of truth in this, but equally it is possible that people will learn from experiences they do not enjoy. As Alliger and Janak comment, "perhaps it is only when trainees are challenged to the point of experiencing the training as somewhat unpleasant that they learn: in such a case learning and reactions might be negatively correlated".[19] I can remember not enjoying my first weeks of differential calculus classes at school as it was far too difficult, but I did

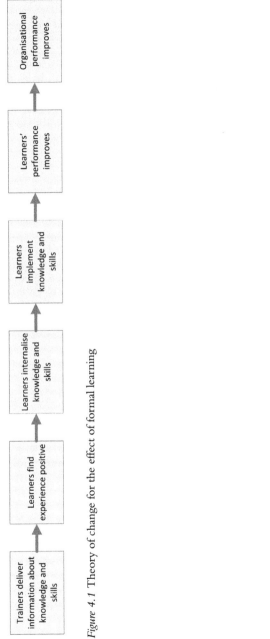

*Figure 4.1* Theory of change for the effect of formal learning

learn enough to pass exams and eventually gain a degree in engineering. But the implication of the causality issue is that if people can learn irrespective of whether they react positively to a learning event, it may be pointless trying to find out what their reaction is.

Nevertheless, as discussed previously, evaluation by measuring reaction has become the most common way of measuring the value of training. This over-reliance on assessing reactions is clearly related to the relative ease with which this can be done: it is very easy to hand around the so-called 'happy sheet' at the end of a workshop and ask people to rate factors thought to be contribut-ing to enjoyment. Such feedback sheets have their value: they can help trainers identify parts of a programme which are less effective and so which need to be strengthened; they provide data which can be used in marketing subsequent delivery of the training; it is immediate data which can be passed to managers and other decision makers showing the 'value' of the training.[20]

But this brings with it a danger that the programme is subverted in order to achieve a positive reaction. More difficult (albeit necessary) technical content may be left out in order to make sure that participants are not overly challenged intellectually. There may be an increasing emphasis on making the training 'fun' so that people respond positively.[21]

Moving on from reaction and learning to consider the causal linkage with behaviour change, again there is little evidence to show that this is true. At this point we now have to consider issues relating to the transfer climate (discussed in more detail in Chapter 9). There are many different issues which will affect whether the learner is able and willing to transfer new learning to their work-place. It is therefore extremely difficult to say with any confidence that failing to change workplace behaviour is the result of inadequate training. A subse-quent improvement in performance may be related to the training, but then it may be difficult to identify what particular aspect of the training is significant. For example, thinking about the lessons learnt from the Hawthorne studies (discussed in Chapter 5), it is possible that the mere fact of attending a training workshop could increase motivation so that workplace performance increases, irrespective of what was actually learnt (or not learnt).

### Ignoring non-training factors

In the previous section we discussed the problems in identifying reliable causal linkages between levels and referred to non-training factors influencing perfor-mance. Kirkpatrick developed his framework on the basis of practical experi-ence in evaluating training programmes but never linked this to any systematic research which developed a model of performance.[22] Although Kirkpatrick suggests inquiring about workplace-related issues which might be affecting the ability to implement new learning in a Level 3 evaluation,[23] the model does not provide any help in analysing issues which might arise as a result of this questioning. It does not, therefore, help an evaluator reflect on factors such as a culture for embracing and encouraging learning within the organisation, organisational goals and values, what type of interpersonal support may be available in the workplace, what the climate for transferring new learning is and whether the learner has the practical resources needed to change their working practices.[24]

Kirkpatrick's omission in not discussing these systemic factors means that training professionals carrying out evaluations are not equipped for considering the impact of non-training issues. Any changes in behaviour or results can therefore only be attributed to the training. Unfortunately, this is not really true, and so the whole process of training evaluation can become discredited.

### Simplifying the outcomes of training

Standard methodologies for designing training programmes recommend that the structure of a formal learning programme should be based on the deconstruction of an overall performance objective. This objective is then broken down through a reductionist process of 'task analysis' into a number of discrete 'enabling objectives', which when performed together create the overall performance. But it is impossible to develop a model for training purposes which perfectly captures the elements of mastery, so training can only be approximate and selective. It also raises the possibility that the function of the training will be to satisfy the requirements of the objectives rather than of the workplace. In the words of the old saying, the tail starts to wag the dog.

Such objectives often also fail to identify the emergent properties of a formal learning intervention. For example, attending a workshop may improve levels of motivation, which is surely a benefit in its own right. Bringing people together in a shared learning experience can help develop social capital within the organisation, which brings benefits to both individuals and the organisation. In the longer term it may be the case that the benefits of such intangibles are more significant than that which is measured by simple knowledge or skill-related objectives.

## The return-on-investment model

The return-on-investment (ROI) model for training evaluation was developed by Jack Phillips in the 1990s.[25] Essentially, it builds on Kirkpatrick's framework by extracting financial results from Level 4 and placing them into a new Level 5. The impetus for this enhancement was the increasing pressure on human resources departments to justify their activities and show a value to training. Because it claims to be able to ascribe a financial value to training, it has become a popular addition to the evaluation toolbox.

As an enhancement to Kirkpatrick, the ROI model suffers from similar weaknesses, in terms of establishing causality, the simplification of objectives and so on. However, the extra task of assigning financial values to outcomes is the chief concern with Phillips's model. While it does provide some suggestions as to how to isolate the effects of a formal learning intervention from other factors, these are limited in effectiveness and rely on a considerable amount of 'guesstimation' on the part of people involved in the process. For example, a participant needs to answer questions such as "What percentage of . . . improvement can be attributed to the application of skills/techniques/knowledge gained in the training program?"[26] How reliable can answers to questions such as these be? It is illuminating that Kirkpatrick himself made the comment, "I almost laugh when I hear people say that training professionals should be able to show benefits in terms of return on investment".[27]

The notion of 'isolating' one factor affecting performance is also antithetical to a systems approach, which is based on an understanding that all factors interact with each other: removing training as a factor influences not only the outcome of performance but many of the other influencing factors as well. As we cannot prove a causal linkage connecting learning and improve performance and are relying on a correlation instead, it is possible that other, cheaper activities carried out within the training event could have achieved the same result. This means that we cannot rely on any return-on-investment calculations, as the initial investment may have been excessive.

There are also ethical objections to deciding the value of training on the basis of financial returns. Reliance on an ROI model may be seen to place the discussion of investment in training at the same level as that of buying a machine and that it represents "an essentially corporatist"[28] view on training. Again, we return to Descartes's duck, that human activity can be likened to a machine and that mind is a separate issue of no concern.

## The organisational elements model

The organisational elements model (OEM) was originally proposed by Kaufman and Keller as an enhancement to Kirkpatrick.[29] They felt that the framework was too focused on training itself and should become more outward looking at the impact of the training on society beyond the organisation but also more inward looking by considering the cost efficiency of the intervention.

A later development of the model proposed six levels:

- Level 1: Input – similar to Kirkpatrick's reaction level but focusing on resources
- Level 2: Process – reaction again, but a focus on the process being followed
- Level 3: Micro (acquisition) – learning
- Level 4: Micro (performance) – behaviour and utilisation of skills and knowledge
- Level 5: Macro – organisational contributions and payoffs
- Level 6: Mega – societal outcomes

From a systems perspective we can see that the OEM questions some boundary assumptions and asks the evaluator to consider the interaction of the organisation with its environment.

## The Success Case Method

The Success Case Method (SCM) was developed by Robert Brinkerhoff, and explicitly rebuts the principles of Kirkpatrick's framework, which he sees as investigating the success of training: rather evaluation should consider how well an organisation *uses* training.

SCM recognises that performance is affected by a host of different factors, some relating to the learner themselves, some from the organisational setting and some from the nature of training that they have received. Brinkerhoff proposes that an evaluation should ask three questions:[30]

1   How well is our organisation using learning to drive needed performance improvement?
2   What is our organisation doing that facilitates performance improvement from learning? What needs to be maintained and strengthened?
3   What is our organisation doing or not doing that impedes performance improvement from learning? What needs to change?

To find answers to these questions the evaluator follows a two-stage process. First, the evaluator sends out a simple one-question survey to all participants in the learning activity, asking them to identify the degree to which they have used their learning in order to make a difference to the business. From this the evaluator can identify a number of both 'success cases', individuals or teams who are seen to have been successful in applying learning, and 'non-success cases', examples in which learning does not seem to have been applied.

The next step is to carry out follow-up telephone interviews with a sample of success and non-success cases in order to explore more deeply what has enabled them to apply (or has prevented them from applying) their learning.

The outputs of the SCM activity are a number of success stories which can be disseminated but also a summary of factors which have been identifying as enhancing or impeding the effect of training.

It can be seen that the SCM has a more systemic quality than Kirkpatrick or its ROI derivative. It attempts to look at a broader range of factors influencing performance and utilises the training as an opportunity to gain access to people in the workplace. However, it has been criticised for not necessarily helping an evaluator to identify what a 'critical success factor' might actually be.[31] The method on its own does not necessarily help an evaluator to understand the interaction among factors, and so while it is a significant step forward there are clearly some ways in which a more rigorous application of systems thinking tools could enhance it.

## Summary

Despite regular criticisms about the difficulties in implementing the Kirkpatrick framework and research which shows its weaknesses, it "remains the bellwether for evaluation decision making in practice".[32] The Brinker-hoff SCM, although potentially more informative if used, is little known. There are a number of other training evaluation methods which have been proposed over the years which have not been discussed here: Stufflebeam's CIPP model (context evaluation, input evaluation, process evaluation, product evaluation), Warr's CIRO (contents/contexts, inputs, reactions, outcomes) and others.[33] However, few of these seem to have gained any traction within the training profession, perhaps because while the designers of the model may have produced something valid, they have not necessarily provided a usable set of tools which can be used to apply the model. This covers both the technical aspects of conducting the evaluation and the more strategic aspects of collaborating with stakeholders (the boundary management issue).[34]

This lack of any significant advances in evaluation methodologies over the 50 years since Kirkpatrick first defined his framework may well be because the training world has found it difficult to escape from reductionist thinking methods which lead us to linear theories of change based on causal linkages connecting learning to behaviour modification.

The lack of evaluation methodologies may be one reason evaluating training is so problematic, but the lack of rigour in the needs analysis process is another. If no needs analysis is carried out, there can be little understanding of the 'real' training need, and so the setting of learning objectives becomes a somewhat arbitrary exercise. If objectives are arbitrary, making decisions about whether or not they have been achieved must also be somewhat arbitrary.

Systems thinking approaches offer a new paradigm and one which may make it easier to draw conclusions about the contributions which training may be making to a performance problem. However, needs analysis and evaluation both need to be done following a systemic approach. Fortunately, the techniques used for a systems-based approach to evaluation are similar to those for a systemically based needs analysis, simplifying the learning needed in order to be able to use them.

The next two chapters look in detail at some of the theory underlying systems thinking, but if you are more interested in looking at practical applications of systems thinking to evaluation, move on to Chapter 10.

## Notes

1 Kirkpatrick, D.L., 1994. *Evaluating Training Programs*, Berrett-Koehler, San Francisco; Kirkpatrick, J., 2007. The Hidden Power of Kirkpatrick's Four Levels. *T + D*, 61(8), p. 34; Kraiger, K. & Culbertson, S.S., 2013. Understanding and Facilitating Learning: Advancements in Training and Development. *Handbook of Psychology*, 12, pp. 244–261; Saks, A.M. & Burke, L.A., 2012. An Investigation into the Relationship Between Training Evaluation and the Transfer of Training. *International Journal of Training and Development*, 16(2), pp. 118–127.
2 Saks & Burke, 2012, op. cit.

3  Bates, R., 2004. A Critical Analysis of Evaluation Practice: The Kirkpatrick Model and the Principle of Beneficence. *Evaluation and Program Planning*, 27(3), pp. 341–347.

4  Hung, T.-K., 2010. An Empirical Study of the Training Evaluation Decision-Making Model to Measure Training Outcome. *Social Behavior and Personality: An International Journal*, 38(1), pp. 87–101; Kennedy, P.E., Chyung, S.Y., Winiecki, D.J. & Brinkerhoff, R.O., 2014. Training Professionals' Usage and Understanding of Kirkpatrick's Level 3 and Level 4 Evaluations. *International Journal of Training and Development*, 18(1), pp. 1–21.

5  Kennedy et al., 2014, op. cit.

6  Torres, R.T. & Preskill, H., 2001. Evaluation and Organizational Learning: Past, Present and Future. *The American Journal of Evaluation*, 22(3), pp. 387–395.

7  Torres & Preskill, 2001, op. cit.

8  Moller, L. & Mallin, P., 1996. Evaluation Practices of Instructional Designers and Organizational Supports and Barriers. *Performance Improvement Quarterly*, 9(4), pp. 82–92.

9  Kirkpatrick, 1994, op. cit.

10  Alliger, G.M., Tannenbaum, S.I., Bennett, W., Traver, H. & Shotland, A., 1997. A Meta-Analysis of the Relations Among Training Criteria. *Personnel Psychology*, 50(2), pp. 341–358.

11  Bates, 2004, op. cit.

12  Lewis, T., 1996. A Model for Thinking About the Evaluation of Training. *Performance Improvement Quarterly*, 9(1), pp. 3–22.

13  Kirkpatrick, 1994, op. cit.

14  Kirkpatrick, 1994, op. cit., p. 54.

15  Holton, E.F., 1996. The Flawed Four-Level Evaluation Model. *Human Resource Development Quarterly*, 7(1), pp. 5–21.

16  Alliger, G.M. & Janak, E.A., 1989. Kirkpatrick's Levels of Training Criteria: Thirty Years Later. *Personnel Psychology*, 42(2), pp. 337.

17  Alliger & Janak, 1989, op. cit., p. 337.

18  Kirkpatrick, D.L., 1996. Great Ideas Revisited. *Training and Development*, 50(1), pp. 56.

19  Alliger & Janak, 1989, op. cit., p. 334.

20  Brown, K.G., 2005. An Examination of the Structure and Nomological Network of Trainee Reactions: A Closer Look at "Smile Sheets". *Journal of Applied Psychology*, 90(5), p. 991.

21  I had a personal experience of this when a contract for delivering training stated that I needed to make sure that the reaction questionnaires recorded a score of at least 3.5 out of 5. One strategy that I employed to try and make sure that I achieved this was to buy a large box of Swiss chocolates at the airport duty-free shop on the way to the venue. By distributing chocolate at regular intervals throughout the workshop I was able to create a positive learning environment(!).

22  Holton, E.F. & Naquin, S., 2005. A Critical Analysis of HRD Evaluation Models from a Decision-Making Perspective. *Human Resource Development Quarterly*, 16(2), pp. 257–280.

23  Kirkpatrick, 1994, op. cit., p. 57.

24  Bates, 2004, op. cit.

25  Phillips J.J, & Stone, R.D., 2002. *How to Measure Training Results*, McGraw-Hill, New York.

26  Phillips & Stone, 2002, op. cit., p. 147.

27  Kirkpatrick, 1994, op. cit., p. 67.

28  Lewis, 1996, op. cit. p. 9.

29  Tamkin, P., Yarnall, J. & Kerrin, M., 2002. *Kirkpatrick and Beyond: A Review of Models of Training Evaluation*, Institute for Employment Studies, Brighton.

30  Brinkerhoff, R.O., 2005. The Success Case Method: A Strategic Evaluation Approach to Increasing the Value and Effect of Training. *Advances in Developing Human Resources*, 7(1), pp. 86–101.

31  Passmore, J. & Velez, M., 2012. SOAP-M: A Training Evaluation Model for HR. *Industrial and Commercial Training*, 44(6), pp. 315–325.
32  Kraiger, K. & Culbertson, S.S., 2013. Understanding and Facilitating Learning: Advancements in Training and Development. *Handbook of Psychology*, 12, p. 253.
33  There is a useful summary of a number of training evaluation models given in Passmore & Velez, 2012, op. cit.
34  Eseryel, D., 2002. Approaches to Evaluation of Training: Theory & Practice. *Journal of Educational Technology & Society*, 5(2), pp. 93–98.

# 5 Key concepts in systems thinking

Chapter 2 introduced some fundamental principles of systems thinking, and in this chapter we now go on to look at some key concepts which are of particular importance in performance improvement. These include:

- how different approaches to systems thinking may be classified
- feedback, how interactions between system entities affect system behaviour
- emergence, how system behaviour can generate unexpected consequences
- causality, how one thing may or may not affect another
- linearity and non-linearity, how cause and effect are not necessarily clearly related
- appreciation, how processes of analysis can create inappropriate solutions
- requisite variety, the importance of considering the operational environment
- single- and double-loop learning, the difference between doing things right and doing the right things
- wicked problems, how the reality of organisational life affects our decisions
- complexity, the idea of dynamic stability and developing the optimum balance between order and chaos.

## Do systems exist?

The issue as to whether or not the real world contains systems troubles some people. While it may be easy to characterise some organised entity such as an organisation as a 'system', it can be much harder to conceptualise loosely connected entities in such a manner. This leads to the concern that systems thinking approaches cannot realistically be applied in such areas, nor can such situations be described as systemic.

As we shall see, one way of classifying systems tools is on the basis of whether we view the world as an actual system or use the idea of a system to consider the world. However, it is important not to get too caught up with this idea (although serious systems people can do just that). For our purposes, when thinking about using a systems approach to look closely at a situation of interest, we can in practice ignore this distinction. There is an old adage, popular amongst systems thinkers, about "confusing the map for the territory".

This draws our attention to the difference between reality and our perception of what it is. There are times when we can indeed view a situation of interest (the territory) as a real system, but there are other times when it is best to simply think that we are looking at a map, at our interpretation of the situation, and to think of this as a system. Adopting this intellectual freedom greatly liberates what we can do with systems approaches.

## Classifying systems approaches

Before going into systems concepts in any detail we need to briefly discuss some general ways of classifying systems ideas. Over the last half century a large number of different approaches to systems have emerged, and while there are common threads across them all, they often have very different underlying philosophies. There is, as in all such disciplines, a vigorous debate which goes on between systems practitioners about the relative strengths and weaknesses of each and about where and how they can be applied and so on. So in this chapter we will review some of these approaches and consider their general relevance to the world of learning in the workplace.

It is useful here to distinguish between what we may call 'approaches', which are more conceptual discussions about each idea, and 'tools', which are practical processes for using systemic concepts. These tools are covered in Chapter 4.

There are many different ways of slicing up and categorising systems approaches, but for our purposes here we will use a classification developed by Mike Jackson[1] (Table 5.1).

*Table 5.1* Classifications of system tools

| Functionalist | Interpretive | Emancipatory |
|---|---|---|
| System Dynamics<br>Viable System Model<br>Social Network Analysis<br>Complexity Theory | Soft Systems Methodology | Critical Systems Heuristics |

### Functionalist approaches

Functionalist systems approaches see situations happening in the world as systems and assume that there are connections between things that happen in real life which drive the systems along. Of the three characteristics of a system, the emphasis here is on *relationships*.

Functionalist systems tools therefore use language related to mechanisms, organisms and so on. Within this domain we will look at:

- System Dynamics, which relies on the generation of feedback loops to explain behaviour
- the Viable System Model, which draws on the ideas of cybernetics and control mechanisms

- Social Network Analysis, which allows us to represent and quantify aspects of social relationships
- Complexity theory, which explores the relationship between order and chaos in a practical system

### Interpretive approaches

Systems tools based on an interpretive philosophy do not consider the real world to necessarily be operating as a system but develop systemic models of the real world and use these to reflect on reality. Within interpretive approaches, the emphasis is on perspectives, and they are particularly useful for data analysis.

Although Jackson describes a number of interpretive approaches, only one will be covered in this book, Soft Systems Methodology.

### Emancipatory approaches

While functionalist approaches focus on relationships and interpretive approaches on perspectives, the emphasis within emancipatory approaches is on *boundaries*: where boundaries are and why they have been set in this way. Emancipatory systems approaches grew out of a concern that functionalist and interpretive systems approaches did not adequately deal with issues of power and control, so emancipatory approaches have political and ethical considerations at their core.

The emancipatory systems methodology described here is Critical Systems Heuristics. It is of particular value in identifying boundaries, for example, in deciding who needs to be involved in a needs analysis process or in deciding on opinions to elicit in an evaluation.

### Simple, complex, unitary, pluralist, coercive situations

As well as classifying different types of systems thinking approaches, it can sometimes also be useful to classify situations in which they may be utilised. Flood and Jackson[2] classified situations in which systems methodologies may be utilised using a two-dimensional grid (illustrated in Figure 5.1).

Situations can be simple or complex. In essence, *simple* situations contain a small number of elements, and there are few, well-defined interactions between elements (for example, a thermostat), whereas *complex* situations contain a large number of elements, with many loosely organised interactions (for example, a human behaviour system).

They can also be:

- *unitary*, where participants in the situation have common interests, by and large agree with each other and follow agreed procedures for resolving the situation
- *pluralist*, where there are similar interests and somewhat divergent beliefs, but compromise is possible and there are agreed procedures for resolution

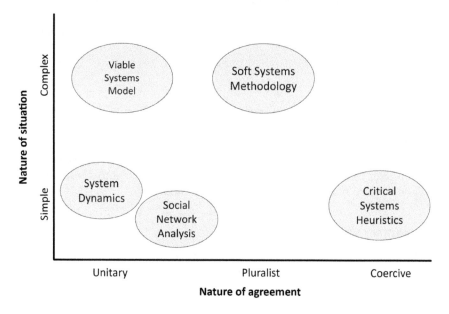

*Figure 5.1* Systems approaches and where they might be used

- *coercive*, where participants do not share a common interest, conflict is likely and resolution may be by coercion

Any of these are possible in an organisational setting. Thinking about situations in which training may be involved, the introduction of a new computer system might be regarded as a simple–unitary situation, whereas developing training for a new policy may be more complex–pluralist in nature. However, training to resolve a serious performance problem may be located within a coercive situation.

Different systems methodologies may be more appropriate for use in particular types of situation. For example, considering the methodologies covered in this book:

- System Dynamics is more suited to a simple–unitary system.
- Viable System Model is useful in complex–unitary situations.
- Social Network Analysis may probably be regarded as most suitable for simple–unitary systems (due to the need for a relatively coherent network in order to gather meaningful data).
- Soft Systems Methodology is useful for complex–pluralist situations.
- Critical Systems Heuristics is suited for simple–coercive situations (as often in such situations conflict occurs between just a small number of actors[3]).

### Which one do I use?

In earlier times there was a class of tradesman who would wander around the countryside from town to town, knocking on doors to see if anything needed repairing. They had no particular specialism or skills other than an ability to mend things using a selection of tools that they carried on their backs. The best word to use to describe the sort of person may be *bricoleur*, a French word which was used by the philosopher Claude Lévi-Strauss to describe someone who was able to use a range of tools to explore a situation. So it is with using systems tools in needs analyses and evaluation. The reality is with these tools that they each have particular strengths in certain situations, and the key thing for a training manager or performance analyst is to be able to pull an appropriate one out of their toolbox and use it to the extent that is necessary to help make sense of a situation.

In the following sections some general ideas will be given as to where each tool may be useful, and in following chapters case studies will show how they can be used in more detail.

## Open and closed systems

The concept of open and closed systems comes from thermodynamics. A closed system is one which operates in isolation from its environment: its elements interact amongst each other but do not draw energy from or radiate energy to the outside world. In a closed system in which elements are moving around, they will slowly become more and more disordered (in thermodynamic terms, their entropy increases) and will eventually settle to a *static equilibrium*, where all activity ceases. For example, if we put two different gases in a closed vessel, the molecules of the gas will move around randomly until eventually there is a completely uniform mixture: this is a static equilibrium, and nothing further changes. If we put people into a closed vessel they will exchange ideas and information until they reach a consensus: if no further information or ideas enter the vessel, their consensus will not change.

By contrast, an open system exchanges energy with its environment. This means that activity can continue, and the system will not move to a static equilibrium, although it may well reach a *dynamic equilibrium*, in other words, behaving in a steady way but with a constant interchange of energy. Somewhat confusingly, this is sometimes described as a system which is operating 'far from equilibrium' (although this is a term which has inconsistent meanings across different academic disciplines).

Human activity systems operate as open systems. Organisations exchange products and information (energy) with their environment, and each individual worker or team does the same, albeit at a different level. One of the constraints of traditional approaches to training needs analysis, the design of training programmes and subsequent evaluation, is that they are based on the assumption of the organisation as a closed system, by neglecting to consider the effects of exchanges with the environment.

## Feedback

As relationships are an integral part of the way systems work, how one entity affects another in the system and what impact that has is a key consideration. This idea of an action producing a reaction is often described as feedback, but in some respects this term is misleading, as it focuses attention on the reaction and may suggest that the reaction always bounces back to the first entity, whereas in practice it often has an impact on other entities within the system.

When we discuss feedback in a systems context, it can be more useful to think about it in terms of the Hindu principle of *karma*. In everyday Western language we think of *karma* as some sort of retribution which we may experience as a result of doing something bad, but the real meaning is more subtle than that. Everything we do creates *karma*, which then affects the world around us and has certain moral consequences for us, positive for good things we do and negative for bad things. As we proceed through life our *karma* accumulates, and in Hindu belief this will then influence what happens in our next cycle of incarnation. So in systems-speak, *karma* is the product of an exchange of information between entities in a system.

*Karma*/feedback operates in many different ways when we are thinking about what to do when improving performance, such as through establishing feedback mechanisms when carrying out an evaluation or when people who have completed a training programme put new information into their workplace environment which will change the way things happen.

The concept of *karma* changing the world around to create new possibilities is central to the idea of a 'wicked problem', which is discussed in more detail in what follows and has profound consequences for performance improvement activities.


## Emergence

In Chapter 2 we introduced the idea of systems creating unintended consequences and defined this as 'emergence'. To give a practical example of this, let us look at the history of the bicycle.

Wheeled transport has been a central feature of civilisation for thousands of years. By the mid-19th century wheels had been put together with a steel frame to create what was called the 'ordinary' bicycle, or what we more commonly know as the 'penny farthing'. This was a difficult and dangerous vehicle to use, and its use was limited to wealthy, athletic young men. However, in 1876 James Starley of Coventry worked out how to combine the newly designed roller chain with the steel frame and wheels to create what became known as the 'safety' bicycle. A few years later John Boyd Dunlop invented the pneumatic tyre, and the bicycle as we know it had appeared.

The new technology revolutionised late-19th-century life. For one thing, women could now ride a bicycle, and it became possible for them to travel away from the villages of their birth. They could therefore meet men from different villages, strengthening the general population by widening the genetic pool for consequent babies and helping women realise that they did not necessarily have to stay at home all of their lives.

> Bicycling has done more to emancipate women than anything else in the world. I stand and rejoice every time I see a woman ride by on a wheel. It gives women a feeling of freedom and self-reliance.
>
> Susan B. Anthony, suffragist

This simple historical tale tells us something about emergence. When Starley and Dunlop first put their mechanical devices together in a particular configuration, the modern bicycle emerged. What they almost certainly did not imagine was that it would play a fundamental part in sexual liberation, another example of emergence and an unintended consequence.

As we saw previously, conventional Cartesian thinking makes us think backwards about how to deconstruct a desired performance in order to create a series of activities which we hope will, when put together, recreate our desired performance. The problem is that this way of thinking does not look forward: when we add all our individual activities together, what other consequences may emerge?

How people behave in a work team is an emergent behaviour. Teams consciously and unconsciously create written and unwritten norms which can regulate what is considered acceptable in terms of dress style, punctuality and work output. Tuckman's well-known four-stage model of group development (forming, storming, norming, performing) describes how groups only start to perform effectively once they have established norms. Conforming to norms can become very important for group members, quite possibly counteracting the effect of attending a training event.[4] This has implications for how effective training can be. For example, when we train staff so that they acquire a higher level of competence, how will that play out in their workplace? Will they become restless and press for promotion or transfer or start looking for a new job? What tensions may this create in the workplace with other, untrained colleagues? A newly trained person may find it is socially unacceptable for them to change their behaviour in the way that the training has recommended.

It is therefore important in a systemically based training needs analysis to develop an understanding of workplace dynamics. This has subsequent implications for evaluation, implications which are often not addressed within conventional approaches to training evaluation. A systemically based evaluation process would look not only at whether learners have achieved the designated training objectives and change their behaviour in the workplace but also at other changes which may have been stimulated by the training activity.

## Causality

Causality describes a process whereby if we do X, Y will happen. In machines, causality is clear: I press the accelerator pedal in a car and the car goes faster; I press the brake pedal and it slows down.

Causality is usually not so clear in a human as opposed to a mechanical system. If a person attends a training course and then returns to work and performs better, what is the causality? The Hawthorne studies of the 1920s are often quoted as an example of the dangers of assuming causality.[5] Researchers at the Hawthorne, New Jersey, plant of the Western Electric Company wanted to see how changes in factors such as light levels and rest periods would affect performance. They increased the lighting and performance went up, so better lighting leads to better performance. But then they reduced the lighting, and performance again went up. They repeated this with other variables, such as cleanliness, timeliness and location of workstations and found the same thing happening. Their conclusion was that what really changed performance was the attention being given to the group of workers in the study rather than changes in working conditions. Later analysis of the survey data suggested that changes in performance were more linked to the workers being given information about their productivity and changes in how they were being paid for their work,[6] but this does not necessarily negate the original conclusions.

So given the difficulty in establishing the cause-and-effect relationship here, how can we confidently connect training and improve performance? A worker's performance may improve after attending a two-day workshop, but how confident can we be that this is because of the skills they have acquired? Maybe they enjoyed two days away from their desk? Maybe spending two days at a health spa would have been equally as effective?

Statisticians have their own views on causality and stress the importance of not confusing it with *correlation*. We may gather evaluation data which shows a clear correlation between attendance at a training event and improved performance, but this does not necessarily show an actual causal relationship.

Causality is implicit within Kirkpatrick's four-level model of evaluation. The assumption is that if people enjoy training they will learn, if they learn they will apply their new knowledge, and if they apply their new knowledge performance will improve. There are three steps of causality here, but in reality none of them can be assumed.

## Linearity and non-linearity

When I am riding my bicycle I know that if I turn the pedals twice as fast I will travel along the road twice as fast: there is a linear relationship between what I put in and what I get out.

However, in systems involving human beings we cannot assume linearity. Training a person so that they can operate a machine faster does not mean that they will indeed operate the machine faster: for many reasons they may decide to work at the same speed as they have always done, so that there is a *non-linear relationship* between input and output. In the commercial world, when Apple reconceptualised a portable computer as a mobile phone (in technological terms a small change) and introduced the original iPhone, this triggered an enormous change within the mobile telephone market.

It is also possible that while we may see a linear cause-and-effect relationship up to a point, eventually certain factors will kick in which will introduce non-linearity. After attending a training course a person's performance may start to increase, but after a certain time other factors start to restrict performance, perhaps group norms, forgetting what they have learnt and so on.

Linearity and non-linearity play an important part in complexity theory, which is discussed below. Perhaps the best-known example of this is the so-called 'butterfly effect', which postulates that the flapping of a butterfly's wings in the Amazonian rainforest can create a disturbance which triggers a chain reaction leading to a massive meteorological event in some other part of the world.

## Appreciation and the dynamics of time

Geoffrey Vickers (1894–1982) was one of Britain's key systems thinkers. He wrote extensively about many different aspects of systems thinking, but the one aspect we shall look at here is one with particular relevance to identifying training needs and evaluation. This is his development of the idea of the *appreciative system*, his description of how we go about making sense of the world around us. In this context, 'appreciation' means how we reflect on a situation and give it some value, based on standards that we hold. Figure 5.2[7] illustrates how an appreciative system works.

People often work in situations in which there is an ongoing flux of ideas and events. Ideas may be corporate policies, characteristics of the customer environment and so on. Events will be particular things that happen or that need to be done, and these will vary from day to day, week to week or month to month.

At some point someone will perceive that there is a problem, that an individual, team or department is not working to the required standards. They will

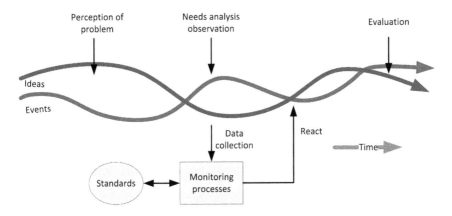

*Figure 5.2* An appreciative system

then ask the training department to carry out a training needs analysis, so they will collect data, analyse this by reference to the required performance standards, make a decision about what kind of training intervention is necessary, design the training and deliver it. Then at some point in the near future the effectiveness of the training will be evaluated.

The problem is clearly shown by Figure 5.2, that the flux of ideas and events keeps changing. For example, suppose we are considering a perceived problem in quality control. Ideas related to quality control constantly change as new technologies make it possible to check for different aspects of quality, while different events are also taking place, such as changes in product design, new products being developed in response to changes in the marketplace and so on. These changes are also not necessarily correlated in any way with each other, and exactly what the changes are may not necessarily be clear. In some professional areas such changes can happen very quickly.

To start the process of designing training to improve quality control we would carry out a training needs assessment, but what the situation is when the training has finally been developed and delivered may be quite different. Who knows, maybe the problem no longer exists? The situation may have changed, rendering the training ineffectual or irrelevant. This all makes the whole concept of formal training and its evaluation problematic. The problem here is, of course, the time delay, in that the time between problem perception and dealing with the problem means that the solution may not be the most appropriate.

This is a problem with the formal training needs analysis process and is one reason it is important that *informal learning* is seen as an important component of any performance improvement strategy. Informal learning is *situated*, in that it is located within the immediate working environment and responds to its particular, current challenges. In this way it cuts out the time delay inherent in the monitoring process.

It should also be noted that the 'standards' being applied here are closely related to the flux of ideas and events and will have been derived by considering what was happening at some point in the recent past. They are therefore not absolute but are based on an analysis of the relationship between the observer and the ongoing flux, so they can change as time goes by. This led Vickers to the observation that what is primarily important for people is the maintenance of relationships, between them and other people, them and what they are doing and so on. He then contrasted this with the 'poverty-stricken' concept of goal setting,[8] which is the basis of much organisational life. Goal setting is inadequate because that is not the way in which people lead their lives. Goals are abstract, and because they are relative to the flux of ideas and events, they are to some extent arbitrary and abstract and, because of the unpredictable causality of life, can become irrelevant. This has a lesson for the design of learning interventions which rely on formally stated learning objectives: can we be confident that these objectives will be relevant throughout the life of the formal learning programme? Perhaps instead of defining objectives by reference to a specific skill, they should instead be defined by the ability to maintain a particular relationship with the environment?

The problem of the appreciative system is a key element within complexity theory, discussed later in this chapter.

## Requisite variety

Ross Ashby (1903–1972) was a practising British psychiatrist whose contribution to systems thinking lay in the field of cybernetics, the study of control mechanisms. Like Vickers, Ashby made many significant contributions to systems thinking, but what is of particular interest to training practitioners is his Law of Requisite Variety.[9]

Variety here refers to the complexity of the situation we are looking at. Returning to our bicycle metaphor, variety in the cycling environment consists of city streets, the open road, mountain trails and the velodrome track. While in theory one bicycle could be used in all of these environments, in order to ride as quickly, comfortably or safely as possible we should use a different design of bicycle in each location. In other words, we need to increase the variety of bicycles available to us to match the variety of the cycling locations.

In general terms, Ashby's Law says that in order to achieve this requisite variety we must either reduce the variety in the environment or increase the variety of our control mechanisms. Applying this to workplace performance improvement we can see that strategies could be designed to:

- simplify the processes that somebody must follow (reducing environmental variety)
- provide clearer information (reducing environmental variety)
- give people the necessary skills to deal with different situations (increasing control variety).

Another lesson here is that variety in the operational environment may not be readily apparent to people working in central functions of an organisation who are away from the front line. It is therefore very important that any needs analysis activity seeks to explore the perspectives of the people who are actually doing the task under examination so that variety can be identified and explored.

## Single- and double-loop learning

One systems thinking concept which has entered mainstream managerial language is that of 'the learning organisation'. Unfortunately, the real meaning of this phrase is often confused: I remember the chief learning officer of a major international organisation proudly announcing that with the launch of a new learning management system, "We are now a learning organisation!" Sadly, it is not that easy.

The concept of organisational learning originated with the writings of Chris Argyris and Donald Schön,[10] although it broke through into mainstream management consciousness in the 1990s with the publication of Peter Senge's *The Fifth Discipline*.[11] At the core of organisational learning is the idea of single- and double-loop learning.

Figure 5.3 shows what is meant by 'single-loop learning'.

In this diagram the process can be anything that the organisation does, perhaps manufacturing widgets. As it manufactures the widgets, it checks them to make sure they are within tolerance and as required and makes adjustments to the inputs to the process as necessary. It is learning how to make better widgets.

Now consider the development in Figure 5.4, which shows what is meant by 'double-loop learning'.

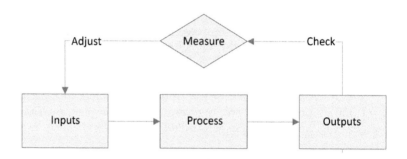

*Figure 5.3* Single-loop learning

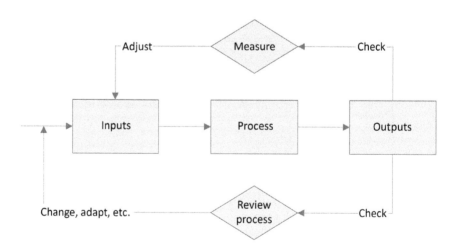

*Figure 5.4* Double-loop learning

Now, as well as checking the quality of the widgets, we question whether we are producing the right widgets or whether we should produce widgets at all. The organisation is now reflecting on its own practice and deciding whether it needs to change.

This seems a simple idea, but double-loop learning can be difficult to do in practice. For example, in training we may evaluate how well a training course has run and, if it has some weaknesses, make changes (single loop), but how often do we make a decision to change the delivery format or stop running the training because the problem is not amenable to training (double loop)?

## Complexity theory

Complexity theory is a field of study which emerged in the 1990s out of the earlier, more excitingly named chaos theory. The study of 'chaos' is often said to have started with research into meteorological patterns, where it was found that making tiny changes to the input conditions in computer models led to wildly different weather pattern predictions – hence the 'butterfly effect'. Subsequent work in other disciplines showed that chaotic patterns would often display an underlying order, and out of this observation grew the field of complexity. It is a field with many different related threads, and it is difficult to define complexity theory precisely, but it provides a way of studying the dynamics created by interrelationships within a system.

Before considering how complexity theory applies to performance improvement it is important to clarify the meaning of certain terms, in particular to distinguish between 'complex' and 'complicated'.

Sending a spaceship to the moon is a *complicated* problem. It requires enormous numbers of algorithms and powerful computers to do the necessary calculations and a sophisticated industrial infrastructure to build the rockets. But if we have the money and get our sums right, the rocket will almost certainly land on the moon.

On the other hand, bringing up a child is a *complex* problem. However well we are prepared, however many books we read, however much money we have and however much time we invest in caring for our child, the end result is quite unpredictable.

So what distinguishes complicated from complex? Paul Cilliers[12] has offered some characteristics of complex systems:

- They consist of a large number of elements which interact dynamically, so that they change over time.
- Interactions are not necessarily physical but can be simply exchanges of information.
- Interactions are rich, in that an interaction between two elements will have some impact on other connected elements.
- Interactions are non-linear, in that a small action by one element can have a large impact on another.

- Interactions may be acknowledged through feedback loops which create similar or different types of interaction.
- Complex systems are open and interact with their environment, drawing in energy in order to survive.
- Complex systems have a history which determines their present condition, and so the future is also dependent on the present.
- Each element in a complex system is only aware of its own behaviour and not of the system as a whole.

From this description we can see how a workplace can be regarded as a complex system. People work together, exchanging information, creating physical and virtual objects (such as values, norms, ideas and so on) and changing their environment. When one person passes some information to another person it will have an impact on them or others: it may make their lives easier or it may make them happy, angry or sad, depending on the nature of the information and the relationship that it indicates between the other people. If one person does something which contravenes a group norm, loops may give them feedback which could be helpful, encouraging or negative but which will in some way change the nature of working relationships.

This dynamic nature leads us to the idea of a *complex adaptive system*. Imagine that we have three people who work together. If one of them receives some training so that they can do their particular task better, what will happen? The outcome may be positive, but this is not guaranteed: the person's new skills may cause jealousy or resentment; they may want to change how things are done and this is not welcomed; the two other workers may not cooperate; there may be a hidden, shared understanding about how well the team should operate and so on. As human beings, the new conditions will lead to a change in behaviour (a new and emergent property), and there will be both predictable and unpredictable consequences. Overall productivity may or may not change, and interpersonal dynamics will adjust to a new state.

Complex adaptive systems are *non-linear*, in that increasing the levels of knowledge and skill of a group of workers does not necessarily mean a proportional increase in efficiency or effectiveness. For example:

- the newly skilled workers may leave the organisation for better-paid jobs, perhaps with competitors
- physical issues in the workplace may mean that they cannot improve their efficiency or effectiveness at all (for example, due to constraints in the equipment they use)
- a small, critical comment by someone in the team could have a huge impact on another person's or the whole team's motivation or behaviour.

What can be said about the emergent properties of complex adaptive systems is that they are often unpredictable and unexpected.

The concept has implications for training evaluation. As the actors in a complex adaptive system interact with each other and the environment and new behaviours emerge, the operating conditions for each actor change. This means that it is possible that the situation which prompted an organisation to design and deliver a training programme may have changed; it may have got better or worse, irrespective of what the training has done. However, the objectives for the training will have been set at the outset of the design project, which means that following a traditional approach to training evaluation, we may be assessing the programme against objectives which are no longer relevant and which may even be damaging to the organisation should the system have evolved in particular ways. We can see that this is the same problem as identified by the application of Vickers's appreciative system approach.

As described previously, complex systems operate far from equilibrium, drawing in energy from the environment and integrating the interactions among different elements to maintain a dynamic stability. In organisational terms we can conceive of these interactions as being such things as customer-facing staff recognising the variety in their operational environment and doing what is necessary to minimise the environmental variety or increase their own control variety. This information (in effect, energy) is fed into the adaptive system of the organisation, and it is then processed in order to become 'best practice'. However, at the same time the centre of the organisation will be developing practice which is needed in order to further the aims of the organisation strategically or to make the running of the organisation operationally efficient. There is therefore potentially a tension between what staff who interact directly with the operational environment think to be necessary and the standardised requirements of corporate headquarters. Mike Jackson[13] refers to this as a tension between 'shadow' and 'legitimate' systems: if the shadow system dominates, organisational practice may become inconsistent and chaotic, whereas if the legitimate system dominates, the overall system moves towards stability and equilibrium and the organisation will become less effective.

Julian Orr's 1996 book *Talking About Machines*[14] was an ethnographic study about how photocopier repair technicians went about their work but which provided the stimulus for significant subsequent research into informal learning and communities of practice by many other researchers. Orr described how nominally the technicians' work was carried out using troubleshooting flowcharts provided in official manuals, but often technicians had to work on machines installed in difficult (and non-standard) environments (noisy, dusty, hot, cold and so on), and they found faults that were not amenable to the standard solutions. The legitimate approach to problem solving was failing. Instead, the technicians relied on each other, sharing 'war stories' and building up a shadow system of informal knowledge that they could draw on when encountering a 'non-standard' problem.

As a second example, I once worked on a training design project aimed at increasing the sales effectiveness of financial advisers. We gathered information on sales techniques from high-performing advisers who described to us how they made their sales in the real world (the shadow system). But when we incorporated this advice into draft training materials and submitted it for approval to the head of training (the legitimate system), she blanched and stopped the project until we made certain fundamental changes. From reading our materials, she had come to realise that the advisers were using techniques which were not, shall we say, altogether compliant with the existing regulatory framework. The shadow system had effectively gone out of control.

What would have been needed in these examples was for there to be a balance between the shadow and legitimate systems, which is described as the *edge of chaos*. In training terms this might be seen as providing instruction which delivers centrally approved content but at the same time enables enough flexibility for staff to be able to cope in real time with the environment's variety. If training staff are to understand how their training is to operate at the edge of chaos they need to have a good understanding of the whole operational context, of how both shadow and legitimate systems work.

This proposition that training needs to support people so that they can work at the edge of chaos raises issues for, amongst other things, the certification of training. Certification is a model drawn from the educational sector, where people study a centrally developed curriculum and need to pass a standardised test in order to receive official confirmation of competence. From a complexity perspective we can see that this makes it very difficult for the content of a certificated course to be flexible enough to meet the variety of demands created by the workplace. The knowledge that staff are certificated to a common, externally verified standard may be reassuring to training managers, but this does not necessarily mean that workplace performance will be optimised. Instead, there is a danger that the end goal of staff members becomes the acquisition of a certificate rather than of learning to carry out their workplace responsibilities to the desired standard.[15]

Complexity theory has become very popular in recent years, but it has been criticised as not actually being supported by real proof of the existence of what it describes and as something of a 'repackaging' of earlier ideas.[16] For example, its discussion of the shadow system dealing with disorder in the environment is very similar to Ashby's concept of requisite variety. Some of the key ideas of complexity theory, that systems can oscillate between stability and chaos in somewhat predictable ways, are based on observations of the natural world (such as meteorological phenomena and forest fire cycles) where the vagaries of human nature are not factors. Also, for our purposes it does not provide a ready-made set of 'tools' which we can use in the needs analysis or evaluation process. Nevertheless, it provides a number of useful concepts to use when considering organisational behaviour.

### Wicked problems

In the previous section we distinguished between complex and complicated in order to develop a clearer understanding of complexity theory. We saw how complexity can be used to reflect on the nature of training design, but now we can take these ideas further into the reality of the workplace by considering the idea of a 'wicked problem', a concept which was introduced by Horst Rittel and Melvin Webber[17]. In a seminal paper, they outlined 10 characteristics of a wicked problem. We can look at them here, and see how a typical workplace performance problem can be seen as wicked.

### There is no definitive formulation of a wicked problem

We will all have experienced the problem of people looking at a situation from different perspectives. How do we describe a problem in the workplace? Because reality is socially constructed, each actor in a system will have their own perspective, and each one will define the problem differently; there is not enough time to do the job; the instructions are unclear; we have not had the necessary training; the other department gets in the way, and so on. Every actor will define the problem in their own way, and each definition has its own validity.

So because there is no single definitive description of the problem, there can be no clear 'right answer'. An initial drawing of boundaries will have an impact on how we describe the situation of interest and what we recommend about solutions.

### Wicked problems have no stopping rule

Because there is no definitive formulation of the problem, there can be no definitive criterion of success. This means that we can never be sure if we have succeeded.

Training programmes are based around learning objectives, but these will be only partial definitions of the problem (which cannot be definitively defined). By choosing appropriate criteria we can almost always show that training is 'effective', for example by basing the evaluation of a workshop on how much people enjoyed it. So even if an evaluation suggests that the objectives have been met, expanding the scope or changing the focus of the evaluation will almost certainly identify people who disagree.

### Solutions to wicked problems are not true or false but good or bad

Again, because a performance problem cannot be described definitively we cannot design a training course which is exactly what is needed so that everything becomes perfect. All we can hope for is that it makes things better in some way.

### There is no immediate and no ultimate test of a solution to a wicked problem

Because performance problems involve multiple relationships between people, equipment, processes, procedures and so on, any change that we make to the people will create a ripple of changes throughout the system, some good and some bad.

We can never therefore say that a training programme is completely successful or unsuccessful. For example, we might evaluate a training programme after three months and find that it seems to have had an impact then find that after 12 months it has caused major problems. Depending on when we carried out the evaluation we could decide that the training had been successful or unsuccessful.

In one evaluation I carried out into the effectiveness of management training programmes for local staff in an east African country, I found that while there was no clear evidence that managerial skills had improved, the trainees thought the programme was very important because it enhanced their self-perceptions of ability when working with expatriate colleagues: the attempt to improve one wicked problem inadvertently proved to be effective at improving another one.

### Every solution to a wicked problem is a one-shot operation

As soon as we implement a change within a complex system, the situation changes. If we stop the implementation the situation will continue to change, but we will not go back to the original situation.

So if we implement a training programme which is ineffectual for some reason, it may make the situation worse than before by making people sceptical about future training. Stopping the delivery of the programme will not restore the situation to how it was originally.

### Wicked problems do not have a finite set of potential solutions

There is an infinitely long list of things that we can do to improve what is happening in a wicked problem. What we identify as a solution to a performance problem is based on the perspectives of people involved in the analysis process, political requirements, practical constraints and so on.

So there are an infinite number of non-training interventions that we could make and possible training programmes that we can design and deliver.

### Every wicked problem is essentially unique

Every situation is different in terms of organisational location, the people involved, the time of year and so on. Similar problems may occur in different organisations, but they will never be exactly the same, as the culture, timing, significance and so forth will all be different.

This means that a solution for solving a performance problem (such as a training programme) which works well in one organisation to deal with a particular issue may be completely ineffectual when tried in another, with a different context. We should therefore be wary of 'off-the-shelf' solutions.

### Every wicked problem can be considered to be a symptom of another problem

Problems are interrelated. What happens in one problem will probably have a knock-on effect in another problem (see Figure 5.5).

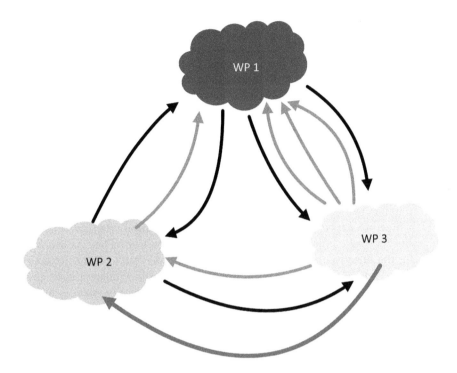

*Figure 5.5* Wicked problems affect each other

So a training programme designed to improve the effectiveness of Department A may be rendered completely ineffectual by problems occurring in Department B. Similarly, Department A's training programme may actually make life worse in Department C. Training which makes the sales process more effective may put pressure on production staff to meet extra demand, which they then cannot meet, making marketing's role more problematic and so on.

Some of the literature on training evaluation suggests that to isolate the effects of training we should have control groups (the idea of the randomised control trial is sometimes regarded as the 'gold standard' methodology for evaluation in general) who do not receive any training so that we can then compare the outcomes.[18] However, because each group of workers is its own complex adaptive system and wicked problem, their behaviour may well change if they are aware of being 'singled out' or excluded.

A needs analysis needs to take into consideration which wicked problems have some form of impact on the performance situation we are examining and to try to assess how significant they are. Training and non-training solutions need to think about what impact they may have not just on our specific situation of interest but on other, interrelated situations.

### How a problem is defined affects the nature of the solution

As there are multiple ways of defining a problem there will be multiple ways of trying to solve it.

If a problem is defined as being due to a lack of knowledge or skill, training will be seen as a potential solution. If the problem were defined as having motivational roots the solution defined would be quite different. We are back to the problem caused by multiple perspectives.

### The planner has no right to be wrong

A person making decisions about actions taken to solve a problem becomes responsible and liable for the consequences.

A training manager therefore finds themselves in a thankless position in which they are expected to implement solutions to improve a situation, but in reality they have little control over what actually happens. They are asked to evaluate the effectiveness of their training programmes, but actually the combined effects of no direct causal relationship, the time delays inherent in designing and delivering training, the dynamics of complex adaptive systems and so on means that using traditional, conventional approaches they will find it hard to demonstrate success.

### What the concept of wicked problems implies

To the reductionist thinker the concept of wicked problems seems extremely daunting. Reductionism requires us to break problems down into simple elements and to tackle each one at a time, but looking at human activity systems as a nest of wicked problems makes us realise that we must be more sophisticated in our analysis and thoughtful in our evaluation.

Each time we implement some form of performance improvement solution, the situation changes. Small, evolutionary solutions may be more effective than one-shot blockbusters. When we look to measure the impact of a solution, we need to look more widely than just an immediate impact and consider how the solution has changed other related wicked problems.

Scenario planning is a technique which has grown out of the recognition of the realities of wicked problems. The traditional approach to planning may be described as rationalistic: we predict the future, define a set of goals to be achieved and implement a strategy that will lead to their achievement. This works with a well-defined and predictable future but can fail miserably if the future does not turn out as expected. Scenario planning, on the other hand, follows a *processual* paradigm.[19] Working within this paradigm, planners consider what likely futures there may be (positive, negative, hostile, friendly etc.) and identify what strategies will be needed in order for the organisation to operate successfully in each future. They then try to identify a strategy which offers the greatest chance of success in whatever future appears. Note the emphasis here on maintaining a relationship with reality rather than working towards an abstract goal, as discussed in the earlier section on appreciative systems.

## Summary

The aim of this chapter has been to explore some key concepts relating to systems thinking and to consider what relevance they may have for training. In subsequent chapters we will be constantly referring to these concepts, so it would be useful before moving on to summarise some of the key observations.

There are three basic approaches to systems methodologies:

* *functionalist*, which see the world as a system (and focus on relationships)
* *interpretive*, which construct the idea of a system in order to reflect on reality (and focus on perspectives)
* *emancipatory*, which focus on power relationships within systems and the implications this has for boundaries.

Which we choose depends on the context, but in practice the distinction between functionalist and interpretive is not necessarily important as long as we recognise the difference.

The chapter continued with a discussion about various concepts which are used within systems thinking. This included a certain amount of repetition and overlaps between different ideas, so to summarise it will be useful to see how we can draw these together in a description of the dynamics of a general organisational performance situation. In conceptual terms this is represented in Figure 5.6.

Within this diagram we have three *wicked problems* (WP 1, 2 and 3). WP 1 and WP 2 represent organisational functions, perhaps production and sales. We can choose to represent an organisational department as a wicked problem because in reality organisations are not composed of a set of smoothly running gear wheels, all driving each other smoothly and silently. Instead, they are jumbles of overlapping and interacting activities, which can never be definitively described, and their performance can never be perfect: it can just be made better or worse.

WP 3 is the operational environment, constantly changing and always with an ill-defined mixture of opportunities and constraints.

Both WP 1 and WP 2 have an impact on the environment through their production and sales activities. These impacts will include *feedback*, the exchange of information, and this is a crucial element to the maintenance of systems. Impacts also change the nature of the wicked problem within the environment, so that the feedback received will constantly be changing. The effects that these exchanges between the wicked problems will be *non-linear*, in that a small change may have a huge impact.

We must also be aware of *causality* existing or not existing. Causality is clear in mechanical systems but can only be inferred in human behaviour systems

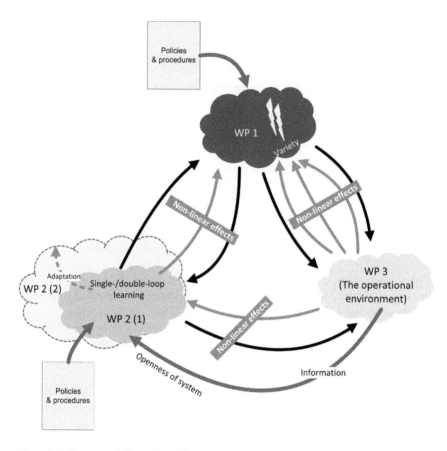

*Figure 5.6* Conceptual illustration of an organisational issue

due to the complexity of the way in which such systems behave. Just because people in WP 1 do something and the nature of WP 3 changes does not necessarily mean there is a causal connection.

The impact of WP 3 on WP 1 is shown as presenting the latter with a variety of challenges with which it must deal. In order to be able to work successfully within the environment, people working within WP 1 have to be able to make as many decisions about what to do as there are challenges presented by the environment. This is the principle of Ashby's *Law of Requisite Variety*.

The ability to deal with this variety will depend on the ability of the people within WP 1 to balance the central requirements of the organisation's policies and procedures with the range of demands that they face. Drawing on complexity theory, they will need to operate at the *edge of chaos*, where they will work optimally if they can achieve this balance. If they cannot achieve this balance, there will be constant tension between the legitimate and shadow systems over getting things done.

Figure 5.6 shows WP 2 as an *open system*, meaning that it accepts information being provided by WP 3. Information represents energy, and this ability to absorb and utilise information means that the actors within WP 2 can continue to operate and reach an appropriate steady level of performance (a dynamic equilibrium). This change in the nature of WP 2 is an example of a *complex adaptive system*, in which the people working in it adapt what they are doing to deal with the new situation and develop a new dynamic equilibrium.

If the actors in WP 2 do absorb information and act on it so that they change the nature of their wicked problem, we may consider that they are practising *double-loop learning*. If they merely continue to improve the same things that they have always done (*single-loop learning*), their survival may be short term.

Changing the nature of their wicked problem is an example of *emergence*: changing configurations within WP 2 as a result of double-loop learning creates a new set of properties or behaviours which the original configuration did not have. Emergent properties may be intended or unintended, desired or not desired.

Because of the wider dynamics of this situation, delivering training to people within a workgroup in WP 1 or WP2 may not have any impact at all if these dynamics militate against it

This conception of organisational activity from a systems perspective has many implications for training, which will be covered in more detail later. One challenge is caused by the dynamic nature of what is happening and the implication that has for analysing training needs. Using the concept of an *appreciative system* we need to remember that the solutions we identify in an analysis are based on what was important at the time of the analysis, not of what is actually important at the time of implementation. The emphasis in finding solutions to performance problems should therefore be in maintaining a desired relationship with reality rather than on developing a static set of skills.

In the following chapter we will look at some specific tools which have been developed to help us work with these concepts.

## Notes

1 Jackson, M.C., 2000. *Systems Approaches to Management*, Kluwer Academic/Plenum Publishers, New York.

2 Flood, R. & Jackson, M.C., 1991. *Creative Problem Solving: Total Systems Intervention*, Wiley, New York.

3 Flood & Jackson, 1991, op. cit.

4 For more discussion about the dynamics of group behaviour, see West, M., 1996. Working in Groups, in Warr, P., ed., *Psychology at Work*, Penguin, London, pp. 359–382.

5 For more information, see: https://en.wikipedia.org/wiki/Hawthorne_effect, accessed 15 April 2016.

6 Gilbert, T.F., 2007. *Human Competence: Engineering Worthy Performance*, Pfeiffer, San Francisco.

7 Based on Checkland, P. & Casar, A., 1986. Vickers' Concept of an Appreciative System: A Systemic Account. *Journal of Applied Systems Analysis*, 13, pp. 3–17.

8 Checkland, P., 1985. From Optimizing to Learning: A Development of Systems Thinking for the 1990s. *Journal of the Operational Research Society*, 36(9), pp. 757–767.

9  Ashby, W.R., 1956. *An Introduction to Cybernetics*, Chapman and Hall Ltd., London.
10 Argyris, C. & Schön, D., 1978. *Organizational Learning: A Theory of Action Perspective*, Jossey-Bass, San Francisco.
11 Senge, P.M., 1990. *The Fifth Discipline: The Art and Practice of the Learning Organization*, Century Business, London.
12 Cilliers, P., 1998. *Complexity & Post-Modernism: Understanding Complex Systems*, Routledge, London, pp. 3–5.
13 Jackson, 2000, op. cit.
14 Orr, J.E., 1996. *Talking About Machines: An Ethnography of a Modern Job*, Cornell University Press, Ithaca, NY.
15 Sfard, A., 1998. On Two Metaphors for Learning and the Dangers of Choosing Just One. *Educational Researcher*, 27(2), pp. 4–13.
16 Jackson, 2000, op. cit.
17 Rittel, H.W. & Webber, M.M., 1973. Dilemmas in a General Theory of Planning. *Policy Sciences*, 4(2), pp. 155–169.
18 Kirkpatrick, D.L., 1994. *Evaluating Training Programs*, Berrett-Koehler, San Francisco; Tamkin, P., Yarnall, J. & Kerrin, M., 2002. *Kirkpatrick and Beyond: A Review of Models of Training Evaluation*, Institute for Employment Studies, Brighton.
19 Van der Heijden, K., 1996. *Scenarios: The Art of Strategic Conversation*, Wiley, New York.

# 6 Tools to help systems thinking

In the previous chapter we looked at some important concepts in systems thinking. In this chapter we will look at some actual systems thinking tools which we can use when carrying out a training needs analysis or a training evaluation. Here we will look generally at how these methods work, and in Chapters 8 and 10 we will draw on the tools to show how they are used in specific training-related situations.

We will look at:

- how to use different types of diagrams to help with our thinking
- System Dynamics, a technique for using feedback loops in order to develop a clear understanding of how a system evolves over time
- the Viable System Model, a tool for reflecting on how an organisation functions
- Social Network Analysis, a way of quantifying and developing a visual representation of the way in which people interact
- Soft Systems Methodology, which helps us to reflect on reality by developing a theoretical model of how a situation might work
- Critical Systems Heuristics, an emancipatory approach which helps us to explore issues of power within a system and to define boundaries.

## Diagramming

Before looking at some specific systems thinking tools, we need to think briefly about one of the most useful generic tools that we can use, which is drawing diagrams. A picture is worth a thousand words, as is often said, and this is particularly important in systems thinking, where we are often grappling with a complicated set of actors and relationships. Rather than try to describe this in words, we can draw a picture.

Drawing diagrams with stakeholders is always useful and can often generate a considerable amount of interest and energy. Depending on the nature of the people you are working with, the activity may need to be approached with some care, as people can become somewhat intimidated by the thought of having to 'draw in public'. However, regardless of drawing ability, the process stimulates discussion, helps clarify confusion and produces a very useful summary of data collected.

So what are some of the diagramming techniques that may be useful?[1] This section describes some generic diagramming techniques, and we shall look at some other techniques which are specific to particular systems tools later.

### System maps

We looked at system maps earlier, when discussing the idea of boundaries (Chapter 2).

Figure 6.1 is a system map drawn to help clarify which organisations were involved in humanitarian activities in a particular country. This diagram was initially created on a flipchart pad using Post-its, which made it easier to move things around. Its creation started by asking stakeholders to identify which types of organisation were relevant to the delivery of various programmes,

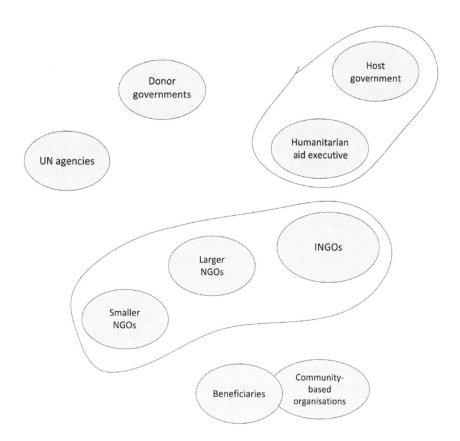

*Figure 6.1* Map of relevant organisations

and so through a process of discussion and negotiation this grouping was decided.

Drawing lines to enclose particular groupings of organisations creates a boundary between a system (inside) and environment (outside). Organisations inside work directly with each other, while organisations in the environment determine the operational context. In this particular system map, the two boundaries drawn create two systems, the non-governmental organisations (NGOs) and the host government agencies, as this was relevant to this particular exercise. Had the exercise been to consider some other aspect of programme delivery, we may have decided to draw a boundary enclosing 'UN agencies' and 'INGOs' (international NGOs) alone.

This shows that which organisations are inside or outside is not necessarily clear and may vary from situation to situation. Drawing a system map therefore helps with stimulating discussion about such things as who is in and who is out, or what are the most important relationships in this particular situation of interest?

### Multiple-cause diagrams

Multiple-cause diagramming is a technique that you can use to capture different factors contributing to a perceived problem. It is similar to the idea of the 'fish bone' or Ishikawa method. As with drawing a system map, you can do it on your own or with groups of people.

Figure 6.2 is a multiple-cause diagram that was drawn to understand some of the factors influencing the implementation of a programme for vaccinating

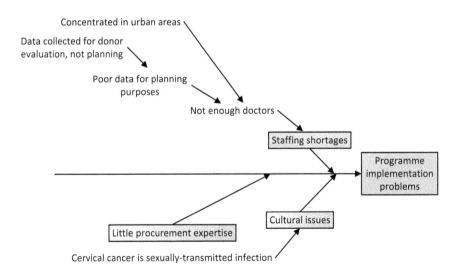

*Figure 6.2* Multiple-cause diagram about implementing a health programme

against cervical cancer in an ethnic minority group. It has been drawn using the Ishikawa structure.

To create a diagram such as this, start with the problem statement and ask, "Why is this happening?" For each answer (and you may come up with several), ask the question "Why?" again. Do this repeatedly to build up a picture of the different factors that are influencing the performance.

Figure 6.3 is a more complex multiple-cause diagram drawn in a less structured style. This explores some of the factors affecting an international company which was operating in the Middle East, where there were issues about expatriates and local staff working together. Creating the diagram showed that problems of inadequate English (the official operating language) amongst local staff and low salary levels were recurrent problems.

Such diagrams may be familiar to readers who have used a root-cause analysis technique for problem solving. When such techniques are used in this way, it is important to note that care needs to be taken not to just identify the key causes coming out of the analysis and find solutions for each one individually. This is reductionism in action and runs the risk of ignoring the relationships between different factors and the possibility of unintended consequences emerging from implementing individual solutions. For example, one problem is that local salaries are not competitive, but simply increasing salary levels may have other implications, such as creating new tensions within the workforce, distorting the local economy and so on. Multiple-cause diagrams should always be used as part of a systemic analysis and not be treated as a way of finding solutions quickly.

### *Influence diagrams*

Influence diagrams are useful when you want to understand more about how the relationships among different factors in a situation work. These may be physical entities, for example, how one group exercises influence over another, or abstract concepts such as funding levels, power, access to information and so on.

Figure 6.4 is an influence diagram showing organisations that are involved in different ways in a programme aimed at helping intravenous drug users. The thickness of the lines indicates the strength of the perceived influence, so here the police and national government are seen as having little influence over the behaviour of the drug user community, with most influence coming from community groups. This might help us understand that the most effective way of taking action to help such drug users would be to focus efforts through community groups rather than health providers, say.

Influence diagrams are similar to system maps, and having drawn one, it is fairly easy to draw the other. Drawing the lines of influence is the main difference: lines have an arrow to show the direction of influence, and we use thicker lines for stronger influence. If the influence flows both ways, draw two separate lines rather than use a line with arrows at each end.

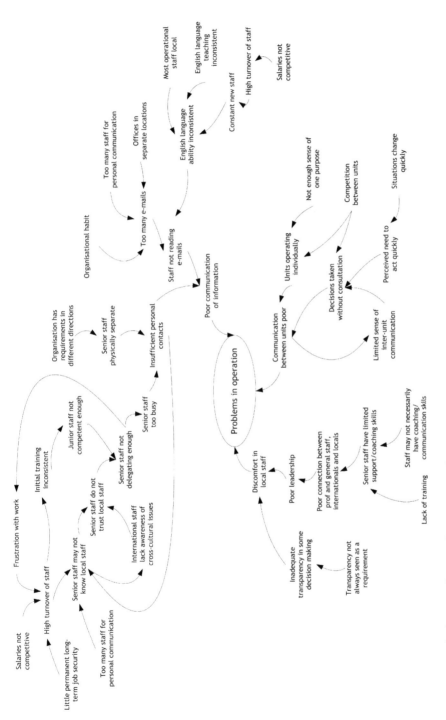

*Figure 6.3* Multiple-cause diagram about operational issues

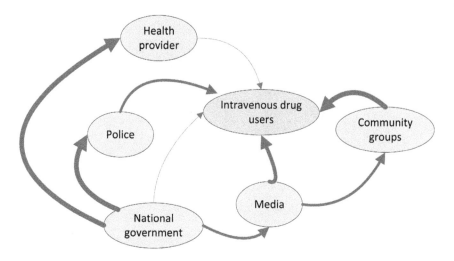

*Figure 6.4* Influence diagram about intravenous drug use

Influence diagrams are somewhat similar to the causal flow diagrams discussed in what follows and which are a key part of the System Dynamics methodology.

## System Dynamics

System Dynamics (SD) is an approach which developed out of work originally done by Jay W. Forrester at the Massachusetts Institute of Technology in the 1950s. As the name suggests, it takes a dynamic look at how situations develop. SD was the systems approach promoted by Peter Senge as 'the fifth discipline'.[2]

SD is a highly graphical method, relying on the development of *causal flow diagrams* which illustrate relationships and feedback mechanisms. Figure 6.5 is a causal flow diagram showing a situation in which a training department offers a training course and monitors its enrolment levels.

Before explaining what it illustrates, we must first explain diagramming conventions within causal flow diagrams. The items shown here are not objects but *levels* relating to aspects of running the training course. So for example, 'Popularity of course' means the level of popularity of the course. A line with an arrow is then drawn to another item, 'Enrolment', which indicates an effect that the first level has on the second level. This line is labelled with a '+' or a '−':

- Arrows with a '+' indicate a *direct* relationship – that is, if a factor increases (or decreases), the factor it influences also increases (or decreases)
- Arrows with a '−' indicate an *inverse* relationship, so if the factor increases (or decreases), the factor it influences decreases (or increases).

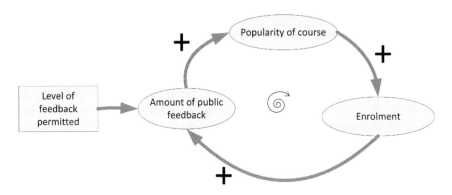

*Figure 6.5* Course enrolment causal flow diagram

Note the similarity of causal flow diagrams with influence diagrams, discussed previously. The nomenclature for such diagrams is not always consistent, and there are some differences between British and American usage. For consistency in this book we will refer to such diagrams as 'influence diagrams' if they are not signed to show the nature of the relationship (direct or inverse) and 'causal flow diagrams' if they are signed.

What does this diagram try to show us? The popularity has a direct effect on enrolment, and the more people enrol for the course the more feedback is provided on the course through the learning management system. Of course, this feedback in turn stimulates popularity, which increases enrolment, increases feedback and so on: this is called a reinforcing loop, and a convention is that this is indicated by a spiral inside the loop showing the direction of operation. Now, it may be that it is not possible to enrol a large number of people, and you do not want to have to continually disappoint people. You therefore need to look at a point in the loop where you can apply some leverage to slow the reinforcement effect down. Clearly, one place to do this is in regulating the amount of feedback that people see about the course. You restrict the amount of feedback, and demand for the course starts to slow down.

You may now see that if you restrict the amount of feedback too much, the loop then starts to send demand for the course into a tailspin. It stays as a reinforcing loop, but demand for the course gets less and less until nobody wants to enrol for it. The level of feedback you permit is therefore a throttle which you can use to control demand.

So wherever you have a reinforcing loop you can always look for a point of *leverage*, where you can control one of the factors in order to regulate the behaviour of the loop. Of course, because in reality a feedback loop will probably contain several different contributory factors, you may find that you have to be constantly opening or closing the throttle in order to maintain an approximately balanced loop.

SD is generally regarded as a functionalist methodology (that is, the world is a system). Where the reality of the world can be quantified in different ways, it becomes amenable to computer modelling, and online software is available which you can use to create dynamic models.[3] Such models can then provide dynamic simulations of behaviour, calculating values for *stock* and *flow*. Stock refers to the level of each factor, while flow describes the rate at which each factor changes. With a computer model you can vary the rates of flow and see what this means in terms of stock levels. For example, here flow would be the rate of enrolment and the stock would be the number of learners enrolled.

As the use of such diagrams has become more widespread, SD has started to be used in an interpretive way to help people reflect on a situation of interest (as a map rather than as the territory). When used in this way quantitative modelling is much less relevant, and this application of SD is sometimes called *qualitative system dynamics*. There is some disagreement within the systems thinking community as to the value of this qualitative approach, but for the non-systems specialist using such diagrams can help physically express mental models and assumptions and explore potential interrelationships and unintended consequences.[4] It is this qualitative use of SD that we will draw on extensively through this and other chapters.

Figure 6.6 is an example of a qualitative use of SD. What does this diagram try to explain? It illustrates one problem that the training community faces, one which was an issue in which Chris Argyris (who, as described in the previous chapter, was one of the originators of the concept of organisational learning) had a particular interest. As he conducted extensive research with successful management consultants in the United States, he noted the tendency for successful consultants to be defensive about their ongoing professional development.

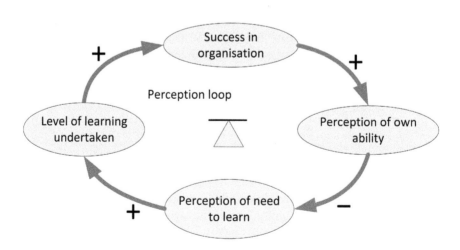

*Figure 6.6* Causal flow diagram showing defensive learning

What we are suggesting here is that as a person within an organisation enjoys higher levels of success (promotion, high pay, status etc.) their perception of their own ability increases (direct relationship). As their perception of their ability increases they may feel they have less need to learn anything new (inverse relationship) and so take part in fewer training opportunities (direct relationship). As their participation in training declines and they acquire fewer new skills their success in the evolving organisation may decline (direct relationship).

This is different to what we saw in the previous diagram, as it shows a tendency to move towards a stable condition – in this case, that an individual's level of success will reach a certain point and then stop. This is an example of what we call a *balancing* loop, which we can show by including a small 'balance' symbol inside the loop.

We can work out what sort of loop we have from the logic of the diagram, but one quick and easy way to do this is to look at the number of minus signs (inverse relationships) in a loop: if there is an even number of these, the loop will be reinforcing, while if it is odd (as in this case) it will be balancing.

Now consider Figure 6.7, in which we are developing the sophistication of the model. Notice also that we have labelled the loops to make it easier to talk about them and have added symbols to indicate that these are balancing loops.

As the individual undertakes less training, they may lose the ability to innovate (Innovation loop), which will have a further direct impact on their success, particularly when compared to other individuals who may be more innovative.

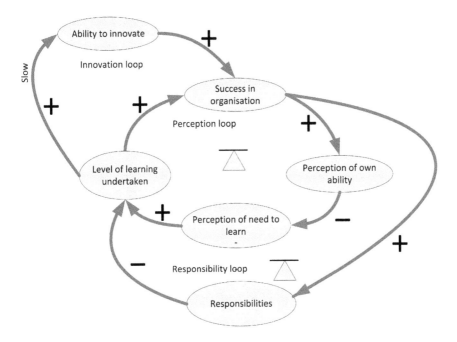

*Figure 6.7* Causal flow diagram showing impact on innovation

Note here that the arrow connecting the level of learning and the ability to innovate has been labelled as 'Slow' to remind us that this effect may not happen as quickly as other effects. Time delays in a causal flow diagram can be very significant, particularly when you have conflicting effects: one loop may produce a reinforcing effect in the short term, but another may exert a link in effect in the longer term.

At this point some readers may be disagreeing with what this diagram shows; they may think that these relationships do not work as shown, that they work the other way and so on. To think this is perfectly acceptable. What we are doing here is trying to create a 'map' of how we think senior people in organisations behave as far as training is concerned. In some cases we will be correct and in others we will not, but what the diagram does is to help us articulate a particular set of possibilities which could be useful as the basis for some discussion.

So, for example, if our analysis is deemed to have some validity, we may wish to consider questions such as:

- What steps can be taken to encourage senior managers to attend training programmes?
- How can the performance appraisal process be adapted to encourage people to continue attending training?
- What can be done to make sure senior staff have enough time to attend training?

SD is a very useful tool to use when thinking about how a number of activities may relate to each other and how things may change over time. For example, in Chapter 4 we discussed a number of possible reasons training evaluation is often problematic. Figure 6.8 is a causal flow diagram which attempts to summarise these issues.

It suggests that we have two reinforcing loops in operation:

- The Expertise loop, where the lack of organisational support is limiting the possibility for developing an expertise in evaluation, which leads to evaluations which are not seen as effective, further reducing organisational support
- The Needs analysis loop, where the lack of support for a quality needs analysis means that training design is inadequate, which further weakens the evaluation process

As with all reinforcing loops, we need to look for points of leverage, where we may be able to provide some input which converts reinforced deterioration into constant strengthening. In this case we may be able to achieve this by providing some improved tools to help the evaluation process. If evaluation is seen as more effective, and it is clear that its effectiveness relies on a quality needs analysis, then more organisational support may be forthcoming.

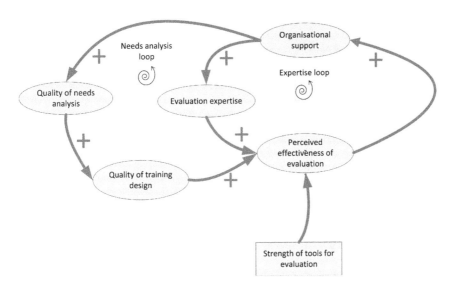

*Figure 6.8* Causal flow diagram linking factors affecting evaluation

The challenge with using SD in a qualitative way is that it is more suited to simple-unitary situations (where there are relatively few, well-organised elements and that there is a good level of agreement between them). This will probably not be the case in human behaviour systems, where the dynamics among participants will be affected by many different factors. So using SD to reflect on such systems should always be seen as more of a sense-making device rather than as a predictor of behaviour.

### Systems archetypes

As people have developed causal flow diagrams to make sense of real-world situations they observe, it has been found that certain patterns keep coming up. These are often known as *archetypes* and are given standard names. The *limits to growth* archetype is a common example and describes a reinforcing loop in which factors are combining to make something constantly improve but in which one variable triggers a slower, balancing loop which interacts with the reinforcing loop to slow it down. For example, consider Figure 6.9, which analyses the impact of a training intervention.

We provide training to a group of people so that their performance increases. This will increase enthusiasm about training, and their desire for learning increases: we have a reinforcing loop which tends to constantly drive performance up. However, while this happens quickly, over time increased levels of

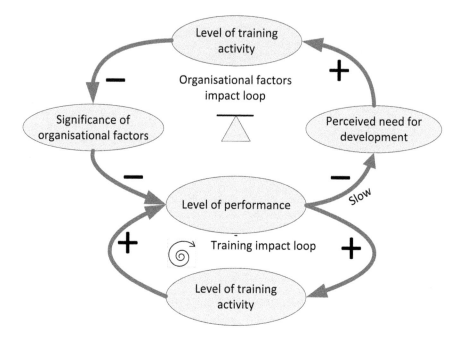

*Figure 6.9* Limits to growth archetype

performance mean that the perceived need for development goes down, and the importance attached to training goes down, so less is done. When this happens the significance of organisational factors affecting the level of performance goes up, and so this will drive the level of performance down. This is a balancing loop (an odd number of inverse relationships), and the overall result on levels of performance will depend on how big the organisational factors become. This particular archetype explains why it is important not to make automatic assumptions that training is an effective long-term solution to any performance problem.

## The Viable System Model

Stafford Beer (1926–2002) was a true British polymath: he worked as a manager in the steel industry, taught yoga, spoke Greek, Latin, Hindi and Spanish and knew Sanskrit, had eight children and also managed to find time to develop the Viable System Model (VSM).

VSM is a cybernetics-based[5] systems approach that developed out of reflections on how biological organisms function. Beer thought about how organisms interact with their environment and proposed a number of interconnected systems which are necessary for survival. He then related this to how

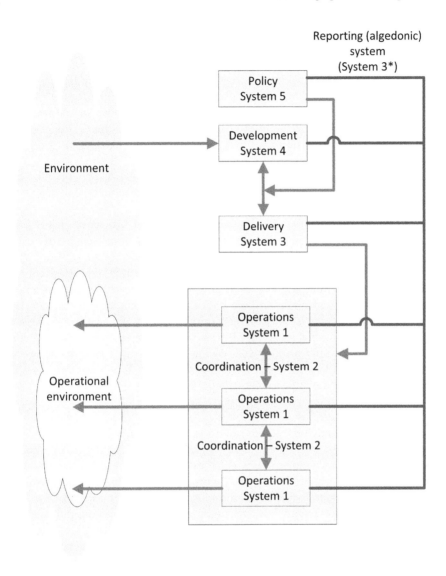

*Figure 6.10* The Viable System Model

an organisation functions, recognising that an organisation is an open system which needs to draw energy from its environment and utilise it in such a way that it constantly adapts to changing environmental conditions.

It is based around the concept of *viability*, which is seen as the ability of an entity to operate on its own by solving problems and making decisions. Refer- ring to the idea of requisite variety (see Chapter 5), such an entity must be able to display enough control variety to respond to the environmental variety which it faces. Starting from these principles, Beer developed the full concept of a viable system, which contains five distinct but connected systems, as illustrated in Figure.

The great strength of VSM comes from the fact that this same model can be used to assess the viability of an organisation's symptoms at different levels. So we can use it to analyse the overall effectiveness of the organisation, of each separate department, each team and each individual employee, should we wish to do so. In most cases we do not need to be as rigorous as this, and depending on the nature of our enquiry, we will probably only want to use the model at one or two levels.

### How the VSM works

It can be somewhat difficult to understand how the VSM works, so to help explain it I will talk about a hybrid biological-organisational system, the married couple.

My wife and I are (usually) a viable organisation. Our purpose is to have a meaningful and fulfilling existence, and to do this we have three primary systems through which we interact with our environment (the System 1s); we supply services to the environment to earn money, we buy fuel (food and energy) and we have a social life. But we have to keep these in balance; if I spend too much time working and writing books I cannot go to the shops to buy food, nor will I have a social life; if I spend too much time socialising I will not earn enough money. So to maintain the balance, my wife and I discuss what we are each doing and make sure we are happy about our work–life balances (System 2 conversations).

The System 1 activities require resources, time and money, and we use System 3 activities to allocate resources (such as by online banking and shopping lists). If the bank account becomes overdrawn or I become exhausted through too much work I need to let my wife know (System 3★, the reporting system).

To make sure our lives remain meaningful and fulfilling we observe the world around us to see how it is developing, and we reflect on this information to see what we need to do in order to adapt (System 4).

Finally our System 5 tells us what 'meaningful and fulfilling' mean to us. Is this about eating good food, enjoying the countryside or having expensive foreign holidays? Based on what we decide at this level we instruct System 4 to gather particular types of data and instruct System 3 to allocate resources differently.

So at the level of 'a couple' all of these systems function, and we are viable. This is usually referred to as the *system–in–focus*. However, each of our System 1 activities must also be able to operate on its own, to make decisions and solve problems, to be viable. If they were not, the whole couple system would be overwhelmed by the environmental variety of work, shopping and social possibilities.

This means that we can go down a level and consider each of these System 1s as having its own internal five interacting systems but at a lower level; in the case of work I have to understand the human resources industry in order to see what skills are needed (System 4), I have to decide what type of work is fulfilling to me (System 5) and so on. This illustrates the crucial feature of VSM, that the structure is *recursive*; in other words, we should be able to see this structure operating at different levels within the organisation because each System 1 at any level must be a viable system in its own right.

So in the organisational context, what are these separate 'systems'? A key thing to understand is that most of the systems in the model refer to information flows and not to organisational functions or departments. We consider functions or departments when examining them as System 1 entities.

For example, we can consider the overall functioning of the organisation. System 1 is the set of activities where at this level the organisation interacts directly with its local, operational environment: at this level this might be Production, Sales and Distribution. Each of these System 1s must be able to manage the variety present in the environment; otherwise the overall system will be swamped with variety-related problems. For example, if sales increase, the Sales department must be able to cope with this and not have to ask the rest of the organisation for assistance. System 1 therefore must be viable in its own right, and in order to do this it must have an appropriate amount of autonomy.

System 2 is the system that coordinates the different instances of System 1 to make sure that they know what each other is doing. At our organisational level this is the system which coordinates Production, Sales and Distribution. If sales increase, System 2 informs Production so that they can make more products and Distribution so that they can arrange the necessary logistics.

System 3 monitors the activities of Systems 1 and 2 and makes sure that they have the resources they need. At the organisational level System 3 ensures that each of these three departments has the information and financial resources that they need.

System 3★ is a 'pain-reporting' (sometimes referred to as the algedonic) system, carrying information back up the system about what is going well or not well. For example, if Sales is finding that sales are going down, it reports back through System 3★ so that System 4 can look more closely at the environment to see if the organisation's purpose is matching the variety that the environment is looking for.

System 4 monitors the environment to make sure that System 1 is doing what is necessary for the organisation to exist.

System 5 monitors the organisational activity to set policies and keep it moving forwards. At the organisational level System 5 will be concerned with the organisation's vision.

As described, we can then apply recursion and move down a level. This means that we can look at the Sales department and analyse the five systems within it. It will have its own System 1s, which will be the different functions within Sales which interact with the environment, such as marketing, invoicing and so on.

### Applying VSM at different levels of recursion

How does recursion show itself in an organisation? At the:

- *organisational* level we see how the organisation as a whole interacts with its environment and develops a structure which facilitates this by having different departments which carry out the organisation's necessary primary functions (for example, production, marketing, research and development).
- *departmental* level, say production, we have different operational functions such as design, manufacturing, assembly, quality control etc.
- *team* level, say for quality control, we have different operational functions such as inspection, record keeping, non-destructive testing and so on.

At whatever level we are working, each System 1 must be a viable system in its own right, which can then be analysed at the next lower level of recursion. It will contain its own Systems 1 to 5 which enable it to be autonomous.

### How to use VSM

How can we use VSM for needs analysis or evaluation? There are two ways in which VSM can be used:

- as a guide to help us set up necessary processes and procedures at each level within the organisation
- as a reference point, so that we can look at how the organisation is functioning as compared to how a viable system would be functioning

For us as training professionals, the second of these is the more useful. When carrying out a needs analysis we can see how well the real-world processes compare with the requirements of a viable system at that level and can then suggest actions which would increase viability. In the case of an evaluation, we can consider the degree to which a training programme contributes to viability at appropriate levels. For example, if working at the organisational level:

- Does the organisation have a clear vision or set of values that it works towards (System 5)?
- Is the organisation monitoring its environment effectively (System 4)?
- How well do internal processes which manage operational functions work (System 3)?
- How well do the different environment-facing functions within the organisation coordinate their activities (System 2)?
- How are the different environment-facing functions actually operating in terms of delivering the organisation's product to its customers (System 1)?

By carrying out the analysis at different levels (say, organisational, departmental and team) we can identify different areas where systems need attention in some way. At higher levels we will typically identify structural issues which need attention, while at lower levels we are more likely to find knowledge- and skill-related issues. The number of levels of recursion is determined by the boundaries within which a needs analysis is set, but in the case of an organisa- tion a three-level recursion is often appropriate, and, as we shall see in later chapters, this corresponds well with the requirements of the needs analysis process.

## Social Network Analysis

It has become a cliché of the early 21st century to say that we are all connected. Through mobile telephones, email and social media where we go, what we see and who we talk to are regularly shared with everyone; family, friends and the security services.

So while we have a fuzzy idea of our connectivity, what does that actually look like? Social Network Analysis (SNA) provides a way for us to do this. When we carry out an SNA we find out from individuals what their relation- ships are with other people. Exactly what we find out about their relationships depends on what we are investigating: for example, we might wish to know who they ask for information, who they give information to, how often they talk to other people and so on.

Then, based on this data, we can construct a diagram, sometimes called a sociogram, which depicts these relationships. Figure 6.11 is an example of a sociogram showing how well 14 individuals at a training workshop knew each other before the event. In such a diagram the individual elements are usually known as *nodes* and the lines connecting them as *edges*.

Note that the nodes in a social network analysis do not have to all be the same type of object: for example, you could have a mixture of individuals, departments and reference documents if you wanted to find out more about how information was being accessed or shared.

So what we can see is that person B has connections with seven other participants, while person D is only connected with three others. This socio- gram also contains other information indicated by the thickness of the lines: the thicker the line, the stronger the relationship, so that while participants C and D only knew each other slightly, A and E knew each other very well.

It is relatively simple to construct a survey which can gather this data, but interpreting it is extremely complex mathematically. However, there are a number of software packages readily available which can process data, create sociograms[6] and calculate indicators which measure certain aspects of the rela- tionship. Here are some examples of possible indicators:[7]

- *Degree centrality*, how many nodes to which each individual node is con- nected. In the example, node A is connected to five other nodes, while node I is connected to eight. In this sociogram, the size of each node is proportional to its centrality.

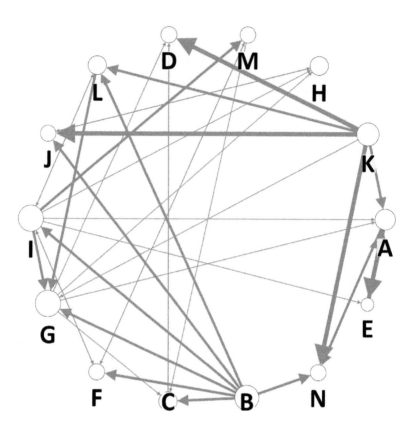

*Figure 6.11* Sociogram showing workplace relationships

- *Closeness centrality*, a measure of the average shortest distance from each node to each other node. The more highly connected the network, the higher these values will be: in our sociogram, person E is not well connected, so connections to many other nodes have to pass through another node, reducing their closeness centrality to 0.037. On the other hand person I, who is well connected, has a closeness centrality of 0.056.
- *Density*, the ratio of the actual number of connections in a network to the theoretical maximum, which indicates the overall level of 'connectedness': the density of the network shown is 0.341.
- *Tie strength*, a measure of the strength of connectivity between two nodes; in Figure 6.11 this is shown by the thickness of the connecting lines.
- *Reciprocity*, the degree to which a relationship works in two directions (for example, if information flows from one person to another only and not in the opposite direction, or if person A says they know person B well but person B says they do not know person A).

SNA can not only be used to explore the nature of interpersonal relationships ("How well do you know person X?") but can also be used to analyse information flows, such as who sends and receives emails to whom or which web or intranet pages are accessed by which people and how often. This makes it possible to develop a much clearer idea about what information circulates within a work group, what people find useful, and so on.

### The value of SNA in performance analysis and evaluation

What value might SNA data have in carrying out a performance analysis or an evaluation? A sociogram shows the relationships between individuals and so can show how information flows. It can help an analyst see a workplace as being a network of interdependent coworkers rather than as a collection of independent individuals and so can shine a light on the nature of relationships and communication within or between teams or departments. This can help with taking action to strengthen informal learning networks and can provide valuable information for developing a better understanding of the learning transfer climate (a concept which is discussed in more detail in Chapter 9) and so help with the design of training initiatives. It can show which people are seen as sources of help or information or wield some form of power.[8]

Sociograms can show individuals who have strong linkages between each other. A highly connected individual (such as K in Figure 6.11) could, for example, be a very useful person to act as a source of information for new processes or information or to act as a workplace coach.[9] Groups of people who form strongly connected networks may bring benefits, as they may share similar sets of values and knowledge, but may limit the possibility for new ideas to enter that particular group, so their performance may be inconsistent with other people.[10] Sociograms can also show cliques, tightly connected groups of individuals who have weak connections with other parts of the network. Such cliques can hoard useful information or act as some form of positive or negative influence on people outside the clique.

Contrasted to this are individuals with weaker connections, who may have different but possibly valuable knowledge to bring to the rest of the network.[11] This applies particularly to people who are on the periphery of one network but who may be well connected with other networks, which means that they have the ability to bring new information in, promoting innovation and helping prevent groupthink.[12] Of course, a sociogram may reveal individuals who seem to be isolated from others, which may raise other issues.

An evaluation carried out using SNA to compare different working groups could provide some useful clues as to differences perceived in the transfer of learning between the groups. This would be a useful independent measure of the learning transfer climate, which otherwise depends to a large extent on self-reporting.[13]

### The challenges of carrying out SNA

SNA has a lot of potential for helping us identify potential causes of poor performance or find ways to better target performance improvement strategies, but it is a challenging technique to employ.

First, there are practical difficulties in collecting the data. Whereas with conventional surveys we can be happy with a 10 or 20% response rate to interviews or surveys, to gather a complete and accurate picture of a social network we must have a 100% response rate. People declining to participate in the survey may be a sign of having too much other work to do, or it may be because they are withdrawing in some way from their work network, which may be highly relevant within the context of the survey. So gathering SNA data can be time-consuming and potentially politically difficult.[14]

We have to make a decision as to whether to analyse an open or a bounded network. In an open network we ask people to identify other individuals in their social network, while in a bounded network we provide a predetermined list of names and ask people to assess their relationship with these others. The two types of network call for a different survey methodology, and the analysis is quite different. Clearly, in an open network analysis there is much more possibility of inconsistency as to who identifies whom.

Perhaps most significantly there are serious ethical issues with SNA data. Conventional surveys can be anonymous so people are free to express their opinions. However, the whole idea of an SNA is for people to identify themselves and to define their relationships with other people. This can be very exposing, and people asked to provide data for a social network analysis can be rightly suspicious about the purposes to which the results will be put. For example, if the survey reveals an individual with very low connectivity, what action might be taken? Whereas in a traditional anonymous survey people consented to providing data, in an SNA survey they are compelled to do so. When data is published it can often be relatively easy for people to identify which nodes represent which individual.[15]

So in conclusion, while the data from a SNA survey can be very useful, in practice it needs to be done with great care and sensitivity.

## Soft Systems Methodology

Soft Systems Methodology (SSM) is an approach developed by Peter Checkland of Lancaster University. Although essentially an applied scientist, he dedicated most of his professional life to finding ways to make sense of the altogether messier world of management. SSM originated in the 1980s, growing out of an action research project in which Checkland was trying to see how to use the systems approaches employed in engineering projects to explore the 'softer' world of organisational issues. SSM is an interpretive systems approach: the methodology is used as a device to help us clarify our understanding about what is happening in real life.

SSM methodology has evolved considerably over the years and now includes a range of tools and techniques which can be used. To help with usability Peter Checkland distinguishes between what he calls Mode 1 and Mode 2 utilisation.[16] Mode 1 sees an explicit focus on the methodology of using SSM, working through the process sequentially, whereas in Mode 2 the situation of interest calls for the selective use of particular SSM techniques to gain clarity as required: in this mode the application of SSM is oriented towards the needs of the problem, so the process followed is much less explicit. The use of SSM within a training needs analysis or evaluation should very much be Mode 2. Readers who would like to study the process in more detail are referred to Checkland's various writings in the Notes section.[17]

For our specific purpose, the useful steps in a SSM analysis are to:

- draw a rich picture of the situation of interest
- develop a root definition (or definitions) of our situation
- draw conceptual models that can be compared to the situation
- use the conceptual model to generate questions which make us think about reality
- use responses to our questions to identify potential actions to take.

### Step 1: Drawing a rich picture

It is often difficult to follow the SSM process when first reading about it, so to help show where we are in the process, we will use this simple flowchart (as in Figure 6.12) at each step.

One of the most significant differences between a human activity system and a mechanical system is the complexity and ambiguity of relationships among elements of the system. It is much easier to capture these complexities in a picture than it is in text, and the idea of a rich picture is to provide some way of portraying key issues in a system. Pictures also help convey a more holistic description of a situation rather than the serial reductionism of a text description.[18]

At this point some readers may be shifting uneasily in their seats at the thought of drawing, but it is important to note that creating such a picture does not require artistic skills, and in fact these can get in the way, as the capable artist seeks to create a thing of beauty rather than concentrating on the capturing of who is involved and describing what they are doing.

*Figure 6.12* Step 1 of the SSM process

Figure 6.13 is an example of a rich picture (which illustrates the level of artistic skill needed), quickly drawn on a whiteboard by the author when contemplating the failure of the England football team in yet another international competition.

At the time when this rich picture was created there was considerable discussion in the English media about the preponderance of foreign players in the Premier League (sports pages), how overseas investors were buying up British businesses and property (financial pages), how British youth had stopped going outdoors to play games (society pages) and the increasing significance of immigration in British politics (politics pages). To create a prose description linking together these related issues would have taken a considerable amount of time (and writing skill), but drawing this rich picture, which provides a useful synthesis of a number of important issues, just took 10 or 15 minutes. Had other people been available at this time, the process of drawing the picture would have stimulated a considerable amount of discussion about what should be drawn first, what is most important, what is not relevant and so on. This discussion itself would have led to an increasing level of understanding amongst all participants of the issues afflicting English football.

Typically, in a needs analysis or evaluation project we would gather some initial data about the situation of interest, such as by talking to people with

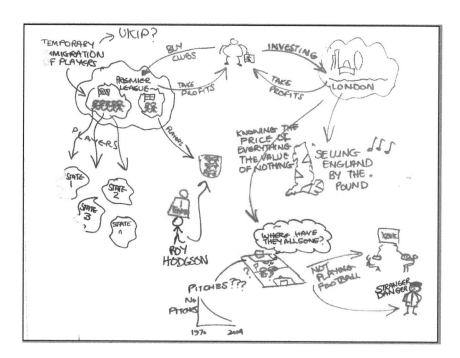

*Figure 6.13* The state of English football

some stake in the situation (managers, operational staff and so on) or carrying out some form of survey. This may well have provided a significant amount of information which needs to be organised in order to make more sense. This is the perfect time to create a rich picture.

So how do we draw a rich picture? Reflecting on these pictures and the processes used to create them, here are some guidelines for drawing rich pictures:

- Find flipchart paper or whiteboards and have different-coloured markers available.
- Where possible, make the drawing process a social activity, where different people with an interest in or knowledge of the situation contribute ideas and discuss what should be included or left out.
- Start by drawing elements (objects, individuals, institutions, concepts etc.) which have some relevance in the situation of interest. Place what seems to be most important at the centre of the picture.
- Draw relationships among the elements. Relationships include flows of resources, lines of communication, conflicts and so on.
- Use graphics wherever possible (for example, currency symbols to show money, crossed swords to indicate conflict etc.).

At first it can seem quite difficult to a draw rich pictures, and like all skills, drawing them requires practice. Some people can find it a little embarrassing to start drawing pictures in public, particularly senior ones. So build up confidence by practice, practice, practice. Every day for the next two weeks find some situation of interest which catches your attention, whether it is a crisis in world affairs, office politics or some family issue, and quickly sketch a rich picture. It soon becomes second nature to capture your perspectives in this way.

Rich pictures are intended to capture as much about a situation of interest as seems relevant; this will include actors, relationships, emotions, environmental factors and so on. This can make it difficult to extract specific pieces of information, so at this stage it is often also useful to draw a system map which just shows the actors. System maps are often useful in Step 2, where we need to create a root definition.

Multiple-cause diagrams can also be useful here. There is often a useful dynamic created between a rich picture and a multiple-cause diagram, where developing the two together can be an iterative process leading to enhanced understanding. As an example, look at Figure 6.14, which is another rich picture, this time put together to capture key issues relevant to deforestation. This was created at an early part of a project looking at how training could be used to help implement forestry maintenance projects.

This is complemented by Figure 6.15, which is a multiple-cause diagram looking at the same topic. The rich picture provided the initial ideas for the topic, and creating the multiple-cause diagram stimulated further discussion about the relationships between different drivers of deforestation.

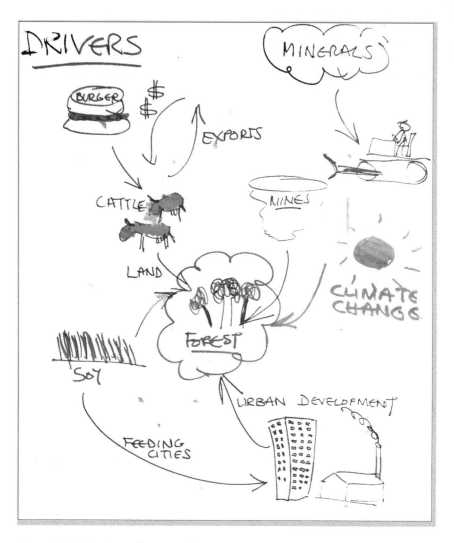

*Figure 6.14* Rich picture illustrating drivers of deforestation

### Step 2: Creating a root definition

Having created a rich picture which provides a visual summary of our situation of interest, the next step is to think more carefully about what our actual concern is and define it as some form of 'transformation'. For example, we have drawn this rich picture (Figure 6.14) because we want to enable some form of transformation relevant to deforestation. Such a transformation will be defined within a 'root definition', a statement which attempts to describe a *purposeful activity* or transformation that we would like to happen in the situation of interest.

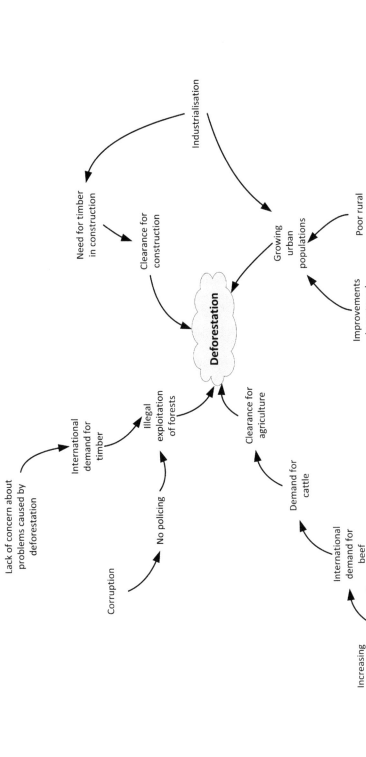

*Figure 6.15* Multiple–cause diagram explaining deforestation

In the SSM methodology we use a particular way of writing this definition, the PQR structure: to do P, by Q in order to achieve R. Within this structure we need to incorporate six distinct elements, which are represented by the acronym CATWOE:

- **C**ustomer(s), the beneficiaries or victims of the transformation T
- **A**ctor(s), the people carrying out the transformation T
- **T**ransformation, the purposeful activity
- **W**eltanschauung, a worldview which sets a context for the purposeful activity
- **O**wner(s), people who have the power to stop the purposeful activity
- **E**nvironment, the outside world which sets particular constraints

Identifying people or entities (the customers, actors and owners) will be easier here if we have created a system map in Step 1.

Within CATWOE, the *Weltanschauung* is of particular importance, as it leads to possible descriptions of transformations. A person's *Weltanschauung* describes their personal understanding of reality, and it derives from their culture, upbringing and experience.[19] In SSM it defines a perspective held by whoever is formulating the root definition and is implicit within it. This is why SSM is particularly useful for pluralist situations, in which people agree there is a need to collaborate to make decisions, but there are a range of possible opinions which may be hard to resolve. Each stakeholder in the situation will have their own perspective, and this perspective can be articulated by their *Weltanschauung*.

Table 6.1 shows some possible worldviews and associated transformations. These three could have been written down by three different people, each of which has a different interest in the situation; for example, these could have been prepared by a politician, an environmentalist and a farmer respectively.

*Table 6.1* Possible *Weltanschauungen* and transformations

| Person holding the worldview | Weltanschauungen | Possible transformation (T) |
| --- | --- | --- |
| Politician | Deforestation is caused by a complex interaction of drivers. | People who do not understand connections are transformed into people who understand connections between drivers. |
| Environmentalist | Managing forest resources is an important part of dealing with climate change. | Forest resources which are not managed are transformed into resources which are managed with reference to climate change issues. |
| Farmer | Agriculture and forestry management are closely connected. | Disconnected agriculture and forestry sectors are transformed into sectors with strong connections between them. |

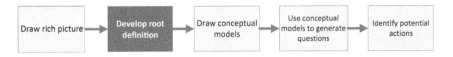

*Figure 6.16* Step 2 of the SSM process

The *Weltanschauungen* are all valid and worthy of consideration, as they each reflect a different perspective based on the observer's interests, experience, values and so forth.

Notice how the transformations here represent both potential training (improving people's understanding) and non-training strategies, showing how the SSM process can broaden our understanding of actions which could be taken. It should be clear that there are many different worldviews and associated transformations which could be included in this situation. This would be expected, as we are looking at a classic 'wicked problem', as discussed in Chapter 5. Exploring this ambiguity and multiplicity is one of the strengths of SSM, as it forces us to question our own (as analyst) perspective and those of other actors. This means that working through SSM may give us a number of different root definitions, each one leading to different perspectives on potential solutions.

We then write a root definition that contains the CATWOE elements and which reflects a particular worldview. Here are the CATWOE elements for the first worldview defined earlier.

| | |
|---|---|
| Customer | National government |
| Actor | People with influence in a particular country |
| Transformation | People who do not understand connections transformed into people who understand connections between drivers |
| *Weltanschauung* | Deforestation is caused by a complex interaction of drivers |
| Owner | National government |
| Environment | State where deforestation is considered to be a problem |

This leads to the following possible root definition:

A system owned by and operated for national government staff which creates an understanding of connections between drivers of deforestation in people with influence by providing learning opportunities in order to better manage national forest resources.

Notice the PQR structure:

| | |
|---|---|
| Do P | . . . which creates an understanding of connections between drivers of deforestation in people with influence . . . |
| By Q | . . . by providing learning opportunities . . . |
| To achieve R | . . . to better manage national forest resources . . . |

As each root definition reflects a particular *Weltanschauung*, we should always seek to create several different root definitions at this stage, each one based on a different *Weltanschauung*.

There are some clear parallels between creating a root definition and defining an overall objective for a training programme, and in fact this process can be very useful as part of the process for developing such an objective. The added value of the SSM process so far is in helping us think through the real issues which the training and other initiatives should be seeking to address. Working through the process several times using different *Weltanschauungen* is to be recommended, even if this is the only part of the SSM process which is used.

### Step 3: Drafting a conceptual model

Now (as shown in Figure 6.17) armed with our root definition, we need to put together a conceptual model (Figure 6.18), a sequence of activities which would allow this to happen.

*Figure 6.17* Step 3 of the SSM process

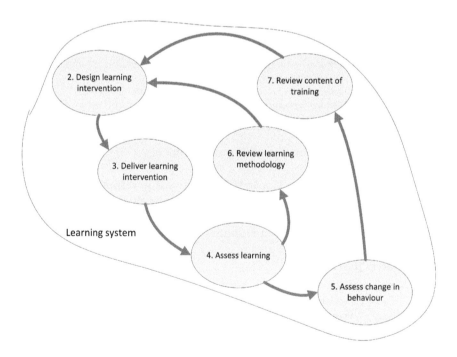

*Figure 6.18* Partial conceptual model for improving understanding

As this model exists at the moment, it has a process built in for single-loop learning: are people changing behaviour in the desired way? However, to complete the model we need to build in double-loop learning, the ability to question whether the change of behaviour is the appropriate change. To do this we add an external quality control mechanism, as shown in Figure 6.19.

This complete conceptual model builds in three levels of quality control:

- *efficacy* – are people developing an understanding? (Step 5)
- *efficiency* – is a learning process such as this the best use of resources? (Steps 7 and 8)
- *effectiveness* – are the people who have completed the learning process developing better policies for managing forestation? (Steps 7 and 8)

Step 5 asks if a single-loop learning process is happening, and Steps 7 and 8 question the whole system, representing double-loop learning.

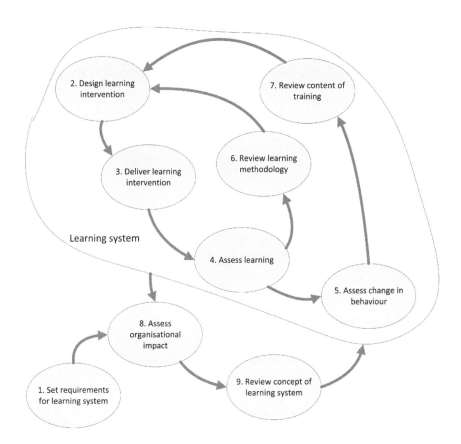

*Figure 6.19* Complete conceptual model for improving understanding

There are some things to note about this model:

- It is only a device to help thinking and does not intend to represent the best or ideal way of doing things.
- It does not describe the process itself but is just a way of reflecting on the process.
- There are many different conceptual models that we could develop, and each one would enrich our understanding.

Conceptual models are usually created using a structure such as in this example, with a core system describing the main transformation and an external quality control process. It should all be kept as simple as possible, with no more than about nine individual steps (remembering Miller's ideas about short-term memory only being able to deal with $7 \pm 2$ items[20]). Each step is numbered, as this helps in the next part of the SSM process.

### Step 4: Comparing the conceptual model with reality

The aim of developing a conceptual model is to compare it with reality, so that we can reflect on what needs to be done or changed. We next therefore (as in Figure 6.20) look at each of the steps in the model and see what questions this raises for us. Table 6.2 illustrates the sorts of questions which are raised at

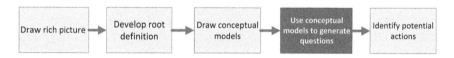

*Figure 6.20* Step 4 of the SSM process

*Table 6.2* Questions arising from the conceptual model

| Step | Question |
|---|---|
| 1 | What is the knowledge and skill needed? |
| | Where will we find the appropriate knowledge and skill to include in the programme? |
| 2 | Who would be suitable for this programme? |
| | What are the entry requirements? |
| | Will people be invited, or will they apply themselves? |
| 3 | What is the best way of transferring knowledge and skills? |
| | What are the practical issues to consider here? |
| 4 | How do we assess learning? |
| | Is there a pass/fail mechanism? |

this stage. Note that this table just includes a very brief selection of possible questions.

This process would be repeated for each of the nine steps and, of course, for each conceptual model developed for the different *Weltanschauungen* considered.

### Repeat steps 1 to 4 as required

By engaging in this structured process of reflection and questioning we have developed a better understanding of the situation of interest and may now want to revisit our rich picture and add more detail. We may have different ideas about what the transformation should be or want to explore a different transformation based on a different *Weltanschauung*. These changes may well lead to different conceptual models and a new set of questions. So we can repeat the process of developing a conceptual model and asking questions, and each time we do this our understanding will become deeper and stronger.

This iterative process and the visual nature of the associated graphics makes using SSM with a group of interested people very easy. Questioning of the process and emerging ideas from different perspectives all adds to the richness of the decisions which come out at the end.

### Step 5: Identify potential actions

Of course, we cannot continue reflection and questioning indefinitely, and at some point we must conclude our analysis and make decisions (Figure 6.21).

If we have worked through the SSM process several times, exploring different perspectives, we should now be in a good position to be able to propose appropriate organisational and knowledge- or skill-related actions to improve our perceived problem and to make practical suggestions about how these can be implemented and monitored.

Because of the systemic basis within SSM we can do this feeling confident that whatever actions we do decide to implement, they will contribute to the effective and efficient functioning of our real world situation of interest.

## Critical Systems Heuristics

When we talk about something as being 'is' or 'is not' we are actually stating an opinion about where a boundary is being drawn – what is included or

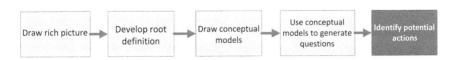

*Figure 6.21* Step 5 of the SSM process

not included. This was something which concerned David Hume, the Scottish philosopher. In about 1740, he wrote:

> In every system of morality, which I have hitherto met with, I have always remark'd, that the author proceeds for some time in the ordinary way of reasoning . . . When all of the sudden I am surpriz'd to find, that instead of the usual copulations of propositions, *is* and *is not*, I meet with no proposition that is not connected with an *ought*, or an *ought not*. This change is imperceptible; but is, however, of the last consequence.[21]

Hume was commenting on the writings of other philosophers but was, in our systems terms, articulating an observation about boundary decisions. Of course, we always need to define some limits to our investigation of the causes of a performance problem or of factors influencing the success of a training programme, but unless we spend some time reflecting on 'ought' we may consciously or unconsciously exclude matters of great significance.

We have seen that one of the principles of systems thinking is the attention paid to multiple perspectives and how if we see human activity systems as a network of wicked problems, all of these perspectives have validity. Selecting which perspectives to explore or exclude therefore becomes an ethical issue, and this is reflected in a field of systems thinking described as *critical systems*.

One technique that has developed in this area which is of particular use in both training needs analysis and evaluation is Critical Systems Heuristics (CSH), a methodology developed by the Swiss academic Werner Ulrich. By 'critical', Ulrich means to encourage us to be reflective about assumptions we are making, and a 'heuristic' is a device which we can use to help us explore aspects of a problem or situation. CSH is particularly useful in helping us explore issues related to power, where particular individuals or institutions make decisions about what is included in or left out of a situation of interest. This applies to all sorts of power. Table 6.3 shows how power may be relevant in a performance analysis or evaluation activity (using the typology developed by French and Raven[22]).

All of these sources of power may have some impact on decisions about the boundaries of the system, and the aim of applying CSH is to think about how this power is operating and if it needs to be challenged in any way.

To apply CSH we look for answers to a set of questions about our system of interest which are defined within a matrix, as shown in Table 6.4.[23] The four rows of questions refer to different groups of stakeholders:

- 'Sources of motivation' are questions about who gets what from the system.
- 'Sources of control' are questions about who has some form of control over the system.

*Table 6.3* Types of power and their manifestation

| Type of power | How it may be manifested in a performance analysis/evaluation |
|---|---|
| Reward power | Based on rewarding a particular course of action. For example:<br>• Allocating resources (time, personnel, budget etc.) for carrying out an activity in a particular way |
| Legitimate power | Power derived from a position of authority. For example:<br>• An instruction delivered by a director or chief executive<br>• Access to information being granted or denied by a manager with authority |
| Referent power | Based on our affiliations. For example:<br>• What the training department always does<br>• A desire to please senior management by delivering a certain type of training or limiting the terms of reference of an evaluation |
| Expert power | Power based on having specific knowledge or skills (or the perception that these are held). For example:<br>• Opinions expressed by senior or experienced people within the organisation that things must be done in a particular way<br>• Certain individuals have specific, in-depth knowledge of a specific subject and so can exert disproportionate influence. |
| Informational power | Power based on access to information. For example:<br>• Individuals may have access to data which is relevant to an analysis or evaluation. |
| Coercive power | Power based on a physical threat. This is perhaps less likely to be an issue in the peaceful world of human resources, but may be present as workplace bullying or harassment of some form. |

- 'Sources of knowledge' are questions about who is involved in decisions about what goes into the system.
- 'Sources of legitimacy' are questions about who is affected by the system.

Comparing answers from different stakeholder groups helps us explore different perspectives held on the system.

A first point to address is that the language used in this table is somewhat opaque and not necessarily accessible or obviously relevant to the world of training. In Chapters 8 and 10, in which CSH is used as a tool for needs analysis or evaluation, we will adapt these original questions and develop a set of practical, easy-to-understand questions which can be used 'in the field'.

Notice that each of these questions is expressed as "ought to be/is": David Hume would be very relieved to find that CSH is forcing us to question our assumptions. The answer to the 'is' form of the question gives us a description of what the situation actually is, but the 'ought to be' gives us a normative answer, what it should be, remembering that answers to 'should be' are also dependent on the perspective of each observer.

*Table 6.4* Questions used in a CSH analysis

| | *What (stakes)* | *Who (stakeholders)* | *Key issues (stakeholdings)* |
|---|---|---|---|
| **Sources of motivation** | 1. Purpose: What is/ought to be the purpose of the system? | 2. Beneficiary: Who is/ought to be the intended beneficiary of the system? | 3. Measure of improvement: What is/ought to be the system's measure of success? |
| **Sources of control** | 4. Resources: What conditions of success are/ought to be under the control of the system? | 5. Decision maker: Who is/ought to be in control of the conditions of success of the system? | 6. Decision environment: What conditions of success are/ought to be outside the control of the decision maker? |
| **Sources of knowledge** | 7. Expertise: What are/ought to be relevant knowledge and skills for the system? | 8. Expert: Who is/ought to be providing relevant knowledge and skills for the system? | 9. Guarantor: What are/ought to be regarded as assurances of successful implementation of the system? |
| **Sources of legitimacy** | 10. Emancipation: What are/ought to be the opportunities for the interests of those negatively affected to have expression and freedom from the worldview of the system? | 11. Witness: Who is/ought to be representing the interests of those negatively affected by but not involved with the system? | 12. Worldview: What space is/ought to be available for reconciling differing worldviews regarding the system among those involved and affected? |

CSH is a very useful tool to use at the start of a performance analysis or evaluation activity. It allows us to either frame or challenge already-established terms of reference.

## Summary

The tools discussed in this chapter provide the basis for the systemic approaches to needs analysis and evaluation covered in later chapters, so before continuing it would be useful to briefly summarise what it has covered.

A number of different types of diagram are useful in systems thinking, including system maps, multiple-cause diagrams, influence diagrams, causal flow diagrams and rich pictures.

System Dynamics uses causal flow diagrams to explore the relationships among different aspects of a situation. These diagrams show direct and inverse relationships which can lead to either reinforcing or balancing feedback loops. Using a qualitative approach to system dynamics can help us to develop causal flow diagrams to strengthen our understanding of a dynamic complex situation.

The Viable System Model is a cybernetics-based approach to understanding how an organisation operates. The VSM is based around a five-system model, which can be applied at different levels within the organisation and which helps us to understand how organisation, departments and individuals interact with each other and their environments.

Social Network Analysis is a mathematical way of quantifying and developing a picture of relationships between individuals or other entities within a particular setting. It can help us understand levels of connectivity and the flows of information around a system.

Soft Systems Methodology is a systematic process we can follow in order to develop a conceptual model of how a particular situation might work. We can then use this conceptual model to reflect on reality and hence decide what might help make the situation more systemically effective.

Critical Systems Heuristics is a technique used to explore power relationships within a situation of interest so that we can decide who or what should be included or excluded from a training needs analysis or evaluation activity.

## Notes

1  The Open University has a very helpful website dedicated to diagramming: http://systems.open.ac.uk/materials/T552/, accessed 30 October 2015.
2  Senge, P.M., 1990. *The Fifth Discipline: The Art and Practice of the Learning Organization*, Century Business, London.
3  For example, see Insight Maker at: https://insightmaker.com/, accessed 17 September 2015.
4  Wolstenholme, E.F., 1999. Qualitative vs Quantitative Modelling: The Evolving Balance. *Journal of the Operational Research Society*, 50(4), pp. 422–428.
5  Cybernetics: "the field of study concerned with communication and control systems in living organisms and machines", www.oed.com, accessed 1 December 2015.
6  This graph was created using NodeXL, a Microsoft Excel template, available at http://nodexl.codeplex.com/.
7  Hatala, J.-P., 2006. Social Network Analysis in Human Resource Development: A New Methodology. *Human Resource Development Review*, 5(1), pp. 45–71; Parise, S., 2007. Knowledge Management and Human Resource Development: An Application in Social Network Analysis Methods. *Advances in Developing Human Resources*, 9(3), pp. 359–383; Van der Hulst, R.C., 2009. Introduction to Social Network Analysis (SNA) as an Investigative Tool. *Trends in Organized Crime*, 12(2), pp. 101–121.
8  Hatala, J.-P. & Fleming, P.R., 2007. Making Transfer Climate Visible: Utilizing Social Network Analysis to Facilitate the Transfer of Training. *Human Resource Development Review*, 6(1), pp. 33–63.
9  Parise, 2007, op. cit.
10  Hatala, 2006, op. cit.
11  Granovetter, M.S., 1973. The Strength of Weak Ties. *American Journal of Sociology*, 78(6), pp. 1360–1380.
12  Granovetter, 1973, op. cit.; Parise, 2007, op. cit.
13  Hatala & Fleming, 2007, op. cit.
14  Hatala, 2006, op. cit.
15  Hatala, 2006, op. cit.
16  Checkland, P., 2000. Soft Systems Methodology: A Thirty Year Retrospective. *Systems Research and Behavioral Science*, 17, pp. S11–S58.

17  Checkland, 2000, op. cit.; Checkland, P. & Scholes, J., 1990. *Soft Systems Methodology in Action*, Wiley, Chichester.
18  Checkland, 2000, op. cit.
19  *Weltanschauung* is a word which has been drawn from the writings of Immanuel Kant, the 18th-century German philosopher, which have provided a key source of inspiration for a number of contemporary systems thinkers, including C. West Churchman and Peter Checkland.
20  Miller, G.A., 1956. The Magical Number Seven, Plus or Minus Two: Some Limits on our Capacity for Processing Information. *The Psychological Review*, 63(2), pp. 81–97.
21  Quoted in Malik, K., 2014. *The Quest for a Moral Compass*, Atlantic Books, London, p. 194.
22  French, J.R.P. & Raven, B., 1959. Bases of Power, in Cartwright, D., ed., *Studies in Social Power*. Institute for Social Research, Ann Arbor, MI, pp. 150–167.
23  Adapted from Ulrich, W. & Reynolds, M., 2010. Critical Systems Heuristics, in Reynolds, M. & Holwell, S., eds., *Systems Approaches to Managing Change: A Practical Guide*. Springer, London, pp. 243–292.

# 7   How do people learn?

This chapter looks at:

*   some different ideas about how people learn
*   what formal and informal learning are
*   the limitations of formal learning
*   the potential benefits of informal learning.

A fundamental reason we design and deliver programmes is to enable people to learn. This is such an obvious statement that it is sometimes easy to make assumptions about the learning process, about how people learn both as individuals and in groups. The aim of this chapter is to present some key ideas about learning from a systems perspective.

## Ideas about learning

Before looking at how learning can contribute to workplace performance improvements, we need to look at some useful ideas in learning and see how they relate to a systems perspective.

One of the most influential and well-known ideas about learning is David Kolb's *experiential learning*.[1] Kolb conceived of learning as taking place through a constant cycle of experience, reflection, conceptualisation and experimentation (Figure 7.1).

So when developing a skill I first try to perform the required task. Having tried it I look at how it has gone and reflect on what worked and what needs to be improved. I develop some sort of mental explanation which explains how to do the task better, and I experiment with this. Based on the new experience I reflect further and refine my explanation, and so on. Through this iterative process I get better and better. We can conceive of this process in a causal flow diagram (Figure 7.2).

This suggests that the more we practice, reflect, conceptualise and experiment, the higher our level of understanding: we have a reinforcing loop, and as long as we keep doing these four things in the right way, things can only get better. In this diagram we have added four potential points of leverage, places

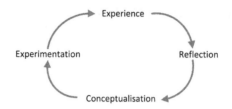

*Figure 7.1* Kolb's learning cycle

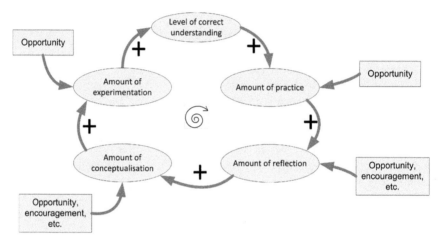

*Figure 7.2* Learning as a feedback process

where we can accelerate, slow down or even reverse this cycle of learning; for example, by restricting opportunities for practice we can slow the rate at which the level of understanding improves, or by changing the way in which someone conceptualises the situation (perhaps through badly executed training) we can even make the level of correct understanding go down.

This provides a clue about one of the limitations of Kolb's model: in systems terms it sees learning as a closed system, not exchanging energy with its environment. This means that eventually it would reach an equilibrium at which it becomes static, and so learning will stop. In human terms it sees the learner as an individual and does not address the way in which a person interacts with (and draws energy from) their environment, for example, by receiving feedback (such as encouragement or criticism) or additional information (perhaps clarification or new information from other people).

Now consider linking several individual learning cycles together (Figure 7.3). Working in the 1930s, the Russian psychologist Lev Vygotsky was greatly interested in how children learnt and proposed that social interactions such as observation, discussion and negotiation were key to helping them learn how to function in their social settings.[2] Applying this to our causal flow diagram, we can see how each person's reflection stage in their learning cycle might link into another's so that they can reinforce each other's learning, and with another, and another. So learning becomes a *social process* of discussion, comparison and clarification of understanding. Each person draws energy (new information and ideas) from their environment, and learning for each individual becomes an open system with energy entering their own system, which they can then share with members of the network. Notice how this relates to the ideas discussed earlier about how reality is socially constructed: each person's understanding contributes to everyone else's.

This aspect of Kolb's theory being concerned with a closed system has implications for one of the significant spin-offs of the learning cycle. What we have described here is a process for learning, but Kolb developed his ideas further to propose that individuals have a preference for a particular part of the cycle: that some people prefer learning from experience while others prefer theory. This proposition became formalised in Kolb's own Learning Style Inventory (LSI), and was adapted later in the Honey and Mumford Learning Style Questionnaire (LSQ). The latter in particular has become extremely popular within management training in the United Kingdom. It easy to see why this is the case:

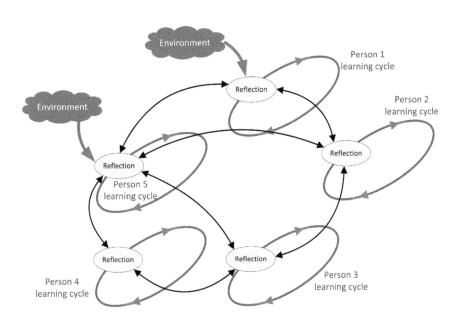

*Figure 7.3* Social network of learning cycles

the questionnaire is easy to administer, gives the respondents a sense of satisfaction in being able to classify themselves in some way and is in some respects quite intuitive.

The contention of learning styles proponents is that we all have a certain preference for the way we learn (and that, by extension, educators and trainers should try to take this into consideration when designing and delivering learning experiences). However, this idea has become quite contentious amongst academics with an interest in learning.[3] For example, people may vary their approach to learning depending on the nature of engagement with the subject matter; subjects requiring a deep understanding will provoke a different approach to learning than those which only have to be understood at a surface level.

But from a systems perspective learning styles theory is problematic because it presents the learner as an individual and detaches them from their social context: learning styles are inadequate because they fail to take account "of the basically political and moral character of social existence and human development".[4] In systems terms, individual learning is a wicked problem surrounded by other wicked problems of our political and social context, and a reliance on psychological theories creates a serious risk of making us see a person's learning as an individual rather than as a social activity. An example is that learners may make a conscious choice for how they learn based on the situation they find themselves in and how they perceive the learning task: for example, when someone is feeling under pressures of work or time they may choose a different learning style, or if they perceive that the assessment of learning will be based on a more theoretical understanding they will adopt a more theoretical approach to learning. This theme will be discussed later when considering the interaction between formal and informal learning.

Returning to our discussion about the learning process, what actually happens in a brain as a result of these individual and social learning processes is much argued about, but one concept (from the work of George Miller[5]) is that as we move through this continual cycle of experience, reflection and so on, we place items we have learnt in short-term memory. This can only hold a very small amount of information (the idea of '7 ± 2' items), but through a process of repetition or reinforcement we increase the size of the items to try to move them into our long-term memory. As this happens we create or modify a *mental model* (a term often attributed to the American psychologist Philip Johnson-Laird[6]) of this particular aspect of reality. A mental model is a cognitive structure which we use to explain how something works or happens. Having a good mental model about some aspect of the workplace means that we feel confident that if we do A then B will happen. We are often not aware that we hold mental models about everything that we regularly do, and it may only be through a social learning activity that we bring the model to conscious attention and review the hidden assumptions on which it is based. Learning is then about amending and internalising this new and improved model.

While engaged in this discussion about learning and memory (and also critiquing some commonly held perceptions about these topics) it may also be useful to briefly discuss what is sometimes known as the 'cone of experience'. This refers to the much-quoted statistic which goes something like "after two weeks we remember 10% of what we read, 20% of what we hear" and so on. While training professionals often refer to this statistic, it may be one of those 'urban myths' which circulate around the training world. For a more complete description of the problem, the reader is referred to various Internet sites which discuss the myth,[7] but briefly these numbers seem to have inexplicably become attached to a structure initially developed by the educator Edgar Dale in 1946, who proposed a number of different ways in which information could be communicated. Dale said nothing about the effectiveness of the methods, but 10%, 20% and so on has been gradually added on and beautiful graphics created in order to explain how increased activity leads to greater retention. So while it intuitively may make some sense, it seems not to be based on any research at all.

To complete this section we should make some reference to the idea of adult learning, which has considerable relevance to the design and implementation of learning interventions. A key figure in the development of ideas around adult learning is Malcolm Knowles, to whom is attributed the development of the idea (at least in North America and Western Europe) of *andragogy*, the theory and practice of adult learning. Knowles[8] argued that learning in ancient times followed andragogic principles: for example, with Socrates developing the Socratic dialogue method, which encouraged learning through a process of questioning and answering with further questions in order to clarify thinking. Then, however, with the development of monastic schools in the Middle Ages learning came to be associated with adults handing down information to dependent children, and this came to be seen as the norm for a learning process.

Knowles proposed seven elements necessary for adult-oriented, andragogical learning:

- Learning should be conducted in an informal, mutually respectful, consensual, collaborative and supportive climate.
- Planning of learning activities should be participative.
- The diagnosis of learning needs should be a mutual process.
- Setting goals for the learning should be negotiated mutually.
- Learning plans should be based on the readiness of the learner and so not be dependent on a course syllabus or a defined 'logical sequence'.
- Activities should be based on enquiry, independent study and experiment.
- Evaluation should be a mutual activity based on evidence collected by the learner.

It is interesting to reflect on the degree to which these elements are implemented in formal learning activities within typical organisations, and this brings us to a discussion of the words 'training' and 'learning'. The verb 'to train' has its linguistic roots in the Latin *trahere*, meaning to pull or draw, and its other derivatives include the noun 'train', describing a wheeled vehicle guided along a fixed path. As such, it has become a metaphor for the process of helping someone acquire or improve knowledge or skill. Metaphors can be very useful in helping us develop mental pictures of what we are describing, but they are potentially dangerous because they can also limit what we can think about.

Discussing 'training' has the potential effect of making us think only about solutions which involve drawing people along a track we build and failing to see other possibilities for knowledge and skill development. In this way training departments may have become attached to the idea that their role is to draw people along a track and to not consider other learning possibilities. At the micro level of delivery, the 'drawing along' metaphor means that inexperienced trainers may fall back on information delivery as a mode of training, reasoning that if they lead people through a long presentation of content, they will absorb everything and be able to utilise it effectively.

'Learning', on the other hand, is more related to the idea of acquisition, and this as a metaphor opens us up to the idea that we can acquire knowledge and skills in a variety of ways. Learning is about more than training. People are learning all the time, from asking colleagues how to do something, spending time with their supervisor in some sort of coaching activity, reading guidelines and manuals and so on. Building on and making these processes more efficient is often overlooked as a 'learning solution' to a needs analysis, even though informal learning is hugely important.

For these reasons you will find that in this book when I discuss activities which can be implemented to improve knowledge and skill, I use phrases such as 'a learning intervention' rather than the word 'training'. At times it may feel irritating or pedantic, but I am doing it to avoid falling into the metaphorical trap of what 'training' is.

## Formal and informal learning

In the previous section we discussed various models which have been used to explain how people learn. However, this discussion did not cover its context, in other words *where* this learning takes place. You as the reader may have imagined any type of context, but when people in a workplace are asked about where and how they learn, they regularly just describe their experiences of formal *training* activities.[9]

This is not actually the reality of learning: studies have shown that most of what people learn in the workplace is actually done through non-formal means. Research carried out by the US government's Bureau of Labor Statistics suggested that 80% of people learn happens through informal means.[10] In recent years the awareness of informal learning has grown, in no small part due to promotion of the '70:20:10' model. Based on research into leadership development carried out by Michael Lombardo and Robert Eichinger,[11] this proposes that 70% of learning is through on-the-job experience, 20% through relationships and feedback and 10% through formal training. It can be seen that in both studies the importance of informal learning is similar, but 70:20:10 downplays the significance of formal learning, although there are difficulties in defining exactly what formal and informal learning actually are in practice.

This distinction is discussed in more detail later in this chapter, but for clarification at this point formal learning at the workplace could include structured coaching sessions, probably on a 1:1 basis but following a plan: ad hoc coaching is more properly regarded as informal learning. Formal learning away from the workplace (the more typical modality) often takes the form of classroom events, such as workshops or lectures, or some form of distance learning, often nowadays mediated through technology, such as by e-learning or webinars. In this context 'at the workplace' should be regarded as really meaning 'engaging within work', as online self-study programmes are often followed while sitting at the physical workplace. However, mentally the learner is usually detached from actual workplace performance when doing this. Informal learning is often seen as learning which is not formal, as described here.

So although the situation is changing, two questions: Why do training functions sometimes not see informal learning as being within their organisational remit, and why do learners not acknowledge the significance of informal learning?

Looking first at training professionals, reductionist organisational structures play a part: the extent of the training department's responsibilities may be formally defined and limited to the design and delivery of training programmes. For example, training has been defined as "the process of acquiring the knowledge and skills related to work requirements by formal, structured or guided means",[12] but this definition goes on to specifically exclude "general supervision, motivational meetings, basic induction and learning by experience".

Designing training programmes may have become an established professional development activity, but 'supporting informal learning' has not, and so there exists little expertise in how to do it. Sometimes informal learning may fall under a knowledge management responsibility, but again there is the risk that this may remain separate from training.

Training mirrors the process we are all familiar with through the schooling system. Attendance at a formal education centre is a legal requirement in wealthy countries, so we become used to the act of receiving instruction. People without any specific knowledge of pedagogical techniques who are asked to 'deliver some training' to other staff almost always default to the delivery-of-information approach they will have experienced at school or university.

The, by definition, informality of informal learning means that it may not actually be recognised by anyone in the organisation as 'their' responsibility. In *Life, the Universe and Everything*, Douglas Adams discusses the concept of the 'somebody else's problem field', a mysterious force which envelops issues which 'are not my problem' and which, when seen as thus by everyone, become invisible.[13] This is often the fate of informal learning.

Many organisations now have a (somewhat misleadingly named) 'learning management system' (LMS), which acts as a gateway to and record-keeper of completed formal training. The name of the system, and the ready access it provides to an individual's record of what training they have completed, creates the perception that this stores all the information that is important to know about learning.[14]

From a complexity perspective, training departments represent an organisation's legitimate system and have a responsibility for ensuring compliance with official norms. They may therefore feel they are caught in a dilemma as to how to strike an appropriate balance between promoting orthodoxy and encouraging learners to develop the autonomy they need in order to respond to operational variety. As far as learners are concerned, people may recognise the training department's dilemma but 'play the game', and even if they feel that a specific formal training activity is not particularly useful, they will take part in order to receive the appropriate recognition.[15] Similarly, learning acquired around the coffee machine is not accorded any value in organisational record-keeping,[16] and will probably not be regarded as significant in performance appraisal activities.

Other factors play a part. People may not understand what is meant by informal learning. It is also possible that the trend within human resources in recent years to refer to 'training' as 'learning' has to some extent hijacked learning as being part of what training does rather than being part of every employee's everyday activity.

## How can formal learning be delivered?

Table 7.1 summarises the main face-to-face ways of providing learning opportunities, along with their strengths and weaknesses. Table 7.2 continues this for ways of providing distance learning opportunities.

Each way of delivering formal learning has its strengths and weaknesses, the relevance of which will depend on many different factors, such as the numbers of people to be trained, geographical dispersion, urgency of the training, complexity of the task and so on. This means that it is unlikely that there will be one method which is clearly superior to all, and most formal learning interventions will benefit from a blended approach, which uses a range of technologies.

Generally, one significant strength is that what is covered in the formal learning process can be carefully designed and structured so that the organisation's approved policies and procedures can be communicated easily, effectively and efficiently. The design of learning processes and materials has been extensively researched over the years, and by using appropriate pedagogical techniques and technologies we can provide high-quality learning experiences for people.

Completion of a formal learning programme means that people acquire a record of completion. This may be anything from a printed certificate to an entry in a learning management system's database, and this record becomes valuable for many different purposes, such as proving competence in an annual performance appraisal exercise, being evidence which can be used when applying for promotion or a new job or as proof of having met some legal compliance

Table 7.1 Methods of providing face-to-face formal learning

| Medium | Strengths | Weaknesses |
|---|---|---|
| Classroom-based | Opportunities to practice real skills. Allows concentration on the learning. Flexibility in terms of pedagogical approaches (for example, can incorporate lectures, group work, role plays, action learning etc., as appropriate). Provides opportunities for social construction of understanding. Collaborative and helps with relationship building. Flexible learning delivery styles. Can be designed and delivered relatively quickly. Makes accreditation or certification much easier. More flexibility about how to carry out assessments. | Can be expensive in terms of bringing participants and trainers together. Expensive for delivering to a large number of people, especially if they are geographically dispersed. Risk of inexperienced trainers relying on a lecture methodology which restricts the possibilities for learning. Complicated to coordinate and organise dates suitable for all. May be difficult to relate workshop to actual performance. Training is a one-shot operation and may not coincide with timing of an organisational need, leading to problems of forgetting and skill decay. |
| 1-to-1, small-group coaching | Close contact between trainer and learner. Meets specific needs. Flexible timing. | Probably needs follow-up to be effective. Dependent on quality of coaching. Accreditation difficult. Commitment of time by learner and coach may be difficult. May need to teach the coach coaching skills. Potential problems of inconsistency from one coach to another. |
| Generic training courses | May be cost effective for larger numbers of learners. External accreditation. Can provide expertise unavailable internally. Can be delivered very quickly if there is a sudden need. | May not be exactly what is needed. Can be expensive. Probably needs follow-up to be effective. May not be culturally appropriate (national or organisational cultures). |
| On-the-job training, demonstration | Close to the real performance. Integrates learning with performance. Flexible timing possible. Builds relationships. | Potentially dangerous/risky to customers, equipment etc. Commitment of time by learner and coach may be difficult. May not be done in a structured way, so that learners fail to understand less obvious aspects of sequence etc. May need to teach coach coaching skills. |
| Distance learning | Cost effective for larger numbers of learners. Consistent quality of training. Variety of delivery options available. Good where training has to be repeated often. Flexible to meet needs of different levels of learners. | Higher initial cost. Quality dependent on strength of design. Less effective for skill-based subjects. Can be expensive to update. |

*Table 7.2* Different types of distance learning approaches

| Medium | Strengths | Weaknesses |
| --- | --- | --- |
| Paper-based | Relatively cheap to design and develop.<br>Flexible delivery.<br>Portable for the learner.<br>Easy to reach large numbers.<br>If delivered in PDF format, can be studied on screen and with a possibility of limited interaction.<br>Does not rely on Internet connectivity.<br>Workbooks may be designed to be useful as reference documentation. | Difficult to train people in more complex skills.<br>Difficult to assess impact on performance.<br>Assessing learning is difficult without other media. |
| Self-study e-learning | Can be stimulating and motivating to learners.<br>Various presentation options available, such as tutorials, simulations and games.<br>Allows centralised recording and monitoring of training.<br>Potentially economical for large numbers.<br>Effectiveness dependent on quality of instructional design. | Can be expensive to develop, especially if incorporating rich media (video, audio etc.).<br>Requires a number of different, specialised skills in order to design and develop it if it is to be effective.<br>Reliant on suitable delivery computers.<br>Learners can find it lonely and/or frustrating.<br>Web-based delivery needs intranet or Internet access.<br>Bandwidth may limit use of multimedia.<br>Reliant on access to a computer. |
| Web-based conferencing technologies | Allows integration of tutor support with flexibility of delivery.<br>Cheap to design, develop and deliver.<br>Can reach multiple locations simultaneously. | Learner participation may be difficult to ensure.<br>Often technical problems in getting started or setting up client software.<br>Bandwidth may be a problem.<br>Needs computers with intranet or Internet connectivity.<br>Time differences. |
| Video | Good for demonstrating desired behaviours.<br>Can be uploaded to the Internet for ready access anywhere in the world.<br>Many people familiar with sites such as YouTube for gathering information. | Passive, so learners may not stay engaged. |
| Audio (CD or podcast) | Flexible delivery options on many types of device.<br>Can be available both online and offline. | Passive.<br>Poor retention, because of limited engagement or chance to practice. |

requirements. Data about course completion is objective and measurable and so can provide good evidence of the quality of a workforce and the services or products that the organisation delivers.

## Limitations of formal learning programmes

The previous section discussed both strengths and weaknesses of formal learning, but the weaknesses were considered more from a practical perspective and as comparisons among potential delivery mechanisms. In this section we will look at formal learning from a systemic perspective in order to reflect on some more fundamental issues.

We have earlier discussed how situations of interest can be seen as having three common characteristics; boundaries, multiple perspectives and relationships (the B–P–R model), and we will examine formal learning from these three viewpoints.

### Formal learning and boundaries

Boundary decisions present themselves in several ways:

- What is an acceptable level of performance, and what is outside this boundary?
- What is the best way of determining what is within the boundary?
- Who should be trained and who should not?
- When is the training appropriate?

Determining the optimum level of formal learning can be difficult. If learning is set at too high a level it may prove too difficult for participants, and they may not be able to integrate the new knowledge and skills into their existing mental frameworks. If it is too low they may become bored or even resentful at having to be there. This might also compound suspicions that senior management thinks that their abilities are lower than they themselves think them to be and that the training is being delivered at a low level because of their low levels of ability. Both problems can arise when mixed-ability groups attend a learning event together.

In order to determine what is within the boundary of acceptable performance we need to assess formal learning in some way, to validate the learning processes followed, to enable the learner to claim their certification or other proof of success, to satisfy regulatory requirements or to provide some broader measure for an evaluation activity.

The danger with assessment is that the emphasis in learning activities can be placed on the need to satisfy the requirements of the assessment, which will not necessarily be the same as those of the workplace. This will be influenced by a variety of factors, including the degree to which the performance can be replicated within a learning setting, the ability of the learning designer to create a true test of performance ability and the relative emphasis placed on the abstracted knowledge and skill as opposed to the real performance. As we have seen, learning becomes a commodity to be acquired. People come away from the workplace to 'be filled', so the learning tends to focus on theoretical aspects of the work and on mental preparation for the skill rather than on actual practice.

Treating formal learning as an individual activity (drawing boundaries through a team) fails to acknowledge that aspects of tacit knowledge may be socially constructed amongst a team of people and so only really have a recognised existence when that team works together. This means that when formal learning is seen as an individual activity (as reinforced by the use of learning management systems, for example) and is undertaken away from the workplace, it fails to take into account those hidden factors which can contribute to improved performance or act to maintain the status quo.

The fourth issue raised is about time-related boundaries: When is the best time to deliver a formal learning intervention? Ideally it should be just at the point where the new knowledge or skill is needed, but this can be very difficult to arrange. Instead, people attend training courses when it is administratively or logistically possible, and it may be some time before they have the chance to practice what they learn. This raises the possibility of forgetting new knowledge and the decay of new skills.

We forget new knowledge (as described by the German psychologist Hermann Ebbinghaus[17]) at an exponential rate unless we take conscious steps to remember it, which would be done by applying new knowledge acquired during a formal learning activity. The same phenomenon applies to skills, where it is often described as skill decay, or fade. The rate at which newly acquired skills decay depends on a number of factors, including how often the new task is practised, the degree of overlearning (making sure people learn more than they actually need to learn[18]) in the original training and the nature of the skill (for example, if it is physical or cognitive). Some research has shown that if an individual is not able to practice a new skill for a period of 12 months after learning it, their performance level will have dropped to 8% of what it was immediately after being trained.[19]

### Formal learning and multiple perspectives

Formal learning usually reflects the legitimate system's perspective on what is desired (to draw from the language of complexity theory). This may be the promulgation of a new policy or set of procedures or training designed to correct what is seen as deviant or otherwise unacceptable forms or levels of behaviour.

The degree to which alternative perspectives are allowed to be included within formal learning depends to a great extent on the design of the learning. For example:

- Distance learning (such as self-study e-learning) usually follows a didactic approach and may not be capable of allowing discussion of anything other than the official message.

- Face-to-face learning may also use didactic, teacher-centred methods and not allow any social construction of understanding which takes into consideration different perspectives of the variety in the workplace.

Complexity theory stresses the importance of operating at the edge of chaos, where the legitimate and shadow systems interact to develop the optimum balance between centrally driven order and the environmentally responsive diversity of the workplace. So while formal learning may not necessarily ignore multiple perspectives, there is a danger that it will if learning programmes are not designed with this in mind.

### Formal learning and relationships

Relationships manifest themselves in several ways in workplace performance. For example:

- There are relationships among individuals working within some form of team and among teams in an organisation.
- There is a relationship between the individual and their operational context.

### Relationships among individuals

Training is often seen as a process of acquisition of knowledge and skills:[20] this has several potential implications:

- Learners are seen as individuals and not working as part of a team, which is the reality of most people in modern organisational life.
- Acquisition of certification for completing the learning becomes valuable as a means of exchange (for a better job, promotion etc.) and may become more valued than the ability to carry out the task to the required level.

Individualisation of learning makes it harder for new and useful knowledge and skills to be integrated into the workplace community's framework of understanding, so it remains as a lone possession, making it vulnerable to being lost if the owner leaves the team.[21] Individualisation mirrors the pressures in modern life which tell us that the key to happiness and success is to have more material goods, so it is easy to make people believe that learning has personal rather than team value. This gives it the potential to drive wedges between members of a team. It also sends a message that performance is based on disconnected individuals doing separate tasks rather than being a team-based collaborative enterprise.[22]

### Relationships between individuals and their operational context

The effectiveness of formal learning rests on an assumption that we can define a required performance precisely and deconstruct it into a precise series of individual tasks, which when replicated away from the workplace reproduce the desired performance.

This assumption that we can 'recreate mastery' by capturing the abilities of an expert was much criticised by the French anthropologist and philosopher Pierre Bourdieu. He distinguished between what he called the *opus operatum*, the finished work, and the *modus operandi*, the way in which the work was carried out, pointing out that when a competent person carries out a task their 'learned ignorance' means that they are unaware of the judgements and adjustments they are constantly making while completing the task. All that an observer can do is create some approximate map of what they see.[23] This is sometimes referred to as 'unconscious competence' in the well-known four-stage model (unconscious incompetence, conscious incompetence, conscious competence, unconscious competence[24]).

To understand this point, think about something you can do very well. Try to define exactly what you do to do what you do. This is almost impossible, as to perform anything at an expert level we have to internalise and automate judgements and decisions to a degree at which they become subconscious. Formal learning away from the place of performance therefore can only ever be an approximation. It may be adequate for learning some initial competence in a new task where explicit knowledge is enough, but it cannot be relied on to develop any degree of mastery.[25]

One reason this is so difficult is the removal of the performance from its context, the working environment which provides many different types of performance support, for example, such things as the presence of colleagues, performance aids, familiar equipment and so on. Note that although we are discussing this here as an example of relationship issues (between the worker and their operational context), it is also due to a boundary decision, that we can separate performance from its context. As John Brown and Paul Duguid commented:

> Training is thought of as the transmission of explicit, abstract knowledge from the head of someone who knows to the head of someone who does not in surroundings that specifically exclude the complexities of practice and the communities of practitioners. The setting for learning is simply assumed not to matter.[26]

Brown and Duguid recognised that training was about the transmission of *explicit knowledge*, which we can regard as knowledge which is recognised and known within the organisation, and exists in some recorded form.[27] However, as well as explicit knowledge, high-quality performance also depends on a knowledge "of beliefs, opinions, sensibilities, styles of doing things, and lore that may be expressed in stories and anecdotes, a glance, a nod, body language or go unsaid".[28] Michael Polanyi[29] described this as *tacit knowledge*, what we know but do not know that we know. Tacit knowledge can be pure knowledge or the knowledge of how to carry out a skill expertly but can also include subconscious aspects such as prejudice, assumptions or attitudes. Tacit knowledge might therefore be regarded as the 'glue' which holds expert performance together and which a reductionist task analysis fails to see.

A key challenge with dealing with tacit knowledge is that while it is essential for optimum performance it is 'sticky' and cannot easily be transferred from one person to another:[30] it can only be acquired by practical experience and the associated social learning processes, which are not present when the learning takes place away from the workplace and other team members. What needs to happen in order to bring tacit knowledge out of the closet is for people who hold it to maintain an ongoing dialogue with others about how to connect it with explicit knowledge: "As the concept resonates around an expanding community of individuals, it is developed and clarified. Gradually, concepts which are thought to be of value obtain a wider currency and become crystallised".[31] Ikujiro Nonaka calls this process of making tacit knowledge explicit 'externalisation'[32] and claims that it is essential if an organisation is to practice double-loop learning, as it leads to constant reconstruction of perspectives and frameworks and the questioning of assumptions.

## How does informal learning happen?

While we were able to provide a reasonably clear definition of formal learning, it is less easy to provide one for informal learning. Of course, we might simply regard informal learning as anything which does not meet the definition of formal learning, but this is not necessarily very helpful. However, Victoria Marsick and Karen Watkins have suggested the following as characteristics:[33]

- It is integrated with daily routines.
- It is triggered by an internal or external jolt.
- It is not highly conscious.
- It is haphazard and influenced by chance.
- It is an inductive process of reflection and action.
- It is linked to learning of others.

Given these characteristics, it is not surprising that informal learning is pervasive: as mentioned previously, perhaps 80% of what we learn at work comes through informal means. Let us explore these suggestions in more detail.

Being integrated with daily routine means that the learning becomes *situated*, to use a term introduced by Jean Lave and Etienne Wenger,[34] which means that it is related to a particular context and is defined within the physical, temporal and organisational constraints of that context. As such, the learner acquires both the explicit and tacit requirements of that particular context, even though they may not consciously recognise that this is happening. Whereas formal learning relies on a principle of *transference*, where the requisite knowledge and skills are passed from 'an expert' to a learner, situated learning works by *participation*, where the learner constructs meaning through a process of social negotiation and clarification. It is therefore highly constructivist in nature, relying on the individual's reflection on their experience and ability to integrate it within existing mental models.

Situated learning is generally a social activity, as it often involves discussion, explanation, negotiation, clarification and so on. One person's learning therefore usually contributes to another's and so serves to strengthen networks of knowledge. However, there will be cases in which situated learning is an individual activity – where, for example, someone learns through reading or individual experimentation. Nevertheless, even such acquired knowledge may well eventually be passed on to others.

Given these characteristics of informal learning, what activities might be seen as examples? Here are some possibilities:

- *Networking*, chance or planned conversations with close or distant colleagues in which some aspect of work is discussed, leading to an improved understanding by one or both parties.
- *Coaching*, in which a more experienced colleague or perhaps supervisor helps someone carry out a new task, explaining the principles of doing it well so that they can subsequently do it for themselves.
- *Mentoring*, or a more strategic form of coaching, in which an experienced person develops an ongoing relationship with someone with the aim of passing on wisdom.
- *Performance planning*, in which periodically someone sits with their supervisor and discusses their experiences over the previous months or year and hopes for the future so that they can develop a plan about what development would be appropriate in the near future.
- *Reflective practice*, a voluntary or required activity (for example, in the case of trainee doctors who regularly work through a structured process of considering cases they have seen and how their decisions were made) in which an individual thinks about their professional practice, its strengths and weaknesses and how it can be enhanced.
- *Self-directed learning*, in which an individual takes the initiative to gather information about or practice doing something which they need to be able to do in their daily work.
- *Self-generated learning content*, in which an individual creates some form of training or reference materials, perhaps as a wiki or in a contribution to a discussion forum, thereby improving their own understanding as well as helping others.

This is not a definitive list, and many other activities can be considered under the heading of informal learning. The key is to acknowledge the many possibilities.

## The limitations of informal learning

There are issues associated with informal learning.

There is no reassurance that it will happen. Because informal learning relies on the operational context, it can only happen when the appropriate context presents itself. So informal learning would be ineffectual for learning:[35]

- about emergency or other exceptional procedures which only happen occasionally, only to certain people or, which when they happen, put people in danger
- tasks which are new or which require specific equipment or machinery
- how to operate in environments which are constantly changing, where learnt abilities may often not be reused

How do you assess competence? Because informal learning is a response to what happens within a particular context, it becomes difficult to carry out reliable assessments. We cannot therefore be sure that someone is competent in all possible contexts. There will also probably not be any formal assessment which can be recorded, for example for satisfying regulatory requirements.

What is satisfactory performance? Because the knowledge about 'satisfactory' performance is socially determined, criteria for this may vary from one team to another: What is acceptable in one office may not be in another. There may also be temporal variations in criteria: what is acceptable at one time may not be acceptable at another.

This may be exacerbated by groupthink,[36] in which all the individuals in a particular context have a similar perspective on how the performance should be carried out, or when external, different perspectives are limited. This can make it difficult for someone to develop a new, improved set of ideas or to question the status quo.

If criteria for performance are not externally defined, decisions about what is or is not acceptable are ultimately determined by who has the most power, which might depend on legitimacy, expert knowledge, access to information or simple coercion (see the discussion in Chapter 4 on types of power).

## Integrating formal and informal learning

In Chapter 2 we introduced the idea of complexity and proposed that organisations needed to be able to organise themselves so that they operated at the 'edge of chaos'. We can now see that formal and informal learning are respectively representatives of the legitimate and shadow systems operating within an organisation. Formal learning represents the standardised, official way of doing things, while informal learning represents local responses to dealing with variety. Each has its advantages and disadvantages, and it is therefore important that within a needs analysis we identify strategies which can bring formal learning interventions and informal learning activities together so that they can develop a synergy.

An analyst must therefore make sure that they develop a good understanding about how informal learning operates within the groups of workers they are looking at.

## Summary

Learning has been conceived of as an ongoing cycle of experience, reflection, conceptualisation and experimentation. If reflection includes eliciting different perspectives from other people, then individual cycles of learning can become a powerful network promoting social learning. Learning and transferring learning to long-term memory results in the strengthening and broadening of mental models, which we construct as a way of making sense of the world around us.

Adult learning is most effective if learning activities are designed to relate to and strengthen existing mental models, through such things as making the learning enquiry oriented and related to the needs of the individual learner.

Learning may be either formal (structured and usually away from the workplace) or informal (unstructured, responding to an immediate need and usually at the workplace). Conventional definitions of 'training' generally exclude informal learning, so it is often not considered as a strategy to employ when seeking to improve performance.

Both formal and informal learning have their advantages and disadvantages, and an effective formal learning strategy should look to find ways of promoting both in order to help an organisation operate at the edge of chaos.

## Notes

1   Kolb, D.A., 1983. *Experiential Learning: Experience as the Source of Learning and Development*, Financial Times/Prentice Hall, New Jersey.

2   Vygotsky, L.S., 1930. *Mind and Society*, Harvard University Press, Cambridge, MA.

3   For example, see Reynolds, M., 1997. Learning Styles: A Critique. *Management Learning*, 28(2), pp. 115–133.

4   Reynolds, 1997, op. cit., p. 124, quoting from Apple, M., 1990. *Ideology and Curriculum*, Routledge, New York.

5   Miller, G.A., 1956. The Magical Number Seven, Plus or Minus Two: Some Limits on our Capacity for Processing Information. *Psychological Review*, 63(2), p. 81.

6   For more information, see https://en.wikipedia.org/wiki/Mental_model, accessed 11 April 2016.

7   For example, see https://sites.google.com/site/thecorruptedconeoflearning/home accessed 29 October 2015.

8   Knowles, M., 1977. Adult Learning Processes: Pedagogy and Andragogy. *Religious Education*, 72(2), pp. 202–211.

9   Clement-Okooboh, K.M. & Olivier, B., 2014. Applying Cybernetic Thinking to Becoming a Learning Organization. *Kybernetes*, 43(9/10), pp. 1319–1329.

10   Frazis, H., Gittleman, M. & Joyce, M., 1998. Determinants of Training: An Analysis Using Both Employer and Employee Characteristics, in *Key Bridge Marriott Hotel, Arlington VA, US Department of Commerce*, Citeseer, Washington, DC.

11   Lombardo, M.M. & Eichinger R.W., 2000. *The Career Architect Development Planner (3rd Edition)*, Lominger Limited, Minneapolis, MN.

12   Definition from the UK's Training Agency, as quoted in Felstead, A., Fuller, A., Unwin, L., Ashton, D., Butler, P. & Lee, T., 2005. Surveying the Scene: Learning Metaphors, Survey Design and the Workplace Context. *Journal of Education and Work*, 18(4), pp. 360.

13   Adams, D., 1982. *Life, the Universe and Everything*, Pan Macmillan, London.

14   Clement-Okooboh & Olivier, 2014, op. cit.

15 Antonacopoulou, E.P., 2001. The Paradoxical Nature of the Relationship between Training and Learning. *Journal of Management Studies*, 38(3), pp. 327–350.

16 Felstead, A., Fuller, A., Unwin, L., Ashton, D., Butler, P. & Lee, T., 2005. Surveying the Scene: Learning Metaphors, Survey Design and the Workplace Context. *Journal of Education and Work*, 18(4), pp. 359–383.

17 For more information, see https://en.wikipedia.org/wiki/Hermann_Ebbinghaus, accessed 11 April 2016.

18 Driskell, J.E., Willis, R.P. & Copper, C., 1992. Effect of Overlearning on Retention. *Journal of Applied Psychology*, 77(5), p. 615.

19 Arthur Jr., W., Bennett Jr, W., Stanush, P.L. & McNelly, T.L., 1998. Factors that Influence Skill Decay and Retention: A Quantitative Review and Analysis. *Human Performance*, 11(1), pp. 57–101.

20 Sfard, A., 1998. On Two Metaphors for Learning and the Dangers of Choosing Just One. *Educational Researcher*, 27(2), pp. 4–13.

21 Parise, S., 2007. Knowledge Management and Human Resource Development: An Application in Social Network Analysis Methods. *Advances in Developing Human Resources*, 9(3), pp. 359–383.

22 Sfard, 1998, op. cit.

23 Bourdieu, P., 1977. *Outline of a Theory of Practice*, Cambridge University Press, Cambridge, UK.

24 The origins of this model are somewhat unclear and disputed, and if the reader wishes to learn more, they are advised to spend a little time browsing the Internet.

25 Felstead et al., 2005, op. cit.

26 Brown, J.S. & Duguid, P., 1991. Organizational Learning and Communities-of-Practice: Toward a Unified View of Working, Learning and Innovation. *Organization Science*, 2(1), p. 47.

27 Preece, J., 2004. Etiquette, Empathy and Trust in Communities of Practice: Stepping-Stones to Social Capital. *Journal of Universal Computer Science*, 10(3), pp. 294–302.

28 Preece, 2004, op. cit., p. 295.

29 Polanyi, M., 1983. *The Tacit Dimension*, Peter Smith, Gloucester, MA.

30 Nonaka, I., 1994. A Dynamic Theory of Organizational Knowledge Creation. *Organization Science*, 5(1), pp. 14–37.

31 Nonaka, 1994, op. cit., p. 15.

32 Nonaka, 1994, op. cit.

33 Marsick, V.J. & Watkins, K.E., 2001. Informal and Incidental Learning. *New Directions for Adult and Continuing Education*, 2001(89), pp. 25–34.

34 Lave, J. & Wenger, E., 1991. *Situated Learning: Legitimate Peripheral Participation*, Cambridge University Press, Cambridge, UK.

35 Lervik, J.E., Fahy, K.M. & Easterby-Smith, M., 2010. Temporal Dynamics of Situated Learning in Organizations. *Management Learning*, 41(3), pp. 285–301.

36 Janis, I.L., 1972. *Victims of Groupthink: A Psychological Study of Foreign-Policy Decisions and Fiascoes*, Houghton Mifflin, Boston.

# 8 Systemic approaches to analysing training needs

In this chapter we will look at two anonymised case studies based on real situations in order to see how to utilise systems thinking tools within a needs analysis process.

The first case study describes a relatively straightforward situation: there is a perception that training is needed to enhance the skills of experts delivering specialised training to clients. In this case study an internal analyst uses Critical Systems Heuristics and Soft Systems Methodology to identify what training would help and what other interventions would be needed to support this.

The second case study is more complex, as this involves an organisational change. Nevertheless, the first reaction within the organisations involved is that the only intervention which is needed is training. This case study shows how to use these previously mentioned approaches and also demonstrates the use of the Viable System Model. This example also shows how a problem presented to a training department can actually start to become a question of organisational development, but how use of the VSM provides a solid structure around which to carry out a needs analysis.

## How a systemic needs analysis works

Explaining how to carry out a needs analysis following systemic principles is not altogether straightforward. There are several reasons for this. First, within a systemic enquiry we are constantly developing and refining our understanding of the situation, and this means that we often have to move backwards and forwards, as illustrated in Figure 8.1.

It is always a good idea to start off with the boundary definition, but then the reflection on different perspectives and relationships between elements of the situation may well cause us to review our initial boundary ideas.

Then we need to remember that workplace problems are wicked, and there are no definitive right or wrong answers, just ones which are better or worse. This potentially means a never-ending search for the best ideas for intervention, and the challenge will be to decide when we have found good enough solutions.

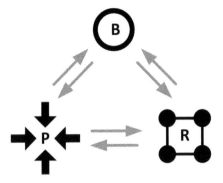

*Figure 8.1* The Boundaries–Perspectives–Relationships model

Third, there are several different systems tools that we can use, and we may find ourselves starting with one and moving to another ... before moving back or onto a third. This is not a bad thing, but it shows a systems *bricoleur* in action, choosing the right tool for the right moment.

This obviously has implications for defining a process to follow for carrying out a training needs analysis. If we are to be true to our systemic principles we must suggest a process which is flexible rather than clearly defined and iterative rather than linear. This is not so easy to do in the linear structure of a book, so I will attempt to propose a somewhat loosely defined process to follow and will, as necessary, suggest points at which hesitation, repetition or deviation may indeed be the best way forward. It is important to remember that this process is based on my own experiences of particular situations of interest, which, as wicked problems, have been unique and with their own characteristics. So what is described here is not definitive practice for all situations, and the reader is encouraged to experiment with finding their own path!

With these words of warning, we will (loosely) follow the process as shown in Figure 8.2.

This process follows double-loop learning principles, in that we are not only collecting data to find an answer to our conception of the situation of interest but also using this data to constantly enhance our perception of what the situation is.

## Case study 1: Weknow Consulting

This is an anonymised case study based on what happened in a real organisation.

Weknow Consulting is a consultancy organisation which provides specialist training and support services to voluntary and public-sector organisations around the world. Such training would help these organisations provide services to their own clients, usually individuals. It employs about 200 people,

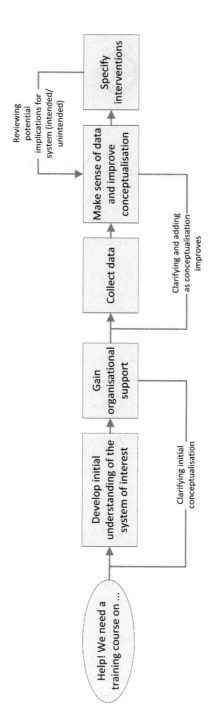

*Figure 8.2* A process for carrying out a needs analysis

approximately half of whom have some form of training responsibility, which could be anywhere between running a half-day course once a year through to spending perhaps 100 days a year training. As well as having their own staff delivering training, they also engage external experts to deliver specialist courses and help client organisations deliver their own training events. The training which Weknow delivers is in quite specialised legal and technical subjects, and to deliver the training required a substantial amount of professional experience and knowledge of the subject.

A problem started to arise when the chief executive started getting feedback from clients that they thought that the training they were receiving was "a bit boring" and that there was a tendency for it to be rather passive and presentation focused. When she discussed this with some of her senior management colleagues, they told her that essentially because of the highly technical nature of the courses, there had to be a lot of reliance on presenting and explaining information. Nevertheless, when sales of courses started to go into a steady decline and she saw competitors increasing their share of the market, she decided that something needed to be done.

The chief executive knew that Lorna, one of the people working in the human resources department, had trained as a teacher, and so possibly understood more about the process of learning and education than more technically specialised colleagues, so she asked her to carry out a needs analysis to see what could be done.

### Develop an initial understanding of the situation of interest

The first step in any needs analysis activity is to develop an initial understanding of what is happening and why people feel there is a problem of some sort. It is very useful at this stage to draw a rich picture which illustrates the elements of the situation (organisations, departments, the operational environment, political structures, systems, equipment and so on) and their relationships (weak or strong, positive or negative). Guidelines on drawing rich pictures were discussed in the section on Soft Systems Methodology (see Chapter 6), but note that although rich pictures have been presented as part of the Soft Systems Methodology process, you do not have to be using SSM to draw a rich picture; it is a very powerful technique to use in its own right.

Based on the brief given to her, Lorna quickly drew out a rich picture (Figure 8.3). She thought that it captured the different actors in the situation and illustrated the problem that had been perceived. In subsequent interviews with stakeholders, she found it useful to show people the picture and see what their reactions were: invariably it provided a stimulating way to start conversations.

### Explore the boundaries of the situation of interest

By looking at the rich picture Lorna was able to appreciate that she needed to think a little bit about the boundaries of the situation in order to decide who

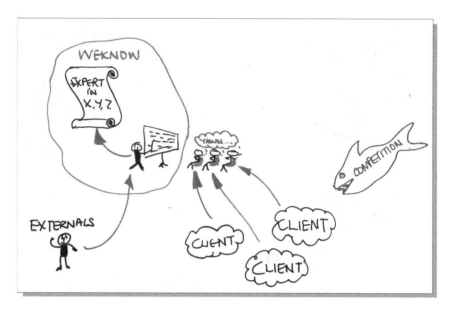

*Figure 8.3* Rich picture of the Weknow situation of interest

needed to be involved in the needs analysis process and who would be part of any eventual training activities.

She decided that Critical Systems Heuristics (CSH) would be a useful technique to help her do this. Gathering the data would also help her improve her understanding of the situation.

When CSH was introduced in Chapter 6, it was noted that the questions presented in the matrix are generic and somewhat difficult to understand, having been written for an academic audience and a general application. What is more useful for our training purposes is to customise these questions (as shown in Table 8.1) to make them more applicable. These customised questions are in the column "Questions to ask in the field".

By finding the answers to as many of these questions as possible, a more complete understanding of the situation of interest can be developed, making it easier to develop a set of more effective proposals for improving the situation. Note that not all of these questions may be relevant, and they may also need to be adapted to suit individual circumstances. One person will not be able to provide all the answers: human behaviour situations are wicked problems, and there will be no single, correct definition of the situation; each interested person will have their own valid perspective on the situation, and there is no 'right' answer.

So Lorna started interviewing various stakeholders to gather more information. She found the expected confusion, ambiguity and little clarity. Her answers

*Table 8.1* Exploring Weknow boundary issues

| CSH question | Questions to ask in the field | Findings |
|---|---|---|
| 1 What is/ought to be the purpose of what people in the situation of interest are doing? | What are the officially stated objectives of the training? What do experts delivering the training see as the objective they need to fulfil? What should the purpose of the training be? | Trainers are delivering courses according to agreed course outlines. People delivering training see their objective as making sure that people complete the end-of-course questionnaire with a satisfactory score. The purpose of the training should be to make sure that client personnel have the necessary knowledge and skills they need in respective subject areas. |
| 2 Who is/ought to be the intended beneficiary of what the people are doing? | Who benefits from the training? Who should benefit from the training? | The primary beneficiaries are client personnel attending the Weknow training courses. Indirectly, people receiving services from the client organisations should benefit. |
| 3 Measure of improvement: What is/ought to be the measure of success of what people are doing? | What are the measures of success for the training? What should the measures of success for the training in practice actually be? | Success in delivering training is measured by scores on the end-of-course questionnaire. Questions are limited to suitability of course content and performance of trainer. External follow-up with course participants by third party could be helpful to probe more deeply. How well client personnel who have received the training perform in practice would be a good measure of the effectiveness of the Weknow training. |
| 4 What conditions of success are/ought to be under the control of the people involved? | What equipment, information and other resources needed for the training do people involved have? What equipment, information and resources should they have? | Course materials are sometimes provided by Weknow, and experts simply follow instructions. Some courses rely on experts' own expertise in the subject. Materials limited to subject matter information and guidance on activities. Experts should have guidance on alternative pedagogical techniques and how to use them. |

(Continued)

Table 8.1 (Continued)

| CSH question | Questions to ask in the field | Findings |
|---|---|---|
| 5 Who is/ought to be in control of the conditions of success of what people are doing? | Who has control over the development of course materials, equipment, information and other resources necessary for delivering the training successfully?<br>Who should have control over these resources? | Subject matter experts internal to and external from Weknow have generally designed course contents, so they have control. Some courses are designed by people who do not deliver training.<br>Someone with pedagogical expertise should have control/oversight of materials, delivery etc. |
| 6 What conditions of success are/ought to be outside the control of the decision maker (Q.5)? | What success criteria are determined by the decision makers?<br>What success criteria are determined by other people?<br>What would be better arrangements for the success criteria? | Success criteria for training (learning objectives, end-of-course questionnaires) are designed by the experts themselves.<br>Evaluation materials ought to be standardised and developed by Weknow human resources. |
| 7 What are/ought to be relevant knowledge and skills for what people are doing? | What are the relevant knowledge and skill areas needed in the training courses?<br>What knowledge and skill areas should be incorporated in the training courses? | Ideas about the training courses focus on technical content, and little thought is given to pedagogical techniques.<br>Skills in training delivery are very mixed; some experts have very little understanding of pedagogical theory.<br>Trainers generally work on their own and do not share much information with other trainer/experts. |
| 8 Who is/ought to be providing knowledge and skills related to what people are doing? | Who provides expert guidance on how to deliver the training?<br>Who should be providing expert guidance? | Nobody provides guidance. Experts are just expected to follow the course materials or be able to develop their own presentations etc.<br>There are no official support services for the trainers, and probably nobody obvious to turn to for any advice.<br>Some training expertise should be available within Weknow.<br>It will be good if there was a 'training delivery expert' available for guidance. |

| | | |
|---|---|---|
| 9 What are/ought to be regarded as assurances that what people are doing is successful? | How do experts find out if what they are doing is successful or meeting requirements? How should experts find out how well they are doing? | Satisfactory scores on the end-of-course questionnaire. No formal system for feeding back information from clients on how courses went. Overall feedback about course performance seems to be done at chief exec-to-chief exec level, which is not very satisfactory as it may all get blown out of proportion. Client satisfaction form (rather than just end-of-course questionnaire) might be useful. Feedback from training expert would be useful, perhaps based on classroom observation? |
| 10 What are/ought to be the opportunities for the interests of those negatively affected by what people are doing? | What channels exist for people affected by the training to comment, provide feedback etc.? Do client companies elicit feedback from their own clients? What channels should exist for people to provide feedback etc.? | There are no systems for eliciting feedback from these people at the moment. If these people do provide feedback, it may not be linked to training. This is a Weknow client issue, but mechanisms for doing this could be explored. |
| 11 Who is/ought to be representing the interests of those negatively affected by but not involved with what people are doing? | Who is affected by the training? Who provides feedback from these people to people delivering the training? Who should be providing feedback? | Staff in Weknow clients who attend training courses then use their new knowledge and skills to help their own clients, so these are the people affected by the training. |
| 12 What space is/ought to be available for reconciling differing worldviews regarding what people are doing among those involved and affected? | What issues do Weknow and their clients see as important as regards services provided to people affected by the training? What should be regarded as important? | Weknow clients seem to be inconsistent as regards eliciting feedback from their own clients. No clear standards of performance regarding service levels. Probably needs a discussion at senior level about how to take this forward. |

are shown in the column "Findings". The situation of interest being considered here is the training system in which Weknow experts deliver technical training to people in client organisations.

Working through these questions should provide very useful data to start the analysis process.

It is particularly important to look for differences between the 'is' and 'ought to' questions, as this is where issues in defining boundaries will come up. For example, when reflecting on Question 9 about finding out about monitoring satisfactory performance, answers to these questions will have a bearing on where a boundary regarding satisfactory performance is drawn and so how the objectives of any subsequent learning programme are defined: Will they be defined by reference to the learning event itself or actual performance in the workplace?

It can be seen that the responses that Lorna has recorded in the table are starting to show a number of areas in which both training (in training design and delivery skills) interventions and non-training changes (such as more for-malised processes for monitoring training delivery) could be useful.

Lorna also started the process of trying to understand what challenges there might be to the transfer of learning: how easy or difficult would Weknow's trainers find it to start using any new knowledge and skills which they were given in a training programme? Learning transfer is primarily affected by three factors: characteristics of the learner, characteristics of the environment in which they will be delivering the training and the design of the training itself. This subject is covered in more detail in Chapter 9.

### Refine the conceptualisation

Lorna was now able to think a bit more about the situation. Her initial ideas about boundaries for the situation confined activities to within Weknow, but she now realised that it would be useful to widen the boundaries to make sure that trainees from client organisations were also involved in whatever actions were taken.

She decided to draw an influence diagram to help her clarify her thoughts about patterns of communication (Figure 8.4).

She identified two systems, the Client and Weknow, but also noted the cli-ents' own clients, who formed the operational environment. She noted that at the moment influence (in the form of feedback about the courses) was delivered to the trainer through the course questionnaires (and this was largely positive although perhaps inconsequential) and via the trainee's chief executive to Weknow's chief executive (which was often negative). She added the role of 'Training expert' to the diagram using dashed lines to show that this did not actually exist at the moment but, if it did, it could provide an advisory and support service to trainers, who seemed to largely work alone. She also noted that there did not seem to be any consistent feedback mechanism about issues

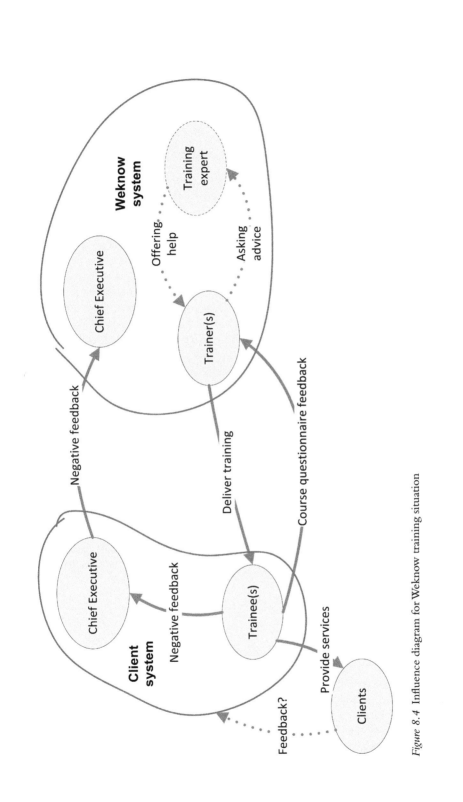

*Figure 8.4* Influence diagram for Weknow training situation

which could have relevance to the training between the clients' clients and the clients themselves.

### Collect data

The next two stages in the process are "Collect data" and "Make sense of the data". This has been done so that the two processes can be described more clearly and should not be taken to mean that these are discrete, sequential activities. Collecting and making sense go on at the same time: collection leads to reflection, feeding into ongoing sense-making processes. This identifies gaps in data, which are filled by more collection, more clarification and so on.

A number of different methods can be used to gather the necessary data: for example, desk reviews of reports and other relevant documentation, surveys, semi-structured interviews, focus-group meetings and so on. There is a substantial literature available about how to conduct these different types of data collection methods, and this is not discussed in detail here. This will be collected from people the initial investigations have shown to be relevant to the situation of interest. It is important to think carefully about boundary decisions and what this means about who should be included or excluded, as this will have an impact on the solutions that we finally identify as being necessary.

What data is collected will of course be determined by the questions asked! The questions listed in Table 8.1 are very useful, as will those in the following sections on making sense of the data.

Lorna decided that it would be useful to look at all of the 'happy sheets', the end-of-course questionnaires, to see what information they might provide, and she also arranged to have some conversations with a number of the organisation's trainers. Although it seemed politically risky, she also realised that it was very important to include clients' staff in this research. She reasoned that talking to them about Weknow's plans to strengthen the quality of their training delivery could actually be good public relations and not a sign of weakness. Those interviews provided very valuable information about what was really happening in the training events.

### Make sense of the data

As she gathered data from the different sources, she realised that she needed to move on to the sense-making stage to see what ideas would emerge from the information she had. She reflected on the different systems thinking tools that were available and wondered which would be most useful. To help her she looked at Flood and Jackson's classification of systems methodologies[1] (which is covered in Chapter 5). Arguably she was looking at something of a complex situation, with several different loosely connected organisations involved, and that in terms of interests about resolving the situation, it was somewhere between unitary and pluralist (largely similar interests but possibly different ideas about resolution). From that analysis, she decided that Soft Systems Methodology would be the most useful approach.

SSM is an interpretive methodology, which means that an imaginary system which describes the transformation the real-world organisation is aiming for is constructed, and this is then used to see how the two compare: does the real world have the feedback loops, control mechanisms and other features which our theoretical system seems to need?

First, it would be useful to briefly review the SSM process. A rich picture is created in order to conceptualise the situation of interest (which has already been done in Figure 8.3). A system map helps to clarify the different actors involved so that the roles they may be playing can be identified (which in effect has also been done in Figure 8.4).

The next thing to do is to think about what worldviews (*Weltanschauungen*) are held by people in the situation of interest and what that means about desired changes. Depending on the boundaries drawn around the situation and who has been included, there can be many different *Weltanschauungen*, as each one can lead to a different perspective and possible ideas. Pragmatically, Lorna realised that the most important *Weltanschauung* was that of Weknow's senior management.

Table 8.2 shows the *Weltanschauung* that Lorna worked from, the associated CATWOE elements and a possible root definition. Note that the root definition follows the SSM convention of the PQR structure: to do P, by Q in order to achieve R. This also incorporates the six CATWOE elements (Table 8.2).

The next stage with each of these transformations is to develop a conceptual model which describes how such a transformation would work in theory so that this theoretical model can be compared with reality, which will suggest

*Table 8.2* CATWOE elements for the Weknow situation

| Element | Response |
| --- | --- |
| **Weltanschauungen** | Increasing the quality of delivery of Weknow's training is essential if it is to hold its market share and maintain its strong reputation. |
| **Transformation** | Weknow training moves from inconsistent practice to a uniformly high level of stimulating, interactive and effective training which consistently receives good feedback. |
| **Customer** | Weknow clients |
| **Actors** | Weknow experts and commissioned external consultants |
| **Owners** | Weknow human resources department |
| **Environment** | Domestic and international public and voluntary sector organisations |
| **Root definition** | A Weknow human resource department–owned system to strengthen the capacity of Weknow's internal and external experts to deliver stimulating, interactive and effective training to clients from the domestic and international public and voluntary sectors so that feedback received is consistently positive. |

actions which could be taken to help the real world function in the same way as the conceptual model.

Figure 8.5 shows the conceptual model which Lorna developed for her situation.

She then spent some time looking at this model and thinking about what questions it raised. As she asked herself each question, she made a note of possible interventions which would be needed (Table 8.3). (Note that for reasons of space, the number of questions presented here is limited.)

Applying the SSM has given Lorna a number of potentially relevant actions which she could consider taking. Because they have come out of this systemic analysis she can with some degree of confidence say that they are *systemically desirable*, as being potentially relevant to the real world system she was modelling.[2] However, she also needs to make sure that these interventions are *culturally feasible* – in other words, will they be acceptable to the people within the situation of interest?

When using SSM as an iterative process, Lorna would have next repeated the exercise for different *Weltanschauungen* and root definitions in order to see what new ideas emerged from the process. However, there is no need to repeat this here.

### Specify solutions

In this case study the use of Soft Systems Methodology has shown how taking into consideration different perspectives, multiple relationships and boundary decisions can help us identify possible solutions to an organisational situation of interest. Well, that may be optimistic: after all, we are dealing with wicked problems, and as discussed earlier, we can never definitively resolve problems of this kind, and all we can do is make things better.

Lorna developed a list of potential interventions (shown in Table 8.4), categorised as knowledge- and skill-related or organisational. Again, we need to remember that this account of the needs analysis process is not complete and that further SSM transformations could be considered. For conciseness within this book, the analysis of systems and possible interventions has not been done as fully as would be the case in a real needs analysis.

When a set of interventions is identified using a systems thinking approach, it is important to think briefly about potential emergent properties of the new learning system: what might unintended consequences be? Here are some possibilities:

- Experts may not want to change the courses they are delivering. How will this be managed?
- Clients may have negative reactions to courses being changed.
- Changes may introduce additional workloads which cannot easily be absorbed.

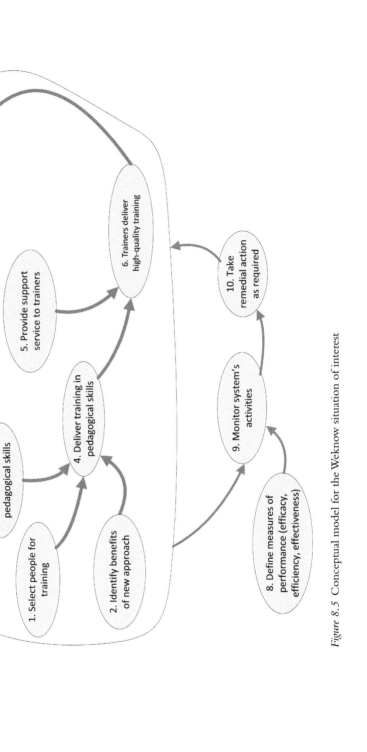

*Figure 8.5* Conceptual model for the Weknow situation of interest

*Table 8.3* Questions prompted by the conceptual model

| Step | Questions prompted | Possible interventions |
|------|--------------------|------------------------|
| 1 Select people for training. | Which people (internal/external) need training? <br> Do we need to establish criteria for receiving training? <br> Do some people need special attention? <br> Should some people be excluded from training? | Senior management decision required on admission policy. <br> Establish list of baseline requirements. <br> Prioritise people who should be trained first. |
| 2 Identify benefits of new approach. | What are the benefits (to trainees, to trainers, to the organisation)? <br> How do we communicate these benefits? | Carry out research into benefits. |
| 3 Select appropriate pedagogical skills. | What pedagogical skills are relevant? | Carry out research into possibilities for pedagogical skills, techniques etc. <br> Design training course incorporating identified pedagogical skills. |
| 4 Deliver training in pedagogical skills. | Who designs and delivers the training? <br> How often is the training delivered? | Identify designated pedagogical skills training manager. <br> Prepare schedule for delivering training based on need, resource availability etc. |
| 5 Provide support service to trainers. | What support needs to be provided to trainers? <br> Who will be responsible for providing this support? <br> How proactive/reactive will this support be? | Include provision of support as part of training manager's role. <br> Establish knowledge management system for supporting trainers. <br> Establish seminar programme for discussing pedagogical skills development. |
| 6 Trainers deliver high-quality training. | How is this quality measured? <br> What evaluation process do we need to have in place? | Review design of after-course questionnaire. <br> Establish monitoring programme for observing training delivery. <br> Set up mentoring scheme to help less experienced trainers. |
| 7 Review training skills being provided. | Are the skills that the trainers are using still relevant? | Formalise review process so that training system is updated yearly (minimum). |
| 8 Define measures of performance (efficacy, efficiency, effectiveness). | How do we know that the system is delivering training which meets clients' needs and expectations? <br> Is this system cost effective? | Agree performance measures with senior management. |

| Step | Questions prompted | Possible interventions |
|---|---|---|
| 9 Monitor system's activities. | How will the effectiveness of the system be monitored? Who will be responsible for monitoring? How will we make sure that the solution stays relevant to all actors? | Agree monitoring system with senior management. Identify independent resource for monitoring. What is the role for the actual trainers in monitoring the overall system performance? |
| 10 Take remedial action as required. | Who will have responsibility for managing the operation of the system? | Identify appropriate resource within human resources for supervising the training manager. |

Thinking these through and making provisional contingency plans is a useful strategy at this point.

Having developed this list of interventions, the next step is to think through how learning interventions would be designed and implemented so that learning transfer becomes more likely. Throughout the needs analysis process Lorna collected data relevant to this, so that by the end of the process she had a good understanding of what type of people were delivering training for Weknow and how accepting their work environment was for implementing new knowledge and skill (the transfer climate) and had given some thought to how learning interventions would need to be designed in order to take these issues into consideration.

We now have a set of potential solutions that would help Weknow transform the quality of the training that it provides to its clients. But what we have in Table 8.4 is just a list of actions to take, and it is not presented in any logical or sequential form. So what is useful to do next is to think through the logic of how these actions would be implemented in order to achieve our ultimate goal. We can do this by formulating a *theory of change* for the programme of knowledge- and skill-related and organisational interventions that we think are necessary.

A theory of change is a description of a mechanism by which we create change[3] and, when developed as an output of a needs analysis, gives us a structure for planning and implementing interventions. It will also be extremely useful when the time comes to evaluate the intervention, as it then provides a framework for examining what did or did not happen during the programme implementation, so that factors contributing to the achievement (or non-achievement) of programme goals can be identified. We will return to the idea of the theory of change in Chapter 10, when we look at systemic approaches to evaluating formal learning interventions.

Theories of change are usually, but not always, represented in some form of diagram. There are many different ways in which this can be done. The simplest is what is sometimes called a pipeline logic model representing a simple linear causal chain connecting inputs, activities, outputs and outcomes. These are

*Table 8.4* Potential interventions in the Weknow situation

| Knowledge- and skill-related interventions | Organisational interventions |
| --- | --- |
| Design training course incorporating identified pedagogical skills. | Senior management decision required on admission policy. |
| Carry out research into possibilities for pedagogical skills, techniques etc. | Identify designated pedagogical skills training manager. |
| Prepare schedule for delivering training based on need, resource availability etc. | Establish list of baseline requirements. |
| Establish knowledge management system for supporting trainers. | Prioritise people who should be trained first. |
| Establish seminar programme for discussing pedagogical skills development. | Carry out research into benefits. |
| | Include provision of support as part of training manager's role. |
| Review design of after-course questionnaire. | Agree performance measures with senior management. |
| Establish monitoring programme for observing training delivery. | Agree monitoring system with senior management. |
| Set up mentoring scheme to help less experienced trainers. | Identify independent resource for monitoring. |
| Formalise review process so that training system is updated yearly (minimum). | Identify appropriate resource within human resources for supervising the training manager. |
| Make sure trainers have the skills to monitor how well overall performance improvement system is operating (situational awareness). | |

the stages normally articulated in a logical framework analysis (a log frame), a technique often used by organisations working in the humanitarian and development sector to define and plan development projects. Such logic models is not adequate for our purposes for a number of reasons: they create the impression that the programme unfolds in a linear sequence (inputs are followed by activities which leads to outputs and eventually outcomes), but in practice, activities, which are represented in the second box of the logic model, may be implemented at varying stages during the project and overlap with outputs and outcomes from other activities; they do not show different, interrelated activities and also do not show any feedback loops needed in order to make the programme work effectively.[4]

Figure 8.6 shows the outcomes chain logic model Lorna developed for these interventions. It tries to show the approximate sequencing and interrelationships between different activities identified as necessary to enable the required changes in Weknow's training delivery. Each activity is expressed as a result, in other words as a completed state, such as "Success criteria for training improvement programme agreed". As well as providing a clearer picture of how the elements will be implemented, the process of creating the logic model is also very useful as a way to review the whole needs analysis process, as it can identify possible gaps in provision and help us think more clearly about what each element might contain.

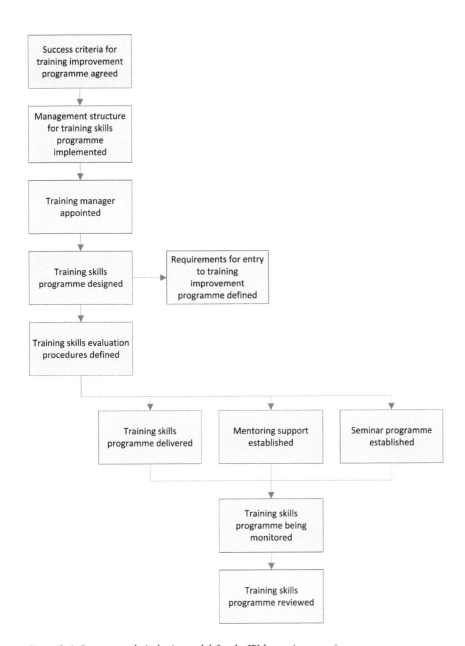

*Figure 8.6* Outcomes chain logic model for the Weknow interventions

Here are some useful guidelines to follow when drawing logic models:[5]

- Make sure the diagram provides a coherent causal model of how the interventions contribute to a particular result.
- Link every result to the overall outcome, and avoid having any 'dead ends'.
- Make sure that arrows do indicate an intended causality.
- Label each item clearly and consistently as a result.
- Use the diagram to show a logical, sequential progression.
- Keep it simple, and focus on key elements; avoid excessive detail which makes the diagram too difficult to understand.
- Keep feedback loops to a minimum to maintain simplicity.
- Avoid unnecessary graphical elaborations; a simple flowchart is perfectly adequate.

Although the logic model diagram should provide a clear explanation of how we intend to implement the programme, a narrative explanation is also often useful, particularly for the stakeholders, who may be more comfortable with text descriptions. We could therefore draft a narrative description of Figure 8.6, which could be something like the following:

> The first stage in this programme to improve the delivery of training within Weknow Consulting is to agree what the success criteria for the programme will be. This should be done in consultation with our clients, so that we become clear as to what their expectations are.
>
> This will help inform the development of a management structure for implementing the programme. It is envisaged that there will need to be a training manager appointed, with responsibility for ensuring the quality of pedagogical skills deployed within our training courses. This person should report to a manager within the human resources department, who will have ultimate responsibility for ensuring the quality of the programme.
>
> The training manager's first task will be to decide what needs to be included within a training programme and to design it accordingly. This may require establishing some selection criteria for enrolment in the training. Design of the training will include developing a robust and effective method for evaluating training delivered under the Weknow Consulting banner and which may involve consultations with clients as well as workshop observations.
>
> Once the graduates from this training programme have started to deliver training, they will need to be supported by various measures, including mentors, more experienced trainers with recognised skills, and a seminar programme, which will provide the opportunity for ongoing discussion with peers.
>
> Operation of the training programme will need to be monitored to ensure that it is meeting the necessary quality levels, and it is recommended that progress be reviewed yearly to ensure that it is achieving the agreed success criteria.

## Case study 2: the Advanced Technology Procurement Agency

This is again a fictional case study, although also based on a real organisation and situation.

The Advanced Technology Procurement Agency (ATPA; not its real name) was established as an inter-governmental organisation in the 1970s and for many years helped developing countries acquire high-technology equipment, such as computer systems, mobile telephone equipment and so on. 'Acquiring' covered a wide range of supply chain activities, including identifying needs, studying the marketplace, procurement, logistics and so on. The rationale for creating the agency was that because expertise did not exist in many countries for making informed decisions about how to acquire high-technology equipment to support economic development activities, it would be useful to have an independent agency which would act as an intermediary. The agency would provide advice to developing countries about what they should be buying and enable them to obtain appropriate equipment at a fair price. This would help them avoid being at the mercy of the sales teams of Western high-technology corporations.

In the early years of the 21st century a consensus was emerging that many developing countries now had more capacity in technological procurement, and that procurement was something which could start to be handed over to national governments. However, the ATPA had over the years built up a considerable body of knowledge about how the advanced technology market worked and had expertise in procurement processes, so it could have a considerable role to play in helping national governments set up procurement systems.

The challenge was that this represented a completely different vision for the organisation and that its staff, who were primarily people with backgrounds in different aspects of supply chain management, were now going to have to operate as advisers and problem solvers.

The call went out: "We need a training course!"

The consultants engaged to design the training course smiled politely and suggested that they needed to explore the situation more fully before coming to any conclusions about what was needed. They decided on the following strategy:

1   Spend some time with the key stakeholders to develop a high-level understanding of ATPA's new role, a key output from which would be a rich picture.
2   Based on information gathered here, along with some other key interviews, they would make some boundary decisions about who needed to be involved further in the needs analysis process.
3   They would prepare an interim report based on their initial understanding of the situation, which would enable them to gather support from senior stakeholders in order to carry out more detailed data collection.

4   They would gather more data and start to make sense of the situation iteratively so that they could start to create a list of suggestions about what was
needed in order to help ATPA fulfil its new mandate.
5   The final output would be a report summarising the challenges facing ATPA
and proposals for both learning-related and non-learning interventions.

To see how this strategy unfolded, we will follow the same process as used in
the first case study (described in Figure 8.2).

### Develop an initial understanding of the situation of interest

As with the first case study, the first step was to develop an initial understanding of what is happening and why people feel there is a problem of some sort.
Again, a rich picture was useful.

Out of an initial meeting with some ATPA stakeholders came the rich picture in Figure 8.7. It shows both the old and new ATPA operating models. In
the old model, governments in low-income countries (LICs) would request a
particular technology and ATPA would source it and arrange for delivery. In
the new model, ATPA's role would be to provide advice to governments, who
would then carry out procurement themselves. It is not a sophisticated drawing,
but the process of creating it with the ATPA team stimulated a useful discussion,
helping clarify various issues.

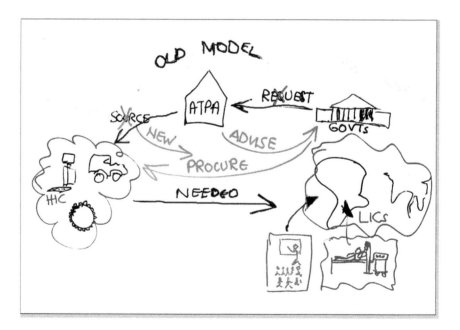

*Figure 8.7* ATPA initial rich picture

At this stage the understanding of the situation of interest was only partial (but, of course, from a systems perspective it can never be complete!). However, this picture was a very useful tool to help the consultancy team start to develop an understanding of the situation of interest, and from this exercise they were able to start developing a list of questions to ask and what issues they might need to consider more closely.

Next, the consultants developed a simple organisation chart to show the functional relationship of the four different teams in the organisation (Figure 8.8).

### Explore the boundaries of the situation of interest

The initial "We need a training course" is in effect an attempt to define the boundaries within which you operate. It is drawing a boundary around required solutions, identifying (but also limiting), for example, who is asked for information. As discussed earlier, boundary issues are related to power in an organisation, and the person who 'needs' the training course will be drawing on the power that they have as a result of things such as their position, their knowledge of the situation or information they hold.

The consultants decided to use Critical Systems Heuristics (CSH) to help with understanding boundary issues and to gather data which would feed back into the initial conceptualisation of the system.

So the team started the process of interviews with stakeholders to gather more information. Based on these interviews, they were able to provide some initial answers to the questions in the CSH matrix (Table 8.5). As in the first case study, the "Questions to ask in the field" are project-specific interpretations of the original CSH questions, and what the consultants found is summarised in the "Findings" column.

Alongside gathering answers to these questions, the consultants also make notes about factors which would be relevant to learning transfer when learning interventions were eventually designed and implemented.

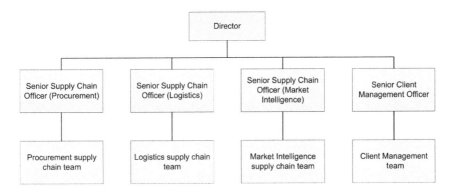

*Figure 8.8* ATPA organisation chart

Table 8.5 Exploring ATPA boundary issues

| CSH question | Questions to ask in the field | Findings |
| --- | --- | --- |
| 1 What is/ought to be the purpose of what people in the situation of interest are doing? | What are the officially stated objectives describing what people should be doing in the new operational model? What do people doing the work see as the objective they need to fulfil? Should these objectives be expressed in an alternative way to make them more meaningful? | The director and senior management team have prepared a report and presentation outlining seven key objectives for the agency. These have not yet been made public. Operational staff are aware that there is going to be a major change in the nature of the work that they are doing and have a general idea as to what this would mean. However, they do not know any detailed plans. |
| 2 Who is/ought to be the intended beneficiary of what the people are doing? | What groups of people are affected directly or indirectly by what ATPA will be doing? Who are people outside the organisation who are affected by the tasks being considered? | Externally, their work affects counterparts working in procurement functions in client governments. The indirect beneficiaries are technology end users. |
| 3 Measure of improvement: What is/ought to be the measure of success of what people are doing? | What are the measures of success for implementing the new operational model? What should the measures of success in practice actually be? | Previously success was measured against criteria such as meeting budgets, time taken from request to delivery etc. No standards have yet been defined for measuring success for the new way of working. They will need to be related to some measure of satisfaction by client governments. |
| 4 What conditions of success are/ought to be under the control of the people involved? | What equipment, information and other resources needed for the tasks do the people involved have? What equipment, information and resources should they have? | Previously ATPA staff spent almost all of their time in their office, with few visits to the field. Logistics related to delivery to site were dealt with by subcontracted local partners. The emphasis was on procedural rather than on relationship-building skills. Within the new model, there will need to be more emphasis on relationship-building with counterpart staff, and so the need for international travel will be greater. Communication systems may need to be strengthened (more use of video-conferencing technology, for example). |

| | | |
|---|---|---|
| 5 | Who is/ought to be in control of the conditions of success of what people are doing? | Supply Chain Officers (SCOs) have not been consulted much about what they think they will need for the new way of working. More consultation is needed. |
| | Who has control over operating procedures, equipment, information and other resources necessary for carrying out the tasks successfully? | The supply chain teams rely on an IT infrastructure for email, telephone etc., which is managed by the IT department. |
| | Who should have control over resources? | ATPA offers a service to client governments which they are free to accept or not. They may therefore choose to work directly with technology suppliers if these can provide a good service. Success may therefore be to some extent out of ATPA's control. |
| 6 | What conditions of success are/ought to be outside the control of decision makers (Q.5)? | A significant part of ATPA's income stream is from a percentage charge on transactions, which is determined by the senior management team on a project-by-project basis. SCOs provide no input into this decision-making process. |
| | What factors affecting people's abilities to work successfully are outside of their control? | |
| | What factors affecting work should be outside of their control? | |
| 7 | What are/ought to be relevant knowledge and skills for what people are doing? | SCOs are almost all recruited on the basis of their experience in different aspects of supply chain management in the technology field. They all therefore have specific types and levels of tacit knowledge gained from experience. |
| | What formal or informal knowledge and skill do people have for carrying out the work? | ATPA-specific explicit knowledge is defined in standard-operating-procedure documents. |
| | What formal or informal knowledge and skill should people have? | Each team's SSCO is seen as the point of reference for dealing with problems which cannot be resolved at SCO level. |
| | What support systems (supervisory, help desks, mentoring etc.) are in place for helping people carry out the work? | There are no standard policies regarding coaching, mentoring etc., and this is dependent on the interests of each senior supply chain officer (SSCO). |
| | What support systems should there be to help people? | As ATPA moves to a new modality of operation there may need to be more sophisticated support systems in place for dealing with the more qualitative type of work. |
| | What new knowledge and skills will be needed? | Environmental variety in the new operational model will be probably significantly greater, but what this variety will be is as yet to some extent unknown. |

(Continued)

Table 8.5 (Continued)

| CSH question | Questions to ask in the field | Findings |
|---|---|---|
| 8 Who is/ought to be providing knowledge and skills related to what people are doing? | Who are the people responsible for implementing the operational model? Who provides expert guidance on how to carry out the work? Who should be providing expert guidance? | Operational activities are carried out by Supply Chain Officers (SCO) working in three teams: procurement, logistics and market intelligence. Each team is headed by a Senior Supply Chain Officer (SSCO). Internally, what the operational teams do affects support functions, such as HR and IT. A small policy team is responsible for preparing new standard operating procedures, and SSCOs are responsible for ensuring compliance within teams. Within the new model it is not clear if existing SSCOs will have the necessary skills in order to be able to support SCO operation adequately. Some expertise in managing complex interpersonal relationships will be needed. |
| 9 What are/ought to be regarded as assurances that what people are doing is successful? | How do people find out if what they are doing is successful or meeting requirements? How should people find out how well they are doing? | The ultimate test of success is that governments choose to use ATPA to support their technology-buying needs. At the SCO level it seems unusual for people to be informed about government-level decisions to start or cancel agreements with ATPA. Relationships with governments are managed by the client management team, who are separate from the supply chain teams. As discussed for Question 3, supply chain teams view their success based on meeting quantitative targets for procurement activities, but these will no longer be relevant within the new operational model. |

| | | |
|---|---|---|
| 10 | What are/ought to be the opportunities for the interests of those negatively affected by what people are doing? | What channels exist for people affected by the work being carried out to comment, provide feedback etc.? What channels should exist for people to provide feedback etc.? | There are currently no channels whereby end users of purchased technology equipment can report back to ATPA on issues with equipment supplied. |
| 11 | Who is/ought to be representing the interests of those negatively affected by but not involved with what people are doing? | Which people affected by the work being carried out provide feedback or comment on what is being done? Which people affected by the work should be providing feedback or commenting? | Much of the equipment bought by governments through ATPA channels is then used by public-sector organisations in country, such as schools, health facilities, police services etc. |
| 12 | What space is/ought to be available for reconciling differing worldviews regarding what people are doing among those involved and affected? | What underlying world views are influencing what is important (e.g. profitability, worker satisfaction, customer satisfaction, sustainability etc.)? What world views should be influencing what is important? How are/should different world views be discussed? | The theory in use for ATPA is that it helps to procure advanced technology at the lowest possible price for its clients. There are apparently views within supply chain teams that this may lead to lower-quality items being purchased (which are less reliable) and that the organisation may have an emphasis on short-term success for itself rather than supporting sustainable development in its client countries. There appears to be limited space for discussion about these strategic issues. |

### Refine the conceptualisation

The CSH process provided the team with a rich amount of information which helped them to both define boundaries for the subsequent exploration and develop a better understanding of why there is a perception of a problem.

Their next step was to draw a system map (Figure 8.9), identifying the key actors in the situation of interest.

In this diagram the functional departments are indicated by rectangles enclosing the actors. Four systems have been identified here:

- the 'SMT system', the senior management team comprising the director and head of the functional departments
- the 'ATPA – Government system' which comprises ATPA plus the governmental procurement departments
- the 'Strategic system', which links the client management team and the client governments
- the 'Operational system', which links supply chain officers and client governments.

In this diagram the shaded rectangles show the 'official', functional boundaries, those between departments. The lines added show boundaries between groups of actors who operate together in some way, generally by sharing information and, in effect, withholding it from those outside the boundary.

What was of interest were the actors which were not linked together within a system. For example, what was the role of the end users? As they were outside the system, their ability to influence what was happening was limited. Although the client governments regarded the end users as being within their system, from the perspective of ATPA they were outside. This could mean that they were not included in any discussions about supply chain issues. Also, what about the administration and IT departments within ATPA? Their role was to provide specific services to the operational parts of the organisation, but it would be essential that they were involved in any discussions about changes to operational aspects which had an impact on what they did.

The map shows the somewhat ambiguous relationship between the Strategic system and the Operational system: the client government relates to two different parts of ATPA in different ways, in one case supplying strategic information and in the other operational information. The team's initial understanding was that strategic data may not be reported back to the operational teams, which could have a negative effect on their performance.

With an initial boundary definition completed, it was now possible to make decisions about who needed to be involved in the data collection, who could provide what sort of information and so on. Clearly it would be important to gather information from a number of different parties. However, it is important to remember that further research may suggest that revising these boundaries is necessary; they are not fixed in stone.

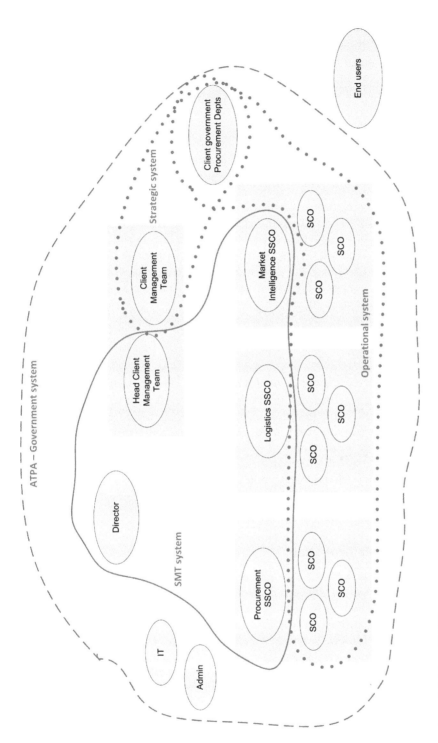

*Figure 8.9* Map of ATPA systems

By completing the CSH exercise the team was then able to complete the third stage of the needs analysis process by preparing an interim report which summarised initial findings and early observations. This was presented to the senior management team, who agreed that the initial findings were interesting and valuable, and this cleared the way for further data collection.

### Collect data

As in the previous case study, the following stages of data collection and sense making went on at the same time. The answers recorded from the Critical Systems Heuristics exercise were useful, as were those in the following sections on making sense of the data, in particular Table 8.6, which looks at questions to ask when using the Viable System Model as a sense-making tool.

One tool which could have been of considerable use in this case study, given the relatively small size of the organisation and its bounded nature, is Social Network Analysis. Using this technique could have thrown considerable light on who is in contact with whom in the organisation and how information flows from one person to another.

### Make sense of the data

When moving on to the sense-making stage, there are some choices as to which systems tools could be used. The choice depends on the nature of the situation being explored, and the classification described in Chapter 5 may be helpful. As participants in the situation of interest probably share a common interest in finding the best way forward, the situation could be described as unitary. As there are a number of different actors and organisations involved, it is a complex situation. This would suggest that both the Viable System Model and Soft Systems Methodology could be useful.

So in this section we shall look at how these two different tools, VSM and SSM, can be applied in the data analysis stage.

### Using the Viable System Model

The Viable System Model is a sophisticated model which we can use to reflect on how organisations operate. As discussed in Chapter 6, one of the reasons VSM so powerful is its recursion: that each System 1 in an overall viable system is a viable system in its own right, and so we should be able to identify the five systems within each System 1. And so on. So to use it in a needs analysis we decide at what level or levels we need to carry out some analysis and then compare what we can see with how a viable system would function. From this we will be able to identify issues which should be addressed in order to improve the performance of concern.

Although powerful, VSM is not a particularly easy model to grasp, and its real-world use has been limited by a shortage of practical guides. However,

Table 8.6 Information for the level 1 recursion

| System | Information to be found | Observations | Possible interventions |
|---|---|---|---|
| 1 | What is happening in the system's environment, how it is operating internally and being managed? What constraints operate on it from senior management? How it is held accountable, and how its performance is measured. | The variety in the operational environment will be significant: the level of expertise in government counterparts will be very varied. Roles will be changing significantly from largely procedural to essentially advisory. Managers' roles may change from being essentially work allocation and progress monitoring to being more collaborative, advising on problem solving etc. Senior management will be very concerned to make sure that the new function works effectively. Current accountability processes will be redundant. New measures are not yet in place. | Job descriptions need to be rewritten. Team-building programmes aimed at helping teams to understand how to operate effectively in the new model. New accountability processes and measures need to be defined. |
| 2 | What may cause each System 1 to oscillate or have conflict with other System 1s or their environment? What System 2 elements work to harmonise or dampen the System 1s? How is System 2 perceived (threatening or facilitating)? | May be problems due to variation in demand from different countries. System 2 was previously linked to supply chain continuity. For example, procurement and logistics needed to maintain close contact in order to ensure efficient transportation of equipment purchased. New role of System 2 less clear, as System 1s will work much more independently. | Development of protocols for relationship among Procurement, Logistics and Market Intelligence functions. Team-building programmes to identify how they will work together in supporting government counterparts. |

(Continued)

Table 8.6 (Continued)

| System | Information to be found | Observations | Possible interventions |
|---|---|---|---|
| 3 | What System 3 components are there? How does System 3 exercise its authority? How does System 3 negotiate with the System 1s to agree resources? Who is responsible for monitoring the performance of System 1s? How is the relationship between System 3 and System 1s perceived (autocratic or democratic)? How much freedom do the System 1s have? | System 3 is exercised through the senior management team, which comprises the director and the Senior Supply Chain Officers. Decisions taken in the team meetings are passed down to each of the operational teams through the SSCOs. How each System 1 operates varies, as each of the SSCOs has their own managerial style, and this seems to vary from quite democratic in two cases to somewhat autocratic in another. This affects how the System 1s negotiate for the resources that they need. System 1 operation has in the past been fairly closely regulated by SOPs, but with the new operating model it will need to be able to operate with more autonomy. This may prove challenging in the short term. | System 3 probably adequate for transition, but needs monitoring. |
| 3★ | How does System 3 monitor what is happening in the System 1s? | The SSCOs monitor the performance of the SCOs against operational objectives, but objectives under the new operating model have not yet been determined. This will be reported back to higher levels in the senior management team (SMT) meetings. | Transition process will create high demand for System 3★, so process needs to be formalised and made clear to all teams. |
| 4 | What System 4 activities are there? How far ahead do System 4 activities look? How effective are these activities in enabling adaptation to the future? To what degree is System 4 open to innovation? | There are two forms of System 4: <br>• The client management team monitors the relationship with client governments and so gathers information about strategic developments. <br>• The market intelligence team monitors the advanced-technology marketplace, making sure that they are aware of relevant technological developments and understanding financial aspects of the marketplace. | Role of market intelligence System 4 will probably stay the same, but linkages with other systems need to be stronger. Strategic-level discussions need to be had about new ways of working and an ongoing monitoring system developed. |

| | Questions | Findings | Recommendations |
|---|---|---|---|
| | Is there any kind of 'operations room' where information is brought together for decision-making activities? <br> How does System 4 relay information to System 5? | Relationship between client management team (CMT) and market intelligence (MI) is not altogether clear and may be affected by possible personality differences. Exchange of information between the two seems to be somewhat ad hoc. <br> Both parts of the systems seem to be open to innovative practice. <br> Information is relayed from System 4 to System 5 within the regular SMT meetings, and through informal channels as necessary. | Role of informal channels needs to be developed, especially during transition phase. |
| 5 | Who is in System 5? <br> How does it act? <br> How does the System 5 ethos affect the perception of System 4? <br> How does System 5's ethos affect the relative perception of Systems 3 and 4? <br> How well are System 5 and System 1 aligned? | System 5 is represented by the senior management team (director, heads of teams). This meets weekly to discuss both short- and long-term issues. <br> The way ATPA has operated has not changed for a long time, and some of the more strategic aspects of System 4, in terms of monitoring the governmental procurement environment, have been allowed to wither somewhat. The emphasis of System 5 has been on maintaining stability within ATPA (through System 3), and the new operating model calls for a radical change in the way it operates. System 4 is going to become much more significant and needs considerable support from System 5. <br> In the past System 5 and System 1 have been well aligned, but System 1 now needs to be brought into line with the new operating model. | Clear articulation of what the new operating model means, its implications and transition arrangements needs to be developed and made public. |

Robert Flood and Mike Jackson have developed a template of questions which can be used as the basis for a VSM–based analysis,[6] and the team adapted these to their particular needs.

### Step 1: Clarify what we need to do

As an organisation which already exists, ATPA has many systems in place for managing what it does. However, its mandate is changing, and it will be increasingly expected to fulfil this new mandate within an existing structure but which will probably need to change in order to cope. The team therefore used VSM to think about what systems would need to be operating for it to fulfil its new mandate and then to see how existing systems related to this in order to identify changes which would be needed.

### Step 2: Identify purposeful systems

The team examined how ATPA operated at several different levels of recursion and started by thinking about the level which seemed to embody the primary focus of the organisation: the various teams that interact with government procurement officials. This is referred to as the 'system-in-focus' at recursion level 1.

We need to define what the purpose of this system is. We can do this using a structure similar to the PQR method described in Soft Systems Methodology, to do P by Q in order to R.[7] In our case we could define this purpose as:

> To provide advice and support in supply chain management by specialist teams in ATPA so that government procurement agencies become sustainable.

As specialist advice will need to be delivered in a number of distinct supply chain subjects, each of these advisory teams will need to be viable systems in their own right, so another level of recursion, level 2, can be added for each team: procurement, logistics and market knowledge. The purpose of each of these systems will be similar to the purpose already defined, but with a narrower focus.

Of course, our level 1 viable system must also be a System 1 in a higher-level recursion, which is referred to as level 0, which would be the broader system of trade to support economic development on a global scale. In our analysis we will focus on levels 1 and 2.

Figure 8.10 shows the level 1 viable system. The consultants looked in more detail at each system within this level of recursion.

### Step 3: Gather information about each system

Table 8.6 summarises what the consultants found about each of the systems at recursion level 1 and what interventions these observations suggested could be

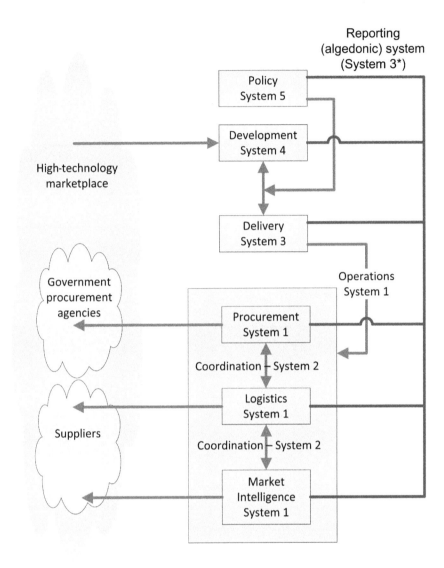

*Figure 8.10* ATPA recursion level 1

useful. Questions in the "Information to be found" column are based on Flood and Jackson's template.[8]

After carrying out this assessment of recursion level 1, the team then looked at level 2, which covered each of the three operational teams. Figure 8.11 shows the model for the Procurement team at this level.

Their findings are summarised in Table 8.7, which follows the same structure as the previous table.

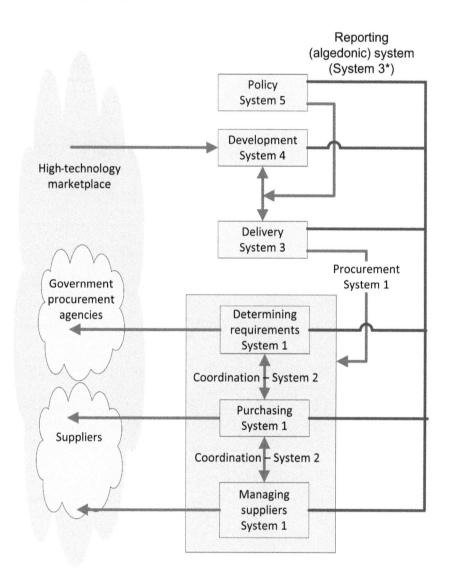

*Figure 8.11* ATPA recursion level 2 (Procurement team)

What did this analysis show? At recursion level 1 (the organisation) the issues which came up and the possible interventions are largely organisational, about developing new policies, clarifying procedures and so on. On the other hand, at recursion level 2 (the team) the need for training appears much more often. Traditional approaches to needs analysis, in which the boundaries are drawn more narrowly and the focus is often on the operational level, tend to generate

Table 8.7 Information for the level 2 recursion

| System | Information to be found | Observations | Possible interventions |
|---|---|---|---|
| 1 | What is happening in the system's environment, how it is operating internally and being managed?<br><br>What constraints operate on it from senior management?<br><br>How is held accountable, and how its performance is measured. | There are three SCOs (supplier management, requirements specification, purchasing) in the Procurement team, all reporting to an SSCO, apparently on an exception basis, so each SCO has a considerable amount of autonomy.<br><br>They are accountable to meet certain targets, based on standard measurable indicators, which are all focused very much around individual contracts.<br><br>Indicators for accountability under the new operating model have not yet been developed.<br><br>Daily work of each SCO will change considerably and will require new skills and knowledge. | Procedures for team-level accountability need to be developed.<br><br>Formal training may be needed for new capacity-building skills.<br><br>Consolidation of technical skills to ensure more standardisation. |
| 2 | What may cause each System 1 to oscillate or have conflict with other System 1s or their environment?<br><br>What System 2 elements work to harmonise or dampen the System 1s?<br><br>How is System 2 perceived (threatening or facilitating)? | The areas of responsibility for each SCO are quite distinct, but they do sometimes come into conflict with each other – for example, where suppliers fail to meet requirements laid down by the requirements specification SCO – and this is attributed to supplier management (or vice versa).<br><br>Harmonisation is normally done on quite an informal basis and depends on the personal relationships between the SCOs. SSCOs will be called on to perform a System 2 function on an exception basis.<br><br>The team see the way System 2 operates as facilitative but acknowledge that when there is a personnel change things can become more difficult until norms are re-established.<br><br>Under the new operating model this three-way division of labour may no longer be appropriate, and each person may need to cover all three areas of procurement. | Team-building activity for clarification about new ways of working together. |

(Continued)

Table 8.7 (Continued)

| System | Information to be found | Observations | Possible interventions |
|---|---|---|---|
| 3 | What System 3 components are there? How does System 3 exercise its authority? How does System 3 negotiate with the System 1s to agree resources? Who is responsible for monitoring the performance of System 1s? How is the relationship between System 3 and System 1s perceived (autocratic or democratic?) How much freedom do the System 1s have? | System 3 is exercised through the role of the SSCO, who in this team is seen as operating in a somewhat autocratic manner. This style of management may be less appropriate for operation under the new model, where outcomes are less clearly measurable. | Team-building activity for clarification about new ways of working together. Coaching skills training may be needed for SSCOs. |
| 3★ | How does System 3 monitor what is happening in the System 1s? | This is done on an informal, exception basis, from SCO to SSCO, and through the SSCO monitoring performance against indicators. In the new operating model this will become much less clear, and System 3★will need to be redefined. | Coaching skills for SSCOs, emphasising two-way dialogue about performance. |
| 4 | What System 4 activities are there? How far ahead do System 4 activities look? How effective are these activities in enabling adaptation to the future? To what degree is System 4 open to innovation? Is there any kind of 'operations room' where information is brought together for decision-making activities? How does System 4 relay information to System 5? | When in System 4 mode, the SCOs are currently very focused on looking at practical, short-term issues affecting current contracts. In the future they will need to transfer this knowledge to government counterparts, but their System 4 activity will then be in identifying capacity-building needs. It is not clear that the current SCOs have the necessary skills to do this. System 4 information should be relayed to System 5 on an ongoing basis, and this process needs to be formalised in some way. | Training on how to identify capacity needs in counterparts. |
| 5 | Who is in System 5? How does it act? How does the System 5 ethos affect the perception of System 4? How does System 5's ethos affect the relative perception of Systems 3 and 4? How well are System 5 and System 1 aligned? | System 5 at team level resides in the SSCO, who determines the operational ethos of the team. Under the new operational model System 5 should promote the importance of support to counterparts and capacity building, but skills in this area are potentially lacking. There seems to be some inconsistency between the abilities of the three SSCOs. | Training for SSCOs on implications of new responsibilities. |

these knowledge- and skills-related needs much more than organisational implications. This ability to operate at different levels shows how useful VSM can be in the needs analysis process: if, for whatever reason, a decision is made to focus on the needs analysis around operational issues, VSM can simply be applied just at that level. However, if a more organisation development–type solution is suspected, it can be applied at a higher level of recursion.

### Using Soft Systems Methodology

Once the analysis using VSM was complete, the consultants thought about developing some alternative perspectives by using another method. So far in this case study we have seen how the team of consultants looked at ATPA *as a real-world system*, composed of activities and feedback loops working together to make the organisation function. This provided very useful information which would lead to various recommendations for potential interventions.

They thought that using Soft Systems Methodology, as an interpretive methodology, could provide some useful alternative perspectives. They would construct an imaginary system which described the transformation the real-world organisation is aiming for and try to see how the two compared: does the real world have the feedback loops, control mechanisms and other features which the theoretical system suggested were necessary? Using an SSM analysis as well as one using VSM could generate new ideas which had not come out of the first analysis.

VSM is particularly suited to unitary situations of interest, which are those in which there are common interests and general agreement on values and means of moving forward. This rests on an assumption that the change in organisational focus is accepted within the organisation and also by those who are affected, which may or may not be true. It may therefore be useful to consider a more pluralist approach which enables us to consider possibly diverging beliefs and different perspectives.

The team had already carried out some of the groundwork for SSM by developing a rich picture and a system map, and the CSH process had identified much useful data. The team were therefore able to establish some different *Weltanschauungen* held by various actors in the situation. This helped them construct root definitions, which described *purposeful activity* or transformations that they would have liked to see in the situation of interest.

Table 8.8 shows some of the *Weltanschauungen* that the consultancy team identified, along with the associated CATWOE elements and possible root definitions for each (following the conventional PQR structure).

The next stage with each of these transformations was to develop a conceptual model, which described how such a transformation would work in theory, so that they could compare this with reality and hence identify actions which need to be taken.

Figure 8.12 shows a possible conceptual model for Transformation 1, and Table 8.9 shows the individual steps, questions prompted by the model and potentially useful interventions.

*Table 8.8  Weltanschauungen* identified for the ATPA situation

| | Transformation 1 | Transformation 2 | Transformation 3 |
|---|---|---|---|
| *Perspective of* | *ATPA* | *Client government* | *Logistics team member* |
| **Weltanschauungen** | Increasing the capacity of governments to carry out their own procurement is a more sustainable strategy than doing their procurement for them. | Managing our own procurement activities will make it easier to buy equipment that meets our needs more precisely. | Changing to an advisory role from one which has been largely procedural is going to be a big challenge for me. |
| **Transformation** | ATPA changes from an organisation which performs services on behalf of governments to one which helps build governmental capacity. | Procurement agency changes from one which does not always obtain the correct equipment to one which always does. | Team member changes from a person who carries out procedural tasks to one who helps somebody else do this work. |
| **Customer** | Client government's procurement departments | End user of technology equipment | Government procurement teams |
| **Actors** | Supply chain teams | Government procurement teams and ATPA | ATPA logistics team |
| **Owners** | ATPA senior management team | Government procurement agency and ATPA | ATPA senior management team |
| **Environment** | International advanced-technology procurement environment | International advanced-technology procurement environment | International advanced-technology procurement environment |
| **Root definition** | An ATPA SMT–owned system to build the capacity of government procurement departments responsible for procuring advanced technology equipment by ATPA supply chain teams so that government procurement is sustainable | An ATPA and government procurement agency–owned system to procure advanced technology equipment by procurement agency teams with the support of ATPA so that end users are consistently satisfied with what they receive | An ATPA SMT–owned system to build the capacity of government procurement teams by ATPA's logistics team so that government procurement agencies are able to manage their own procurement |

As in the previous case study, using SSM has given us a number of relevant and systemically desirable ideas, but it is again important to make sure they are feasible within the context of the situation. This is particularly important in this case study, as we are seeking to impose a major change in the way in which the people in the supply chain teams work: asking them to change from people who are comfortable with administrative, procedural-based tasks to coaches and trainers may be culturally very challenging.

The teams then repeated this process (drawing a conceptual model, identifying questions to be asked and suggesting possible interventions) for other identified transformations, but this is not shown here.

### *Specify solutions*

In this case study, the combined use of Critical Systems Heuristics, the Viable System Model and Soft Systems Methodology have shown how considering different perspectives, multiple relationships and boundary decisions can help us

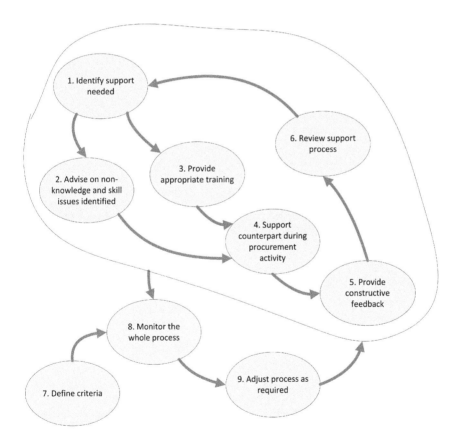

*Figure 8.12* Conceptual model for Transformation 1

*Table 8.9* Issues raised by conceptual model and potential interventions

| Step | Questions prompted | Possible interventions |
|---|---|---|
| 1 Identify support needed | Will supply chain teams have necessary analytical skills? Will supply chain teams be able to identify issues not related to knowledge and skill? | Training programme on needs analysis. Guidelines/reference materials on challenges in supply chain process and potential solutions. Community of practice on needs analysis and solution identification. |
| 2 Advise on non-knowledge and skill issues identified | Will teams be able to suggest non-knowledge and skill actions to take? | Links in with Step 1 interventions. |
| 3 Provide appropriate training | What training skills do supply chain teams have? | Audit training skills within supply chain teams. Deliver training and coaching skills training to supply chain teams. |
| 4 Support counterpart during procurement activity | How much support will be needed? Will this require face-to-face support? | Develop protocols to cover support procedures. |
| 5 Provide constructive feedback | Do supply chain teams have coaching skills? Is there a relevant feedback model already used within ATPA? | Links in with Step 3. Agree standard feedback model and implement within coaching training. |
| 6 Review support process | How do we know how well the process has worked? What systems are in place for monitoring the quality of these support processes? What is role of SSCOs in the process? | Develop protocol for the review process, including roles for ATPA and government counterparts. See how coaching and support relates to existing competency framework and make necessary changes. Formalise procedures and criteria for review process. |
| 7 Define criteria | How do we know if the new ATPA operating model is building capacity in government procurement agencies? Who will be involved in setting the criteria? | Gather benchmark data from government agencies. Agree success criteria with governments and end users. |
| 8 Monitor the whole process | How will the effectiveness of the capacity building be monitored? Who will be involved in the monitoring process? | Establish monitoring procedures and responsibilities. Formalise procedures and criteria for monitoring process. Consider situation awareness training for different staff needs. |

| Step | Questions prompted | Possible interventions |
|---|---|---|
| | Can people at each level become more situationally aware so that they constantly monitor performance? What does sustainability mean in this context? | |
| 9 Adjust process as required | How will changes be made? Who will be responsible for implementing changes? | Allocate overall responsibility for managing capacity-building process. Decide on timelines and milestones for updating processes. |

identify possible solutions to an organisational situation of interest in order to make everything all right. Well, that may be optimistic: after all, we are dealing with wicked problems, and as discussed earlier, we can never definitively resolve problems of this kind, and all we can do is make things better.

We have developed several lists of potential solutions and next need to synthesise these in order to produce a coherent set of recommendations. Table 8.10 consolidates the potential interventions identified by this systemic enquiry (but remembering that the account here of the needs analysis process is necessarily concise and incomplete: for example, further SSM transformations could be considered).

As in the previous case study, it is useful at this stage to briefly reflect on possible unintended consequences and, if necessary, to consider how these could be managed. This helps stop them becoming a nasty surprise if they do emerge!

Having developed this list of interventions, the next step was to think through how learning interventions would be designed and implemented so that learning transfer becomes more likely. Throughout the needs analysis process the consultants had collected data relevant to this, so that by the end of the process they had a good understanding of what type of people were going to be involved in training, what the transfer climate would be like and how learning interventions would need to be designed in order to take these issues into consideration.

Finally, how these various interventions would be implemented needed to be thought through, and this was then captured within a theory-of-change logic model (as discussed in the previous case study).

Figure 8.13 shows an outcomes chain logic model for this transformation. Again, a narrative description capturing this model was developed:

> It is first essential to agree success criteria for ATPA's new operational model with clients. This will make it possible for us to define the required new behaviours for ATPA staff so that we can design training activities and develop necessary policies, operating procedures, guidelines and reporting and monitoring systems.

*Table 8.10* Possible interventions to support the ATPA transformation

| Knowledge- and skill-related interventions | Organisational interventions |
|---|---|
| SCOs:<br>• Training in capacity-building skills (needs analysis, training, coaching etc.)<br>• Consolidation of existing technical skills to ensure more standardisation<br>• Guidelines/reference materials on challenges in supply chain process and potential solutions<br>• Training in relevant situational awareness so that they can adapt their activities as appropriate<br>SSCOs:<br>• Coaching skills training<br>• Training on managerial implications of new responsibilities<br>• Training in capacity-building skills (needs analysis, training, coaching etc.) (as SCOs)<br>• Training in relevant situational awareness so that they can adapt their activities as appropriate<br>Individual supply chain teams:<br>• Team-building activity for clarification about new ways of working together<br>• Establish and support community of practice on needs analysis and solution identification<br>Joint supply chain team level<br>• Team-building programmes aimed at helping teams to understand how to operate effectively in the new model | Relationship with client governments:<br>• Gather benchmark data from government agencies<br>• Agree success criteria with governments and end users<br>• Develop protocol for review processes<br>Development of guidelines:<br>• Procedures for team-level accountability<br>• Development of protocols for relationship among procurement, logistics and market intelligence functions<br>• Protocols to cover support procedures<br>• Formalise procedures and criteria for internal and overall monitoring processes<br>• Allocate overall responsibility for managing capacity-building process<br>• Rewrite job descriptions<br>• Agree and implement standard feedback model<br>• Integrate with existing competency frameworks<br>Strategic actions:<br>• Strategic-level discussions need to be had about new ways of working and an ongoing monitoring system developed<br>• Clear articulation about the new operating model means, its implications and transition arrangements |

The next stage would be to implement formal learning activities, which will include building the capacity of the supply chain teams to provide capacity-building services themselves. It will also be necessary to make sure that they have a high level of the technical skills related to supply chain management which are necessary. Team-building activities centred around the new operational model will be needed in order to make sure that people develop a shared, consistent understanding and buy in to the concept and are comfortable about what their new roles will be. Senior supply chain officers will also need to receive coaching skills training to make sure that they can provide the necessary support to their teams.

If this is all done, then the new knowledge and skills delivered during training should be transferred effectively and efficiently to the workplace so that they can be integrated and sustained during the early years of the new model.

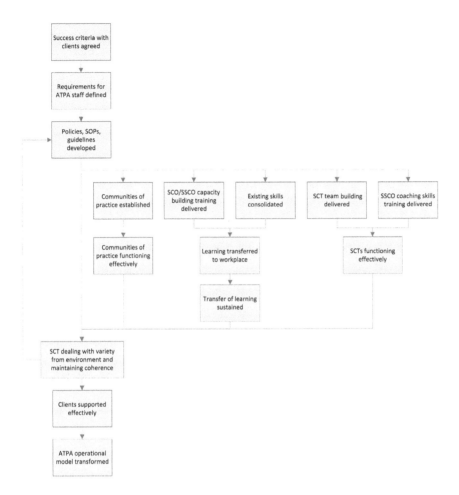

*Figure 8.13* Outcomes chain logic model for ATPA interventions

As well as formal training, steps must be taken to establish, nurture and provide ongoing support to informal learning networks, such as through communities of practice and other activities which can help people develop strategies to deal with the constant developments which can be expected from the client group. The ethos of the organisation should be that it operates at an 'edge of chaos', successfully integrating central policies with the variety of demands created by the environment. This will require a constant monitoring and updating of central policies and guidelines.

If we can achieve this then we should find that our clients are being supported effectively in their own supply chain activities and that ATPA's operational model will have been successfully transformed.

## Summary

Before carrying on to the next chapter, it would be useful to briefly summarise this needs analysis process based around systems-based methodologies.

1   Draw a rich picture to develop an initial understanding of the situation of interest.
2   Use Critical Systems Heuristics to gather data and identify boundaries within the situation.
3   Based on your boundary decisions, gather further data using appropriate techniques.
4   Use the Viable System Model or Soft Systems Methodology (or both) to make sense of the situation and to identify further data needs.
5   Based on your VSM or SSM analysis (or both), identify interventions which are systemically desirable and culturally feasible.
6   Classify them as knowledge- and skill-related or related to organisational structure and procedure.
7   Develop a theory of change which shows how the interventions will be implemented and how they contribute to the desired result.

As the focus of this book is on training, it is important to next give particular attention to how the knowledge- and skill-related interventions should be developed further. This means taking into consideration the wide range of factors which influence the effectiveness of learning opportunities, and this topic is covered in depth in the following chapter.

## Notes

1   Flood, R. & Jackson, M.C., 1991. *Creative Problem Solving: Total Systems Intervention*, Wiley, New York.
2   Checkland, P. & Scholes, J., 1990. *Soft Systems Methodology in Action*, Wiley, Chichester.
3   Funnell, S.C. & Rogers, P.J., 2011. *Purposeful Program Theory*, Jossey-Bass, San Francisco.
4   Funnell, & Rogers, 2011, op. cit.
5   Funnell, & Rogers, 2011, op. cit., pp. 278–290.
6   Flood, & Jackson, 1991, op. cit.
7   Checkland, P., 2000. Soft Systems Methodology: A Thirty Year Retrospective. *Systems Research and Behavioral Science*, 17, p. S27.
8   Flood & Jackson, 1991, op. cit.

# 9 Specifying learning activities

In this chapter we shall look at:

- how to make it more likely that learning will be transferred
- practical steps which can be taken to encourage informal learning
- how to integrate formal and informal learning activities.

## Improving the likelihood of learning transfer

In Chapter 8 we looked at how a systems-based approach to needs analysis can, if appropriate, generate a list of ideas designed to improve the application of knowledge and skills in a situation of interest. However, the next stage is to give some careful thought as to how to specify how these learning interventions (a generic term which we will use to describe both formal and informal learning initiatives) will be delivered or supported so that people can indeed apply what they learn in their workplace.

Recommendations for implementing learning interventions may be based on 'what has always been done', but this may not necessarily be the ideal way forward, so this chapter will therefore look at the factors which influence 'learning transfer'. This is a concept which embraces three distinct stages of applying learning:[1]

- How likely is it that something learned during an intervention will actually be applied in the workplace?
- Will its use be generalised into everyday practice?
- Will this application and generalisation be maintained for an appropriate period of time?

Learning transfer is the process whereby what has been learned in some sort of formal or informal activity is applied in the workplace.

The theory of change underlying learning transfer is illustrated in Figure 9.1. This is quite intuitive and, as is discussed in more detail in Chapter 4, is the theory underlying conventional approaches to evaluating training. However,

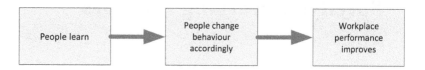

*Figure 9.1* Theory of change of learning transfer

although it makes sense, in practice things are not necessarily so simple, and the chain of causality may not actually work so well.

In order to understand why this theory of change may not be completely reliable, we need to think about what factors influence the causal connections. Three main factors have been proposed which have an impact on how well learning is transferred to the workplace:[2] the characteristics of the learner, design of the learning intervention and the 'learning transfer climate', a term used to describe how receptive the workplace environment is to newly learned skills and knowledge. Various systemic models have been proposed to explain how these three factors contribute to individual and organisational performance,[3] and Figure 9.2 draws on these to create a causal flow diagram.

Before looking at the elements of the model in more detail, it would be useful to explore the idea of how this works. The characteristics of the learners need to be taken into consideration when designing the learning intervention, and developing a target group profile is a key part of a thorough needs analysis process. The quality of the intervention will be good if there is a good match between its design and the characteristics of the learners. This quality will then contribute to both the motivation to learn and the motivation to transfer.

However, what is particularly influential in this diagram is the transfer climate, as it potentially has an impact on most factors in the feedback system. For example, it will affect both the motivation to learn ("What's the point in learning this? We don't do it this way in my office".) and the motivation to transfer ("Implementing these new ideas in my office is going to be very difficult. I'm not sure it's worth the bother".). It will also have a direct impact on the actual level of workplace performance in terms of determining the possibility of change. And finally it will (or should) have an impact on the design of the learning intervention: the needs analyst should develop a good understanding of the characteristics of the workplace environment so that they can specify an intervention which will be effective within its constraints. And of course, other components of the recommendations should be about changes to the operational aspects of the environment which would have a positive impact on performance, irrespective of learning.

If a learning intervention is well designed, there should be a positive impact on both the motivation to learn (it takes into account learners' characteristics) and the motivation to transfer (it takes into account environmental characteristics). These will both have a positive impact on the level of learning transfer, which should then improve the level of workplace performance. It would be

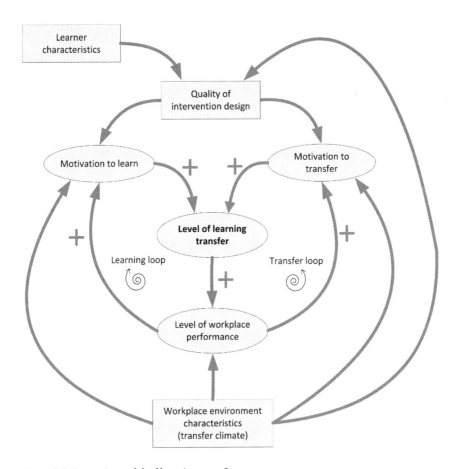

*Figure 9.2* Systemic model of learning transfer

hoped at this stage that this improved performance would feed back into the motivation both to learn and to transfer, creating two reinforcing feedback loops which would benefit future or ongoing learning activities.

Also, however, the level of workplace performance is affected greatly by the transfer climate created by the operational environment, as this will determine the degree to which new skills can be generalised into everyday use and maintained over an extended period of time.[4]

### Learner characteristics

It is important to develop as broad a picture of the people who will receive the training as is possible. There are many different areas that need to be explored.

Two primary factors are age and gender. There is little evidence that biological differences between men and women have any effect on their ability to acquire new knowledge and skill,[5] but the issue of age is more significant. In general, it would seem that as age increases the ability to learn new skills decreases, people become less willing to take part in training activities (possibly due to a fear of failure), they find it harder to integrate different sources of information and the amount of time needed to learn increases. With an older target group it is therefore more important to offer self-paced and well-structured training programmes.[6] Younger people have grown up in a highly technological environment and are often very comfortable with the idea of immediately searching for information as and when they need it, perhaps through YouTube videos, and so may be less dependent on the need for formal learning activities.

Possibly the most significant characteristics of an individual learner which influence transfer is their cognitive ability, or how well they can learn.[7] This is why it is useful to understand what level of educational qualifications the target group typically has (although it is noted that this is not necessarily a totally reliable indicator of cognitive ability given the variety of factors which can influence any individual's ability to negotiate a formal educational system).

Personality traits are significant.[8] A popular model for describing personality characteristics is the 'Big Five', often referred to by the mnemonic CANOE (or the anagram OCEAN). This stands for:

- Conscientiousness: self-discipline about doing things
- Agreeableness: being cooperative and compassionate
- Neuroticism: level of emotional stability
- Openness: appreciation of new experiences, curiosity
- Extraversion: energy and seeking company

As with all models of this type there is ongoing debate as to how reliable the whole Big Five model is, with both critics and proponents. For example, the model is largely based on analysing people from Western cultures, and studies on Chinese, Korean and Japanese populations have found some differences: agreeableness and openness were not significant, but there was a sixth characteristic described as 'maintenance of interpersonal and inner harmony'.[9]

Within the CANOE model, most of the factors seem to have some implications for learning transfer.[10]

- Conscientiousness makes it more likely that people will be motivated to learn and then to transfer this new knowledge.
- Neuroticism seems to contribute to anxiety about trying new things, so people who score more highly on this emotional instability scale may find it harder to transfer learning.
- Openness to experience increases the likelihood that people will value practising new skills.
- Extraversion seems to help people feel more comfortable about demonstrating new skills, particularly where techniques used during learning interventions employed active techniques which extroverts enjoyed.

There is less clarity as to the role which agreeableness plays in learning transfer.

Within a thorough needs analysis, therefore, it could be useful to either carry out some personality testing or look for previous testing that has been done within the organisation on this target group. One of the most popular ways for doing this is through the Myers-Briggs Type Inventory (MBTI). Although this is based on four somewhat different ways of grading personality types, some attempts at correlation have been made.[11] From this it has been proposed that Conscientiousness corresponds to Judging on the Judging-Perception (JP) MBTI scale and Openness to Intuition on the Sensing-Intuition (SN) scale. There is a good correlation between the two systems as far as Extraversion-Introversion is concerned (the MBTI's EI scale), but the MBTI has deliberately avoided considering personality types which might be considered as problematic, in other words, Neuroticism.

In a culturally diverse workplace national cultures may be significant. Culture may be defined as "the collective programming of the mind that distinguishes the members of one group or category of people from others".[12] Cross-cultural psychologists have identified a number of 'cultural dimensions' which make it possible to compare differences in behaviour among national groups. Not all of them are necessarily relevant to the question of learning transfer, but some possibilities are discussed here. It is beyond the scope of this book to provide lists of countries and their different ratings against cultural dimensions, but if the reader feels this is relevant to their situation, they should consult the various references given at the end of the chapter.

People may be regarded as being on a spectrum from *individualism to collectivism*,[13] characterised by the relative importance of the interests of the group of which someone is a member as opposed to those of the individual. Arguably, a person who comes from a collectivist culture may find it harder to transfer learning they have acquired as an individual when they return to their work group, because group norms make it harder to transfer learning without extensive negotiation. Training a group may therefore be more effective than training just an individual.

In some cultures it is much harder than in others for an individual to question orthodoxies in their workplace. So a junior person fresh with new ideas may return to their workplace but find it difficult to implement them because of older, more senior members of staff 'who know best'. In cultures where challenging authority is acceptable, learning transfer may be easier, but in cultures where age or seniority decides everything, introducing new ideas may be extremely difficult. This is most dramatically illustrated in comparisons which have been drawn between airline pilots and surgeons. In both arenas, the cockpit and the operating theatre, the pilot or consultant is in charge and it can be difficult for subordinates to make changes or even point out errors.[14] This characteristic has been called *power distance*,[15] and as examples, it is described as low in countries such as the United Kingdom but high in China and the Arab world.

A third dimension which may be significant is the distinction between *universalism and particularism*,[16] which considers how people apply rules; for example, in the case of learning, recommendations or guidance which has been delivered in a training programme. People in a universalist culture (for example Australia or the United States) would see this guidance as applying to everyone, whereas people from a particularist culture (for example, China or Russia) would make exceptions based on the particular relationship they had with someone; for example, if a person was a friend they would not necessarily expect them to follow the same rules. It follows, therefore, that learning transfer may be less even in a particularist culture, where people would make decisions about what new learning to apply based on relationships within the workplace.

Culture is a complex subject and is often susceptible to stereotyping: it is most important to remember that not every British person will be happy challenging authority, nor will every Chinese person bend the rules for a family member. There are also a significant number of cultural dimensions which have been proposed by different writers, and there is not always consistency between what they may imply in any given situation.[17]

Self-efficacy is important. This describes how much an individual believes in their ability to do something, and this has been shown to be strongly correlated with a motivation to learn and to deal with difficulties along the way.[18] Self-efficacy is not a given personality trait: measures to improve self-efficacy could and should be built into every training activity.

A learner must be willing to engage in the training process. An idea called the 'theory of reasoned action'[19] proposes that people are more likely to engage in voluntary activities (such as enrolling for a training programme) if they are interested in utilising the outcomes of the activity. Therefore, in the context of training, the value of the training must be 'sold' to learners, so that even before starting the learning process they want to improve their performance. A key factor here may be previous experiences of training: if they have attended training that they have thought to be ineffectual or 'a waste of time' the chances that they will engage in new training interventions are reduced. An important question in the training needs analysis is, therefore, how interested in professional development are people in the target group? This variable is often called *learner readiness.*[20]

Figure 9.2 includes both motivation to learn and motivation to transfer. Vroom's expectancy theory[21] provides a way to understand how this motivation may occur. Expectancy theory proposes that people are motivated to do something if the outcome is sufficiently attractive, so motivation is actually a two-way agreement: one party offers an incentive, and if this incentive is attractive to the other party, there is motivation. So in order to decide what is necessary to increase motivation in these two areas, we need to understand what learners will find attractive. This will vary from individual to individual and depends on personality and cultural preferences.

At the level where the training takes place, each learner's motivation will be influenced by thinking that:

- their efforts will result in learning

- what they learn can be transferred to the workplace, given what they know about the transfer climate in their workplace[22]
- the new knowledge and skills will result in some reward, which can be intrinsic (for example, satisfaction from doing a job better) or extrinsic (for example, financial or increased opportunity for promotion) reward,[23] or both

Motivation will be related with their commitment to work. People who are highly committed to what they do will be more motivated, and this will also be influenced by a variety of other factors, such as perceptions that they will be encouraged to use new skills, that their co-workers are also committed and that these new abilities will contribute to better organisational performance.[24] Commitment may also mean ambition to do well and move upwards in the organisation, which can also be a strong motivator for engaging with learning opportunities.[25]

### *Key questions for developing a learner profile*

To summarise what has been discussed so far, Box 9.1 contains a list of useful questions to ask when developing a profile of a target audience.

---

**Box 9.1 Useful questions for developing a learner profile**

How many people are involved?
Where are they located?
What is the age profile?
What is the typical educational profile?
Have any personality profiles (e.g. MBTI) been developed for the people involved?
What is the cultural makeup? What issues about diversity or cultural preferences might this imply?
What is a typical commitment to high performance?
How interested are people typically in professional development activities?

---

### *Workplace environment characteristics*

The characteristics of the workplace environment determine the *learning transfer climate*, which is a somewhat nebulous concept describing the atmosphere within a workplace which supports or constrains the ability to apply new knowledge and skills.[26] It is an emergent property of the workplace system, created by policies, procedures and attitudes prevailing in both the immediate work team and the organisation and will be different everywhere. For example, the transfer climate in private- and public-sector organisations can be completely different, due in part to different expectations about connections between performance and progress.[27]

Constantine Kontoghiorghes suggests a number of general areas which will define the nature of the transfer climate.[28]

The *sociotechnical system* covers issues to do with how the organisation operates and is structured. Does it have a flat or a hierarchical structure? What is the degree of employee involvement in making decisions about how the organisation works? What opportunities are there for advancement? Do people share information and is there a team ethos?

*Job design* looks at the nature of the work that people do. Is the work seen as important, how much autonomy do people have, and does the work make it possible for people to use the best of their abilities?

It is important to consider *quality management* issues. Are people committed to high-quality performance, and what importance is attached to customer satisfaction?

A fourth factor is whether the environment encourages *continuous learning*. To what degree are people encouraged to develop professionally, and is the idea of ongoing learning a priority? Are people rewarded for learning that they do?

Within all of these factors the supervisor is crucial.[29] What supervisors do affects the behaviour of people who report to them: they define what is acceptable and unacceptable behaviour, operate a reward system which sets constraints on what people can and cannot do, act as role models, determine what is or is not important and can be "sources of knowledge and skills or the brokers of knowledge and skills that their subordinates need to be successful on the job".[30] Supervisors therefore need to play a multidimensional role in encouraging learning, and it is essential that they are engaged in the whole formal learning intervention, both before and after the learning takes place.

Work using social network analysis techniques can offer further insights into transfer issues. Helpful feedback on performance can have a positive impact on learning transfer, and it has been observed that it is more likely that transfer takes place when people have more connections which could generate feedback.[31] Conversely, receiving a lot of feedback from a single person may have a negative impact, strengthening the observation that an atmosphere in the workplace which encourages the social construction of understanding *between groups*, rather than between pairs, is more effective in promoting transfer.

All of these factors come together to create a transfer climate which will affect the degree to which people can apply new learning when they return to their workplace.

### Design of the training

It is not the intention of this book to discuss how to design training: this is a vast subject, and the reader should look at the extensive literature already available on this subject.

What is important to stress here is that knowledge about the learners' characteristics and the learning transfer climate must be incorporated in the design process. As is mentioned in many different places throughout this book, systems approaches place a great deal of importance on context (who the learners are and what their transfer climate is): what works in one context may not work in another.

Within the literature on the design of formal learning activities, there is often an emphasis on the psychology of learning as an individual (as discussed in Chapter 7).[32] This can lead to an emphasis on designing formal learning activities which are pedagogically effective but may neglect issues to do with learning transfer. This means that it is important that the design of formal learning should incorporate activities which can help people think through the practicalities of transferring their learning.[33] For example, the learning event should include opportunities to practice applying the new knowledge and skill in an environment as similar as possible to the actual workplace. What is the transfer climate that they operate within and how can they overcome negative aspects? Knowledge and skills which help people to monitor their learning and subsequent performance and decide what is needed in order to improve these are known as self-regulatory,[34] and it is essential that these are included as part of the formal learning intervention. This means encouraging people to reflect on what happens in their workplace, what possible barriers there may be to transferring learning and how they can overcome these.

As well as developing self-regulatory skills, the boundary for designing formal learning interventions should also be drawn widely enough so that it includes developing both pre- and post-training activities. Pre-training activities include providing structures for sessions that an individual can arrange with supervisors or peers to discuss what training they are going to be undertaking so that they can discuss operational priorities, plans for implementing the learning on their return and so on. Post-training activities would be such things as specific projects that the individual can work on which enable them to practice their new skills, buddying arrangements with other learners, coaching sessions with their supervisor and follow-up activities with the trainer. Supportive post-training environments have been shown to have a very powerful effect on encouraging learning transfer.[35]

## Auditing the learning transfer system

If we are going to adopt a systemic approach to specifying a formal learning intervention it is essential that we develop as clear an understanding as possible of the transfer climate. This needs to take into consideration a large number of complex issues and so is not easy. However, one tool which can make this easier is the Learning Transfer System Inventory® (LTSI).[36] Elwood Holton and his team have developed a questionnaire[37] which generates a profile of a transfer climate against 16 categories, which are represented within the conceptual framework in Figure 9.3.[38]

Table 9.1 provides an explanation of what this diagram means.

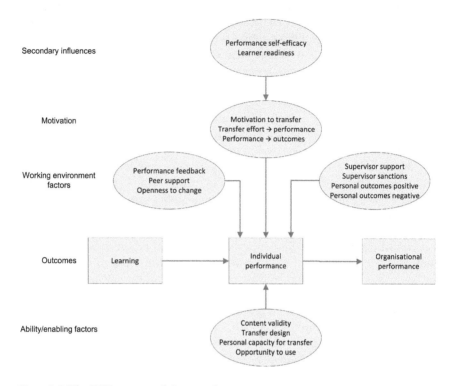

*Figure 9.3* The LTSI conceptual framework

When the questionnaire is used, it generates a score for each of these cat-egories, which are then classified as indicating severe barriers, barriers, weak catalysts or catalysts for learning transfer. So it can be seen that the LTSI can provide a very useful tool for developing a picture of the transfer climate for a formal learning intervention. Armed with the information from the survey, it would then be possible to think about a strategy that could be used to make the transfer of the learning as effective as possible.

## Encouraging informal learning

By definition, informal learning cannot be organised or provided, so the role of the organisation must be to encourage it in some way through providing resources such as time, investment or people which can keep the pot of learning stirred. Here are some ideas which can help this happen.

### Encourage critical reflection by each individual

As people's abilities grow, the amount of tacit knowledge they hold also grows, and it is important that this is externalised so that it can be crystallised and become part of what people know in the workplace.[39]

*Table 9.1* Explanation of LTSI categories

|  | *Category* | *Explanation* |
|---|---|---|
| Secondary influences | Performance self-efficacy | The belief that an individual holds about their ability to change their performance |
|  | Learner readiness | How prepared people are to participate in the learning |
| Motivational factors | Motivation to transfer | The effort exerted in using the new skills and knowledge |
|  | Transfer effort → performance | The expectation that the effort devoted to transferring learning will change performance |
|  | Performance → outcomes | The expectation that changes in performance will lead to a valued outcome |
| Environment | Performance feedback | The feedback that an individual receives about their performance |
|  | Peer support | How much colleagues reinforce and support learning on the job |
|  | Openness to change | How much group norms resist change |
|  | Supervisor support | How much supervisor supports learning on the job |
|  | Supervisor sanctions | What expectation there is that applying new knowledge and skills may lead to negative reactions from a supervisor |
|  | Personal outcomes positive | How much applying the training results in positive outcomes |
|  | Personal outcomes negative | How much people believe that not applying new skills will lead to negative outcomes |
| Ability/ enabling factors | Content validity | How much the learner judges the training to be relevant to the job |
|  | Transfer design | How well the training has been designed so that it can be transferred |
|  | Personal capacity for transfer | How much time and energy people have to make the changes necessary to transfer the learning |
|  | Opportunity to use | The level of resources available for using the new skills |

Although the concept of learning styles has been critiqued elsewhere in this book (see Chapter 7), the process of completing some form of learning styles or personality questionnaire can be a powerful experience in helping people think more analytically about 'what they are doing when they do what they are doing', in particular about how they learn in the workplace.

Developing a culture of reflective practice is also important. This means to encourage people to reflect both on what they are doing when they are doing it (reflection in practice) and what they have learnt afterwards (reflection on practice). It should operate at two levels:

- How can I do what I am doing better (which is single-loop learning)?
- Is what I am doing the best thing to be doing (double-loop learning)?

Double-loop learning means that the learner reflects on how what they are doing relates to their operational environment and how appropriate their current practice is. This might be described as a form of situational awareness, and helping people learn how to be more situationally aware should be a key component in any formal learning intervention.

Figure 9.4, which is an adaptation of previously developed models,[40] illustrates the process of reflective practice.

The practitioner (P), faced with a situation of interest (S), draws on the framework of ideas (F) which they hold. This will be based on previous experience, their education and so on. This leads them to choose a certain method or methods (M) from their toolbox, which they then apply to S. But reflection on how M interacts with S leads P to review their F and so go back to the toolbox to look for different or additional Ms. So the process of interacting with the situation of interest leads to a relational dynamic which enhances both the framework of ideas and the tools available for dealing with such a situation.

Reflective practice should be a standard part of working culture in any organisation, but often the pressures of 'getting the job done' squeeze out moments of reflection. It should be a standard part of the design of any formal learning intervention to encourage reflective practice and show people how to do this when they return to the workplace. It is also good managerial practice to spend time with work teams to see what individuals are learning so that it can be incorporated within standard team practice.

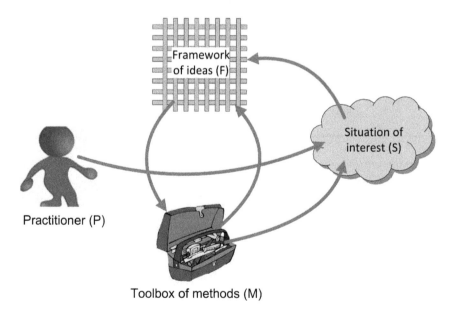

*Figure 9.4* The dynamic nature of reflective practice

### Promote innovation in the workplace

Learning cannot happen in places where people always do what they have always done, so it is important that the workplace becomes somewhere where exploring new and better ways to respond to the variety presented by the operational environment is encouraged. Supervisors must play a key role in creating an appropriate climate for new, improved practice.

### Encourage social aspects of informal learning

Much social learning happens individually, where people do their own reading, research or experimentation to find better ways of doing things. The potential problem with this is that the learning becomes framed within the individual's solitary perspective, so it is possible that they develop blind spots about what is right or wrong, effective or ineffective and so on.[41] Structures therefore need to be created or spaces enabled where individual learning can be surfaced and discussed, perhaps the forum of regular team meetings or events specifically set up to discuss ongoing informal learning.

Social media technologies are also relevant here. Social networking sites, wikis and blogs, for example, provide online spaces in which people can exchange ideas and look for information.

The choice of how informal learning can be socialised will depend on various factors, such as the size of the workplace, its geographical dispersion and even the age profile: older workers may be less familiar with or interested in using social media technologies than their younger counterparts. For example, some research into preferences for seeking work-related information shows that the perceived value of looking at websites for information was higher for younger age groups than for older ones[42] (Figure 9.5).

### Create space for informal learning

One objection that is almost always raised when proposals are made about activities such as personal or professional development is that people are too busy, that there is too much pressure to get things done, and there is just not enough time to do anything else. Unfortunately, that is a reality of life in many (most?) organisations today. But what this actually says is that we are too busy doing what we have always done to think about how to do things better, and this is not a recipe for organisational learning.

Creating space for something as nebulous as informal learning is always going to be difficult, but relies on both top-down and bottom-up pressure. Through creating an organisational culture which welcomes learning (and as a theory-in-use and not just as an espoused theory, to refer to the dichotomy identified by Chris Argyris[43]), senior levels within an organisation should make informal learning and continuous improvement a priority. At lower levels, workplace teams should be prepared to set aside periods of time

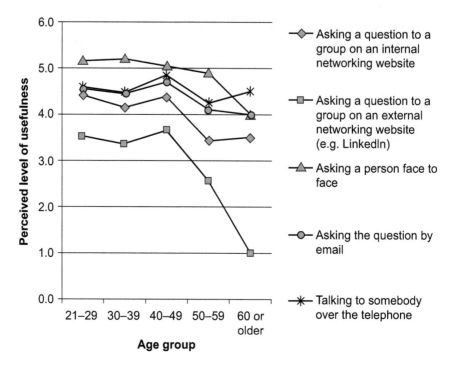

*Figure 9.5* Preferences for seeking information by age

each week in order to review ongoing issues and consider what new ideas have been developed or could be developed in order to manage them more effectively.

Training departments can play an important role in this through influencing both up and down within the organisation. It will not be easy to do this, but what important things ever are?

### Establish and support communities of practice

Communities of practice have existed in one form or another for centuries, but current interest in how they work within modern organisations has been developing since the 1990s, inspired in no small measure by Orr's previously quoted work with photocopier technicians.[44] Subsequent work by academics such as Jean Lave and Etienne Wenger[45] has done much to raise interest in communities of practice as a way of formalising social learning networks.

However, in many organisations communities of practice are regarded as something of a failure, and a comment frequently made is something like, "We used to have a community of practice, but nobody uses it any more". But not everywhere, and there are many examples of organisations which have successful and effective communities of practice and which really help promote organisational learning. So it would be useful to spend a little time exploring what the concept of a 'community of practice' means and what are the distinguishing characteristics of successful ones.

A community of practice has been defined as a "group of people who share a concern, a set of problems, or a passion about a topic, and who deepen their knowledge and expertise in this area by interacting on an ongoing basis".[46] Such communities may be permanent or temporary, being created or creating themselves in order to meet the requirements of a short-term organisational activity. They may be formally defined as communities, which means that they have an awareness of their own existence, or be much less formal learning networks, where people would not necessarily describe themselves as being part of a community of practice.

The community will contain members who have varying levels of expertise, ranging from 'experts' to 'novices', and, to use Lave and Wenger's terminology,[47] novices will be on a trajectory leading them towards becoming expert members (as illustrated in Figure 9.6). They are participating in the community in two ways, through social interaction and by the learning which they are doing.

Learning within a community of practice is not seen in a traditional master–pupil relationship but as *participation*, happening through a set of relationships which enable learning through interaction and engagement, developing a shared understanding of the topic of mutual interest. Note that there is nothing in this explanation which defines the boundaries of a community of practice: it does not need to have a formal membership, and it is not determined by the existence of a technological infrastructure, and to varying extents all of us in our professional lives are members of communities of practice in a variety of forms.

The working of a community of practice can be considered through a complexity perspective. Viewed this way a community of practice is a complex adaptive system, continuously evolving and adapting to the needs of its

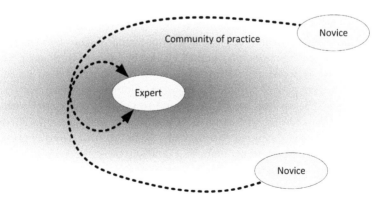

*Figure 9.6* A community of practice as a trajectory towards expertise

participants and the environment. As the environment introduces new demands, the topics of conversation and nature of activity within the community adapt appropriately.[48]

Communities of practice can bring many benefits to organisational life. First, they strengthen the amount of *social capital* within the organisation. Social capital is that quality generated within a group of people through the strength of its networks and relationships between participants.[49] Personal connections lead to greater levels of trust and increase the possibilities for sharing knowledge, cooperating and coordinating activities for mutual benefit.[50] This brings benefits to both the organisation (through the sharing of information and generation of new knowledge) and to the individual, through promoting their own individual learning and increasing their opportunities for promotion or other advancement, for example.[51]

Related to the idea of social capital is that communities of practice can create social norms, implicit or explicit standards about what behaviour is accepted or not accepted. For example, in the context of learning they can establish the norm that 'it is okay not to know' and that asking questions which potentially display ignorance is acceptable and welcomed.[52]

The concept of requisite variety was discussed earlier (see Chapter 5), where the need for organisations to be able to exercise enough control variety to manage the operational variety was explained. It is much easier for a functioning community of practice to be able to generate the necessary control variety than it is for individuals working alone. It is also highly likely that separate communities of practice will overlap, with individuals being members of different communities. By exchanging information both within and across the boundaries of communities, the possibility of developing innovative ways of managing variety is greatly enhanced.[53]

There are potential issues associated with communities of practice, however. A primary one relates to the danger that a community may become too restricted in terms of its membership or organisation. If it develops too strong an idea of its own identity, it may find it harder to recognise alternative perspectives and become subject to groupthink.[54] Here it is useful to think about Granovetter's concept of *weak and strong ties*.[55] This work looked at how people in working class communities found job opportunities and showed that the most important connections that people made for finding work were what could be classed as 'weak ties' with people at the periphery of their social network, as these were people with access to other, different networks. Family members and close friends (the 'strong ties') were too closely connected with the individual's own setting and so were of less help in finding work. These original ideas have been extended within Social Network Analysis to explain how it is important that people maintain and develop weak ties with people who can bring new information and different perspectives into a situation. Reliance on strong ties runs the risk of developing limited perspectives and an inability to generate innovative responses to new situations. People who provide links between different communities (so-called boundary spanners[56]) are therefore extremely important.

From a complexity perspective, as communities of practice will probably exist as part of the shadow system within an organisation, they may establish norms which are to some extent out of alignment with those of the legitimate system. Also, the informality means that there may be multiple definitions of expertise, so that there is no single, agreed definition of 'best practice'. In such situations decisions about mastery may be based on power relations: who is most powerful (for whatever reason) decides what is right, and this may not necessarily be healthy or appropriate.[57]

However, with appropriate guidance and organisation, communities of practice can overcome these potential difficulties and prosper. Which brings us back to the original observation, that experience with communities of practice has often been disappointing. What distinguishes successful, thriving communities from those which wither away and die?

There needs to be a clear domain of interest: the activities of the community should be based around particular knowledge or skills areas of direct relevance to the members.[58] This will contribute to but does not guarantee a perceived sense of dynamism within the community. Community members need to feel that the community is developing and thriving, generating new knowledge of interest, and that they themselves are benefiting from this. This means that the community needs to adapt to new situations and be flexible in what it does and that it evolves in order to constantly engage existing participants and draw in new ones.[59] Dynamism and involvement can be a virtuous circle. The more people are engaged, the more dynamic the community comes, and participants can at the same time perceive their own social capital being strengthened.

Operation of the community needs to be sensitive to cultural factors of both national and organisational culture. In terms of personal, national culture, it has been suggested that communities work most effectively when people share a similar cultural outlook, in particular where they have a more collectivist (as opposed to individualist) perspective. Power distance, the characteristic of a culture where deference is paid to people with greater social status, may also make knowledge sharing within a community more difficult.[60] In some cultures the issue of 'face' is important, and people place great importance on not doing anything which could cause them or others to lose face. In the context of a community of practice, publicly asking what might be seen as a 'silly question' or offering advice which most people see as incorrect could be a way of losing face.[61]

As regards organisational culture, it is suggested that communities of practice may prosper better in organisations which have an existing tradition of open communication and collaboration[62] and where hierarchical structures are less significant in determining the worth of opinions.[63] This may be more possible in flatter, more networked organisations rather than in those with a strong bureaucratic structure.[64]

Personal and organisational cultures come together to create a set of norms which determine acceptable behaviour, and it is important that the community take some action to formalise a 'code of conduct' which determines what is and is not acceptable. For example, in competitive workplace environments, asking a question which other people think shows naiveté or ignorance could lead to ridicule, and such behaviour could very quickly close down open discussions within the community. A code of practice should therefore state clearly that such behaviour is not acceptable and that people who break the code will be subject to some form of sanction. In essence, a community of practice is a network in which relationships are based on trust, and everything that is done within the community and to manage its activities should be done in order to develop trust between participants.[65]

A dynamic, relevant community of practice becomes of more value to the organisation, and it is easier then to assign resources to supporting it. Earlier writings on communities of practice saw them as autonomous, self-driven entities, but this has given way to a realisation that, in common with other open systems, they need to be supplied with energy from their environment and that the energy provided by community participants may not be sufficient.

This organisational support needs to take several forms. There needs to be some form of leadership, exercised through a steering group composed of a representative from management and community members. The steering group will make sure that the community stays focused within its knowledge domain, that it remains active and that trust among participants is promoted.[66] It will need to establish the code of conduct and make sure that participants observe it and also to make people aware of the dynamism within the community to maintain motivation.[67] For example one thing that the steering group could do on a regular basis is to organise some form of face-to-face or online event involving a recognised expert in the domain of interest, perhaps from outside the organisation, who could deliver a presentation, run a seminar or simply take questions from community members.

As well as support in the form of human resources, the organisation also needs to provide an infrastructure through which the community can maintain contact, for example through some form of social networking media.

Ongoing organisational support is essential. It provides official status to the community and shows that taking part is a valid way to use working time. But it is not enough for an organisation to simply provide a technological platform, as once the initial curiosity and interest has faded away it is quite likely that the community will cease to function in any effective way.

## Integrating formal and informal learning

So far we have discussed formal and informal learning as separate activities, and to a large degree they are. However, it is possible and highly desirable to find ways to integrate the two so that they can develop synergies.

For example, formal learning activities can be designed so that they encourage subsequent development of informal learning networks. Distance learning courses should include activities which encourage learners to interact with colleagues to discuss topics covered within the learning materials so that they can strengthen their professional relationships with these people. Workshops should be designed so that they promote trust among participants, for example by incorporating specific team-building activities or through using pedagogical techniques which encourage social construction of understanding.[68]

Members of informal learning networks, such as participants in communities of practice or coherent workplace teams, should be brought together from time to time in formal face-to-face events, where the agenda is self-generating and based around the need to share information and generate a common understanding of knowledge. This challenges the underlying ethos of formal learning within many organisations which is based around the method of 'learning as acquisition', which sees a primary aim of formal learning as for individuals to gain certification. Instead, self-generated agendas for learning promote 'learning as participation', where the focus is on creating a shared understanding of a subject.[69]

Workshops should always encourage participants to engage in reflective practice when they return to their workplace so that it starts to become an integral part of everybody's working culture.

## Summary

Specifying learning activities needs to take into consideration three main factors: the characteristics of the learner population (in particular age, typical cognitive abilities, personality profile and cultural characteristics), the nature of the workplace environment (which will determine the transfer climate) and the design of the learning intervention (which should take the previous two factors into consideration).

The transfer climate is often overlooked during the needs analysis and solution specifications stage, but it should always be considered. Using a tool such as the Learning Transfer System Inventory will help identify which learning and organisational strategies should be employed to increase the probability that learning will be generalised and maintained.

Informal learning can be encouraged by acknowledging its existence and creating organisational space for it to happen. One way of doing this is to support the development of informal learning networks, such as communities of practice.

## Notes

1  Baldwin, T.T. & Ford, J.K., 1988. Transfer of Training: A Review and Directions for Future Research. *Personnel Psychology*, 41(1), pp. 63–105.

2  Baldwin & Ford, 1988, op. cit.; Kontoghiorghes, C., 2004. Reconceptualizing the Learning Transfer Conceptual Framework: Empirical Validation of a New Systemic Model. *International Journal of Training and Development*, 8(3), pp. 210–221.

3  Baldwin & Ford, 1988, op. cit., p. 65; Kontoghiorghes, 2004, op. cit., p. 212.

4  Baldwin & Ford, 1988, op. cit.

5  Salas, E., Tannenbaum, S.I., Kraiger, K. & Smith-Jentsch, K.A., 2012. The Science of Training and Development in Organizations: What Matters in Practice. *Psychological Science in the Public Interest*, 13(2), pp. 74–101.

6  Colquitt, J.A., LePine, J.A. & Noe, R.A., 2000. Toward an Integrative Theory of Training Motivation: A Meta-Analytic Path Analysis of 20 Years of Research. *Journal of Applied Psychology*, 85(5), p. 678; Salas et al., 2012, op. cit.

7  Colquitt, LePine & Noe, 2000, op. cit.

8  Salas et al., 2012, op. cit.; Colquitt, LePine & Noe, 2000, op. cit.

9  Yang, K.S. & Bond, M.H., 1990. Exploring Implicit Personality Theories With Indigenous or Imported Constructs: The Chinese Case. *Journal of Personality and Social Psychology*, 58, pp. 1087–1095, reported in Hopkins, B., 2009. *Cultural Differences and Improving Performance*, Gower, Farnham.

10  Rowold, J., 2007. The Impact of Personality on Training-Related Aspects of Motivation: Test of a Longitudinal Model. *Human Resource Development Quarterly*, 18(1), pp. 9–31.

11  McCrae, R.R. & Costa, P.T., 1989. Reinterpreting the Myers-Briggs Type Indicator from the Perspective of the Five-Factor Model of Personality. *Journal of Personality*, 57(1), pp. 17–40.

12  Hofstede, G. & Hofstede, G.J., 2005. *Cultures and Organisations: Software of the Mind*, McGraw-Hill, New York, p. 4.

13  Hofstede & Hofstede, 2005, op. cit.

14  Leslie, I., 2014. How Mistakes can Save Lives: One Man's Mission to Revolutionise the NHS. *The Economist*, http://www.newstatesman.com/2014/05/how-mistakes-can-save-lives.

15  Hofstede & Hofstede, 2005, op. cit.

16  Trompenaars, F., 1993. *Riding The Waves of Culture: Understanding Diversity in Global Business*, Nicholas Brealey International, London.

17  For a more comprehensive treatment of how to take culture into consideration in a needs analysis, the reader is referred to Hopkins, B., 2009. *Cultural Differences and Improving Performance*, Gower, Farnham.

18  Colquitt, LePine & Noe, 2000, op. cit.; Salas et al., 2012, op. cit.

19  Hurtz, G.M. & Williams, K.J., 2009. Attitudinal and Motivational Antecedents of Participation in Voluntary Employee Development Activities. *Journal of Applied Psychology*, 94(3), p. 635.

20  Hurtz & Williams, 2009, op. cit.

21  https://en.wikipedia.org/wiki/Expectancy_theory, accessed 14 April 2016.

22  Noe, R.A., 1986. Trainees' Attributes and Attitudes: Neglected Influences on Training Effectiveness. *Academy of Management Review*, 11(4), pp. 736–749.

23  Kontoghiorghes, 2004, op. cit.

24  Kontoghiorghes, 2004, op. cit.

25  Colquitt, LePine & Noe, 2000, op. cit.

26  Rouiller, J.Z. & Goldstein, I.L., 1993. The Relationship Between Organizational Transfer Climate and Positive Transfer of Training. *Human Resource Development Quarterly*, 4(4), pp. 377–390.

27  Holton, E.F., Bates, R.A. & Naquin, S., 2000. Large-Scale Performance-Driven Training Needs Assessment: A Case Study. *Public Personnel Management*, 29(2), pp. 249–268.

28  Kontoghiorghes, 2004, op. cit.

29  Baldwin & Ford, 1988, op. cit.

30  Brinkerhoff, R.O. & Gill, S.J., 1994. *The Learning Alliance: Systems Thinking in Human Resource Development*, San Francisco, Jossey-Bass, p. 134.

31  van den Bossche, P. & Segers, M., 2013. Transfer of Training: Adding Insight Through Social Network Analysis. *Educational Research Review*, 8, pp. 37–47.

32  Saks, A.M. & Belcourt, M., 2006. An Investigation of Training Activities and Transfer of Training in Organizations. *Human Resource Management*, 45(4), pp. 629–648.

33 Bhatti, M.A., Battour, M.M., Sundram, V.P.K. & Othman, A.A., 2013. Transfer of Training: Does It Truly Happen?: An Examination of Support, Instrumentality, Retention and Learner Readiness on the Transfer Motivation and Transfer of Training. *European Journal of Training and Development*, 37(3), pp. 273–297; Grohmann, A., Beller, J. & Kauffeld, S., 2014. Exploring the Critical Role of Motivation to Transfer in the Training Transfer Process. *International Journal of Training and Development*, 18(2), pp. 84–103.

34 Gegenfurtner, A., 2011. Motivation and Transfer in Professional Training: A Meta-Analysis of the Moderating Effects of Knowledge Type, Instruction and Assessment Conditions. *Educational Research Review*, 6(3), pp. 153–168.

35 Baldwin & Ford, 1988, op. cit.; Hurtz & Williams, 2009, op. cit.; Saks & Belcourt, 2006, op. cit.; Salas et al., 2012, op. cit.

36 Bates, R. & Coyne, T.H., 2005. Effective Evaluation of Training: Beyond the Measurement of Outcomes. *Online Submission*, http://eric.ed.gov/?id=ED492371, accessed 20 July 2016; Holton, E.F., Bates, R.A. & Ruona, W.E.A., 2000. Development of a Generalized Learning Transfer System Inventory. *Human Resource Development Quarterly*, 11(4), pp. 333–360.

37 For more information, see http://www.ltsglobal.com/index.html, accessed 18 November 2015.

38 Adapted from Bates & Coyne, 2005, op. cit.

39 Marsick, V.J. & Volpe, M., 1999. The Nature and Need for Informal Learning. *Advances in Developing Human Resources*, 1(3), pp. 1–9; Nonaka, I., 1994. A Dynamic Theory of Organizational Knowledge Creation. *Organization Science*, 5(1), pp. 14–37.

40 Checkland, P., 1985. From Optimizing to Learning: A Development of Systems Thinking for the 1990s. *Journal of the Operational Research Society*, pp. 757–767; Ison, R., 2010. *Systems Practice: How to Act in a Climate-Change World*, Springer, London.

41 Marsick, V.J. & Watkins, K.E., 2001. Informal and Incidental Learning. *New Directions for Adult and Continuing Education*, 2001(89), pp. 25–34.

42 Hopkins, B., 2016. *What You Learn or Who You Meet? How Training Workshops Contribute to Establishing Communities Of Practice*. M.Sc. dissertation, Open University, Milton Keynes, United Kingdom.

43 Argyris, C., 1991. Teaching Smart People How to Learn. *Harvard Business Review*, May–June, pp. 99–109.

44 Orr, J.E., 1996. *Talking About Machines: An Ethnography of a Modern Job*, Cornell University Press, Ithaca, NY.

45 Lave, J. & Wenger, E., 1991. *Situated Learning: Legitimate Peripheral Participation*, Cambridge University Press, Cambridge, UK.

46 Wenger, E., McDermott, R. & Snyder, V.M., 2002. *Cultivating Communities of Practice: A Guide to Managing Knowledge*, Harvard Business School, Boston, MA, quoted in Scarso, E., Bolisani, E. & Salvador, L., 2009. A Systematic Framework for Analysing the Critical Success Factors of Communities of Practice. *Journal of Knowledge Management*, 13(6), pp. 432.

47 Lave & Wenger, 1991, op. cit.

48 Borzillo, S. & Kaminska-Labbé, R., 2011. Unravelling the Dynamics of Knowledge Creation in Communities of Practice Though Complexity Theory Lenses. *Knowledge Management Research & Practice*, 9(4), pp. 353–366.

49 Hatala, J.-P., 2006. Social Network Analysis in Human Resource Development: A New Methodology. *Human Resource Development Review*, 5(1), pp. 45–71.

50 Putnam, R.D., 1995. Bowling Alone: America's Declining Social Capital. *Journal of Democracy*, 6(1), pp. 65–78.

51 Bailey, A., 2013. Once the Capacity Development Initiative is Over: Using Communities of Practice Theory to Transform Individual into Social Learning. *The Journal of Agricultural Education and Extension*, 20(4), pp. 429–448.

52 Preece, J., 2004. Etiquette, Empathy and Trust in Communities of Practice: Stepping-Stones to Social Capital. *Journal of Universal Computer Science*, 10(3), pp. 294–302.

53 Borzillo & Kaminska-Labbé, 2011, op. cit.
54 Nahapiet, J. & Ghoshal, S., 1998. Social Capital, Intellectual Capital, and the Organizational Advantage. *Academy of Management Review*, 23(2), pp. 242–266.
55 Granovetter, M.S., 1973. The Strength of Weak Ties. *American Journal of Sociology*, 78(6), pp. 1360–1380.
56 Tushman, M.L., 1977. Special Boundary Roles in the Innovation Process. *Administrative Science Quarterly*, 22, pp. 587–605.
57 Romer, T.A., 2002. Situated Learning and Assessment. *Assessment & Evaluation in Higher Education*, 27(3), pp. 233–241.
58 Scarso, Bolisani & Salvador, 2009, op. cit.
59 Borzillo & Kaminska-Labbé, 2011, op. cit.
60 Bhagat, R.S., Kedia, B.L., Harveston, P.D. & Triandis, H.C., 2002. Cultural Variations in the Cross-Border Transfer of Organizational Knowledge: An Integrative Framework. *Academy of Management Review*, 27(2), pp. 204–221.
61 Ardichvili, A. et al., 2006. Cultural Influences on Knowledge Sharing Through Online Communities of Practice. *Journal of Knowledge Management*, 10(1), pp. 94–107.
62 Retna, K.S. & Tee Ng, P., 2011. Communities of Practice: Dynamics and Success Factors. *Leadership & Organization Development Journal*, 32(1), pp. 41–59.
63 Preece, 2004, op. cit.
64 Inkpen, A.C. & Tsang, E.W., 2005. Social Capital, Networks and Knowledge Transfer. *Academy of Management Review*, 30(1), pp. 146–165.
65 Preece, 2004, op. cit.
66 Garavan, T.N., Carbery, R. and Murphy, E., 2007. Managing Intentionally Created Communities of Practice for Knowledge Sourcing Across Organisational Boundaries: Insights on the Role of the CoP Manager. *The Learning Organization*, 14(1), pp. 34–49.
67 Probst, G. & Borzillo, S., 2008. Why Communities of Practice Succeed and Why They Fail. *European Management Journal*, 26(5), pp. 335–347.
68 Hopkins, 2016, op. cit.
69 Sfard, A., 1998. On Two Metaphors for Learning and the Dangers of Choosing Just One. *Educational Researcher*, 27(2), pp. 4–13.

# 10  Systemic approaches for evaluating training

This chapter looks at:

- the benefits which systemic approaches can bring to evaluating formal learning interventions
- the principles underlying a systemically based approach to training evaluation
- why it is important to develop a formal learning evaluation policy
- how to carry out formative evaluations of learning interventions
- how to use theory-based evaluation approaches to evaluate formal learning
- how contribution analysis can help assess the relationship between learning and performance.

## Why use systemic approaches to evaluate training?

In Chapter 4 we looked at traditional, approaches to evaluating formal learning interventions and identified a number of weaknesses. Before starting to describe a systems-based approach to such evaluations, we need to look at how they need to be able to deal with the major weaknesses we identified in existing approaches.

### Wicked problems in the workplace

If we look at a performance-related situation of interest as a wicked problem, we see that there is no right answer, just an infinite number of possibilities, some of which are better than others. So we can never identify a 'perfect' set of solutions, and there is always the possibility for making things better. Also, as soon as we intervene in a wicked problem, its characteristics change and it is no longer the same problem. Our intervention will also have had implications for other, interconnected wicked problems.

So an improved evaluation process needs to be able to take into consideration that the criteria which seemed to be important at the outset may not be relevant by the time the evaluation takes place. It also needs to be able to reflect on unintended consequences so that, irrespective of what has happened in our specific situation of interest, we can identify and evaluate any positive or negative consequences that may have happened elsewhere as a result of the intervention.

### Simplistic theories of change

Although some of the less well-known evaluation models do try to take the complexity of the workplace into consideration, the reference model, Kirkpatrick, assumes a simplistic chain of causality. Looking at workplace behaviour from a systems perspective has introduced the idea of the wicked problem, where each human behaviour issue that you consider is the result of a different but interconnected wicked problem. We have also considered the implications of humans working in a complex adaptive system, where the dynamics of a workplace team have potentially very significant impacts on the degree to which people can transfer learning. So for a new approach to evaluating formal learning to be systemically appropriate, it has to be designed around systemic principles and use systems-based methods.

### Causality cannot be assumed

If I take some dominoes and stand them up in a line next to each other and flick the end one over towards the next one, I can be reasonably sure that, one by one, they will all fall over. Causality is fairly clear. But what if I do this outside, where the wind is blowing, or if the dominoes have uneven, non-square ends and are unstable when they stand up? If I now flick the end one, maybe the wind will stop them from falling over, or maybe they will fall over just through the vibration of me being near. In the case of human behaviour, we can never be sure that what we do will lead to a specific outcome or that an outcome is due to a particular intervention. John Mayne, who has written about the idea of contribution analysis, suggests that all we can do is *infer* causality, and not specifically attribute it.[1] This inference needs to be based on sound evidence:

- There is a reasoned and plausible theory of change connecting events or activities.
- The events or activities actually take place as intended.
- There is evidence to show that the described change actually happens.
- Other potential contributory factors have been assessed and shown not to be significant or that the contribution was acknowledged.

Our systemic approaches therefore need to reflect on these four criteria before being able to claim that a formal learning intervention has had a particular effect.

### Limited methods of assessment

Most current training evaluation activities use a limited number of methods for evaluating formal learning interventions and have a restricted concept about what is significant. For example, as research quoted earlier shows, there is a heavy reliance on the level 1 reaction questionnaire, the 'happy' sheet. This however, on its own, tells us little other than reassure the trainer that the learners were 'happy'. Actual learning may be assessed by some form of test, perhaps administered by computer, but this often focuses on declarative knowledge, which may have little bearing on the development of higher-order levels of ability. Learning which is harder to assess, such as skill development or changes in attitudes, but which is arguably crucial in developing mastery, is little evaluated.[2] So systems approaches need to offer more sophisticated methods of assessment than we currently have.

As well as making it possible to avoid these limitations, systems approaches can also offer a number of other benefits.

### Ability to scale up and consider wider implications

Tools such as the Viable System Model are based on a recursive principle, so that we can move up a level from the system-in-focus of the evaluation and consider both how factors at that level may be having an impact on the effectiveness of the formal learning intervention, and how the intervention may be affecting higher level operations.

### Emphasis on viability and dealing with variety

Requisite variety, the ability to balance control and environmental variety, is a key principle in systems thinking. It also places a great deal of importance on the relationship of a situation of interest with its environment, so that our evaluation can develop a good picture of how the learning intervention is affecting this relationship.

### Incorporation of multiple perspectives

Workplace situations of interest are wicked problems, and so there is never a single, universally agreed definition of what the problem is. This makes trying to determine the value of an intervention particularly difficult, as different people will see different problems and so have different conceptions of value. There may also be issues of power involved in what is happening, but tools such as Critical Systems Heuristics can help to explore this.

### Acknowledging the dynamic aspects of performance

Traditional approaches to evaluation often attempt to measure impact at some agreed time after the training has been completed, but what is the right time? Soon after training there may be higher enthusiasm and so greater impact, but this may not be sustainable, so the measurement of impact is unreliable. The longer we leave the evaluation the more likely other factors will have an impact on performance.

### Looking forwards and not backwards

Within traditional approaches to training evaluation we often look for changes in behaviour and overall performance and then try to draw conclusions about what role learning interventions may have had in these. In a sense this is back to front: assessing causality is difficult to do, and we have little idea about the dynamics of changes in behaviour. Conversely, the systems thinking approach that we will follow in this chapter works forward, helping us see how learning has contributed to changing behaviour and performance, making causal connections much clearer and helping us understand how the situation may continue to unfold over time.

So approaches to evaluation where we take a snapshot of performance at a given time after the training intervention may ultimately be meaningless: performance may be at any stage in a vicious or a virtuous circle. Systems thinking can help us explore the dynamic nature of levels of performance.

## A systemic model for training evaluation

To create a systemic model for training evaluation we will use Soft Systems Methodology to create a conceptual model of what training is about and then see how this can be applied in reality.

The first step is to create a root definition by identifying the elements in the CATWOE mnemonic.

| | |
|---|---|
| Customer | Person needing to learn |
| Actor | Person with a responsibility for providing learning opportunities |
| Transformation | To change people who cannot perform a task to the required level into people whose performance improves the output of their workplace |
| *Weltanschauung* | Training can help people contribute more to the performance of the organisation where they work |
| Owner | Person with responsibility for training |
| Environment | An organisational setting |

Following the familiar PQR (to do P, by Q in order to achieve R) structure, a possible root definition could be:

> A system, owned by the person in the organisation with responsibility for training and implemented by training staff, for enabling people in the organisation to learn how to carry out tasks that will improve the output of their workplace.

From this we can develop a conceptual model which we can then compare against reality (see Figure 10.1).

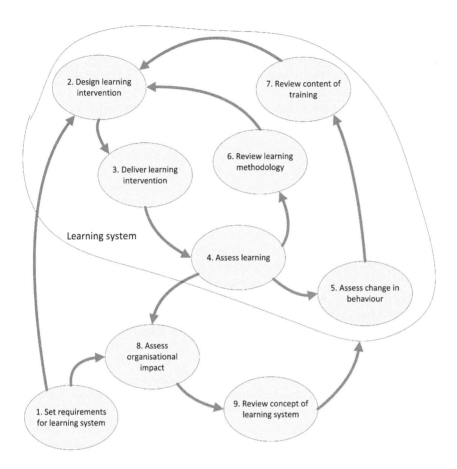

*Figure 10.1* A conceptual model for the process of ensuring learning

We then work through each step in the model, thinking about how this compares with reality:

- Step 1: what are the requirements for the learning system? This should be determined by the needs analysis: if this has not been done, it is in practical terms impossible to evaluate the success of the learning intervention in changing performance satisfactorily.
- Steps 2 and 3: we can assume that these are done.
- Step 4: assessing learning. Do we have assessments of learning which:

  - assess learning of knowledge, skills and necessary attitudes?
  - are valid (actual tests of the objectives of the learning)?
  - are reliable (consistent across different times and learners)?

- Step 5: assessing change in behaviour. What actions do we need to take to gather the necessary data?
- Step 6: review learning. Based on what we learn in Step 4, we may need to make some changes to learning methodologies.
- Step 7: review content. Step 5 may suggest that the content of the learning intervention needs to be reviewed.
- Step 8: organisational impact. How might this be measured or assessed? How reasonable is it to expect an observable change in organisational performance?
- Step 9: learning system concept. Based on what we have learned about the whole learning system, particularly in terms of changes in behaviour and impact on organisational performance, what changes do we need to make about the whole learning system?

From this model we can see that there are the three points at which we need to gather data: Step 4 for assessing learning, Step 5 for assessing changes in behaviour and Step 8 for assessing organisational impact. These correspond to Kirkpatrick's Levels 2, 3 and 4, but what about level 1, the reaction sheet? The value of this was critiqued earlier, but changing the focus of the questions in such a survey can form an important part of the data collection for Step 5: questions which ask for perceptions about the learning transfer climate can provide important data for understanding subsequent changes (or lack of changes) in behaviour.

Returning to some basic principles in systems thinking, what we have identified here corresponds closely to what the anthropologist and philosopher Gregory Bateson described as Learning I, II and III.[3] Learning I is simply the acquisition of new understanding, Learning II is learning about the process followed for this learning, while Learning III describes an awareness of how learning happens, which opens up the possibility for changing this. It should be noted that there are similarities between Learning I and II and single- and double-loop learning. Relating this to our systemic model, we can identify three key questions which a systemically based training evaluation should seek to answer:

- Is the content being learnt? If not, we need to review the methodologies used.
- Is the content the right content? If we do not have the desired change in behaviour, we need to question the content of the learning.
- Is the concept for the learning intervention right? If there is no impact, a change either in behaviour or in organisational performance, we need to question if the whole concept of the learning intervention is correct. Is the intervention needed at all?

Evaluation then comes down to three key words: *learning*, *content* and *concept*. This structure is summarised in Figure 10.2.

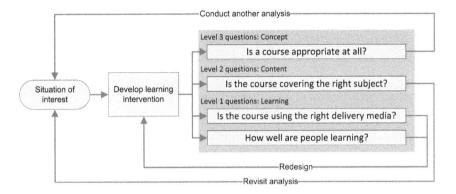

*Figure 10.2* Levels of evaluation

In conventional training language, the 'learning' question corresponds to a *formative* evaluation, referring to those activities aimed at improving the process of implementing the formal learning intervention. The 'content' and 'concept' questions relate to *summative* evaluations, in which we are interested in making observations about the overall effectiveness of the learning intervention in improving performance.[4] Content and concept do not refer to different levels of evaluation: they are both questions which can be answered by examining the impact of the learning intervention in the workplace.

Figure 10.3 shows how this model can work in practice. Every evaluation commission includes a formative evaluation as a basic requirement. This provides answers to the questions about whether people are learning and if the learning medium is appropriate. The question about learning is answered by an appropriate assessment test, and information on effectiveness of the medium comes in part from analysing the results of the assessment tests and also from a reflection survey carried out with the learners.

This reflection survey replaces the familiar reaction sheet. As discussed previously, questions about emotional reactions to a learning event are of uncertain value, but it is really important to use the opportunity of having the learners actually within the formal learning event to ask them questions which will be of value. What is useful at this point is to find out what learners think about the content of the training and learning techniques used and how these can contribute to transfer of the learning to the workplace. Even if there is to be no summative evaluation, finding out about perceived barriers to transfer can be useful in helping redesign activities within the training activity.

If there is to be no summative evaluation, a report is written at this point with appropriate conclusions and recommendations. If there is to be a summative evaluation, further research and data collection will be necessary in order to find out if there has been an appropriate change in behaviour and if there has been any perceived impact on organisational effectiveness. This research,

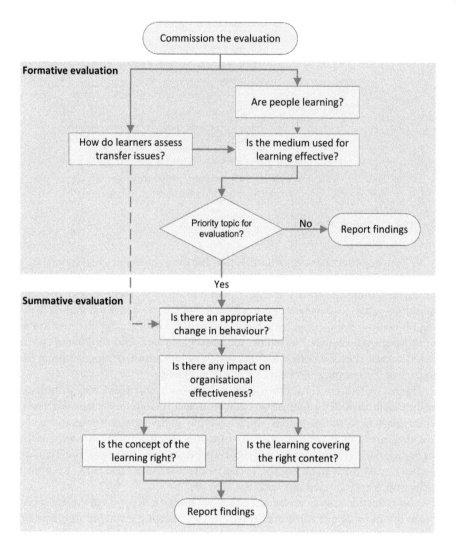

*Figure 10.3* A systemically based model of training evaluation

combined with the data from the reflection survey, will help us obtain answers to the questions about the correctness of the overall concept of the learning and if it is covering the right content.

## Establishing a learning evaluation policy

In most organisations it will not be possible to fully evaluate all formal learning interventions delivered, so there need to be some criteria for deciding which ones to examine in more detail. It is also important to think about the purpose of the evaluation: is it to see if people are achieving the desired objectives, to find out if the design objectives are still valid or to consider whether or not the whole intervention is valid? To do this a formalised learning evaluation policy is needed.

Marjorie Derven suggests that such a policy should be based on five principles.[5]

### Focus on priorities

The policy should cover how to decide if evaluations should be carried out at the formative or the combined formative and summative levels. In practical terms carrying out a formative evaluation is relatively straightforward: the learners are in place, either within the classroom or at their computer, so gathering the necessary data should be straightforward.

However, a summative evaluation is much more complicated and resource intensive. Such evaluations have to look at complex issues of behaviour change and organisational impact. So consider if the learning intervention has been for a high-priority, strategic initiative or if it has involved a large number of participants. How expensive has it been? Has an important stakeholder requested a thorough evaluation? By considering the resources available, how many complex evaluations can be carried out each year? For other formal interventions, carry out simpler evaluations of learning or reaction.

### Define who will be involved

The policy should make it easy to decide who should be consulted during the course of the evaluation. Some of these people will be easy to identify, for example, budget holders or people who are accountable for the performance related to the intervention, but the policy should also encourage evaluators to 'think outside the box' and reflect on the boundaries identified during the evaluation process. This is where the boundary analysis aspect of Critical Systems Heuristics is of value, in particular the 'who' questions.

### Foster shared responsibility

The silo mentality which comes from reductionist thinking can often make the responsibility for formal learning interventions sit squarely with the training department. However, systems thinking tells us that this is a fallacy and that performance is affected by multiple causes and that the effectiveness of formal learning is also subject to many influences other than the design of the intervention itself. Effective boundary analysis and looking at performance as part of a cybernetic system (such as through using VSM) can help reposition 'training' as part of a broader, organisational dynamic.

Alternatively, an overarching, organisation-wide 'evaluation department' could assume responsibility for the evaluation of learning-related activities as part of its remit. This could also help to make sure that learning-related interventions are seen in a more system-wide context rather than being 'buried' within the training department.

### Use resources efficiently

Evaluations can consume time and money, so it is essential to work as efficiently as possible. The policy should encourage evaluators to see what relevant information already exists and to use the tools available as efficiently as possible.

### Make evaluations lead to plans for action

There is no point in carrying out an evaluation if the results will not be used to improve something, even if it is to discontinue the intervention. Make recommendations for action a key requirement of an evaluation.

Another issue which a policy needs to address is who carries out the evaluation. Broadly speaking, there are two possible types of evaluator: an independent, external consultant or an internal stakeholder. Independent, external evaluators have the advantage that they should not have any vested interests in declaring the intervention to be a success or a failure, but their externality means that it can be difficult for them to understand the subtleties of the performance they are investigating – for example, the way tacit knowledge plays a role or the political dimensions behind what people do. External consultants are also sometimes engaged in order to show that 'something is being done', even if the results of the evaluation may not be used.

Alternatively, if a stakeholder conducts or is involved in the process, there is certainly a danger of bias affecting the evaluation activities, even if subconsciously. Unavoidable natural preferences may also make it more likely that the evaluator will suffer from confirmation bias, where they value evidence which supports their initial opinions more highly than evidence which contradicts this (although this may also apply to external evaluators). However, there are some important advantages which can be gathered from seeing the evaluation as an internal learning experience. Involvement in the design and implementation of the evaluation will mean that they buy in to the process and may well be more interested in seeing the lessons which come out of the evaluation process being implemented. The processes of gathering information and clarifying understanding will lead to social learning and development of higher levels of both explicit and tacit knowledge regarding the situation of interest.[6]

It may be the case that for higher-priority evaluations a team approach is valuable, where an external evaluator works with an internal stakeholder. This has the potential for capturing the advantages of both internal and external evaluation approaches, as well as providing a valuable learning opportunity for the stakeholder. However, in such cases the external party needs to take care that they are not unduly influenced by any preconceptions or partialities expressed by the stakeholder, and there would need to be terms of reference which define each person's role.

The policy should also provide clear guidance on how to carry out both formative and summative evaluations. This could be in the form of templates such as how to carry out routine evaluations of formal learning activities (workshops, e-learning courses and so on) and an explanation of the principles of carrying out a summative evaluation, which will need to be less prescriptive.

## Carrying out formative evaluations

Formative evaluations cover learning. Referring to the Kirkpatrick framework, this is level 2, and we have seen how useful it would be to change the focus in typical level 1 assessment from 'reaction' to 'reflection'. This should ask people to comment on issues which are more important and useful than emotional reactions to the learning event.

These are related to learning transfer issues such as self-efficacy, perceived utility[7] and perceptions about how easy it may be to transfer learning.[8] The following are examples of the types of questions which could be asked in a questionnaire given to participants in an event or in an online survey. Note the similarity between these questions and the LTSI framework described in Chapter 9.

### *Self-efficacy*

| How confident do you feel about applying what you have learnt in this training in your workplace? | Not confident at all | | | | | | | | | Very confident |
|---|---|---|---|---|---|---|---|---|---|---|
| Subject 1 | O | O | O | O | O | O | O | O | O | O |
| Subject 2 | O | O | O | O | O | O | O | O | O | O |
| Subject 3 | O | O | O | O | O | O | O | O | O | O |
| Subject 4 | O | O | O | O | O | O | O | O | O | O |

### *Utility*

| How useful do you think the subjects covered in this training are likely to be in your workplace? | Not useful at all | | | | | | | | | Very useful |
|---|---|---|---|---|---|---|---|---|---|---|
| Subject 1 | O | O | O | O | O | O | O | O | O | O |
| Subject 2 | O | O | O | O | O | O | O | O | O | O |
| Subject 3 | O | O | O | O | O | O | O | O | O | O |
| Subject 4 | O | O | O | O | O | O | O | O | O | O |

### *Perceptions about the ease of transfer*

| | Very easy | | | | | | | | | Very difficult |
|---|---|---|---|---|---|---|---|---|---|---|
| How would you assess the ease or difficulty of applying what you have learnt in this workshop to your workplace? | O | O | O | O | O | O | O | O | O | O |

Decide how much you agree or disagree with the following statements.[9]

|  | Do not agree at all | | | | | | | | | Completely agree |
| --- | --- | --- | --- | --- | --- | --- | --- | --- | --- | --- |
| This event has motivated me to apply my new knowledge and skills in my workplace. | O | O | O | O | O | O | O | O | O | O |
| If I apply what I have learnt in this event my performance will improve. | O | O | O | O | O | O | O | O | O | O |
| If I apply what I have learnt in this event the performance of my team will improve. | O | O | O | O | O | O | O | O | O | O |
| People in my workplace regularly offer each other constructive feedback to help performance. | O | O | O | O | O | O | O | O | O | O |
| My workplace team is open to changing what it does if it will help us perform better. | O | O | O | O | O | O | O | O | O | O |
| My supervisor will support me in applying my new knowledge and skills. | O | O | O | O | O | O | O | O | O | O |
| I have the resources (time, equipment etc.) in my workplace which will help me apply my new knowledge and skills. | O | O | O | O | O | O | O | O | O | O |

This could be followed by open questions asking for further information about perceived barriers to learning transfer, for example:

- If you do think it could be difficult to transfer your new knowledge and skills to your workplace, please explain why this may be the case.
- How relevant has the content of this training course been to your everyday work?
- How could the effectiveness of this training course have been improved?

### Guidelines for evaluating learning

It is important to carry out some assessment of how much people have learnt from taking part in a formal learning intervention in order to find out how effective the pedagogical design of the intervention is.

This is normally done by asking participants to complete some form of assessment test, perhaps paper based (if in a classroom event) or an online, multiple-choice type for distance learning. This may also follow on from a pre-test which participants complete before attending the event: this can provide a useful measure of how much learning has taken place. While this data is valid and useful, it is important to remember that such assessments often only examine the cognitive aspects of learning and do not attempt to explore improvements in skill levels or changes in attitude.[10] Without careful question design, there is also a tendency for tests to focus on simple, declarative aspects of knowledge and not to explore participants' ability to apply knowledge.

While declarative knowledge is important, it is only a starting point on the journey to proficiency. For declarative knowledge to be useful, people need to integrate it into new or existing mental models related to the work that they do. Assessments therefore need to show that people can relate what they have just learnt to existing, relevant work-based mental models so that they can show that they know how to apply it, for example, by examining a complex, practical situation and explaining how new knowledge is relevant within this.[11]

Acquisition of skill should be assessed using some relevant practical test which measures aspects such as speed of performance, what errors are made, how well an individual can generalise the skill across different but related situations and so on.

Assessments of attitudinal learning will almost certainly rely on self-assessment measures, such as how the individual's perception of the importance of a subject has changed, what motivation they have for further developing their levels of skill and how confident they are about applying the skill (their self-efficacy).

Enhancing the assessment-of-learning process to encompass more than the very limited testing of declarative knowledge acquisition clearly has significant implications for the design of learning interventions but is necessary if the formative evaluation is to be able to claim that learning has been achieved.

## Carrying out summative evaluations

While formative evaluations examine the process of carrying out the formal learning intervention, the aim of the summative evaluation is to see what the outcome of the intervention is (Levels 3 and 4 in the Kirkpatrick framework). Outcomes as far as a formal learning intervention are concerned are:

- the *generalisation* of learning (how it has been transferred into the workplace and affected operational performance)
- *maintenance* of the new behaviours over a period of time (Level 3)
- the effect that this has on performance of the team, department or organisation (Level 4)

This will allow us to see if both the content of the training and its design concept are right.

It is at this stage that we start to run into significant problems. There are two main challenges. First, logistical: How do we make adequate contact with the participants in the formal learning event? And second, analytical: How can we establish any sort of causal connection between the learning and changes in behaviour?

### The logistics of a summative evaluation

We can first deal with the logistical question which, although it is often seen as a difficult technical obstacle, can be dealt with as long as there is enough organisational support for carrying out the evaluation. The obstacle is usually seen as the problem of making contact with learners once they have 'returned to the wild': how to gather information from them about how they applied their learning; how to triangulate these opinions by gathering data from supervisors and other potential sources; and what the impact on performance at various levels has been.

The key issue here is about what support the organisation is prepared to offer in order to encourage people to support the summative evaluation process, and this is a major reason a summative evaluation should only really be carried out for priority interventions. To provide support, senior management must require their teams to cooperate with the evaluation process by responding to surveys and making time available for follow-up interviews as necessary. Gathering the data can still be a hard and frustrating process, but with higher-level support for carrying it out it should be somewhat easier.

Often the most effective way to carry out such research is by first sending participants and other parties a link to an online survey and following this up with telephone or face-to-face interviews with people who indicate within the survey that they would be prepared to take part. While it is fairly obvious that participants need to be involved in this evaluation process, it is also important to gather information from their supervisors. As discussed earlier, when looking at the issue of learning transfer, we saw how the role of the supervisors is crucial in facilitating the transfer process, and they also have a part to play here in providing a different perspective on the degree to which the participant has actually changed their behaviour and what impact this has had. There is evidence to suggest that involving workplace peers in this evaluation process can also be of value.[12] Such ratings not only provide additional triangulation data on changes in behaviour and effects on performance, but also peer assessment can have a positive influence on feelings of trust within work groups. It should be noted, however, that if peer feedback is unusual in the organisation's culture, it should be used with some caution and its purpose be explained clearly in order to avoid suspicion or a lack of cooperation.

Questions exploring impact should cover three areas: what changes the formal learning intervention has stimulated, what has helped or hindered the transfer of the learning and what other, unexpected consequences have arisen as a result of applying the new knowledge and skill.[13]

The following are some basic ideas for questions which can be adapted for use within a survey or in follow-up semi-structured interviews. It should be noted, however, that there are some other evaluation activities discussed later in this chapter which also raise various questions that should be incorporated within this survey activity.

### Questions for participants:

- How has attending the [name of programme] changed what you do?
- What examples can you provide of applying your new knowledge and skill?
- How has this benefited you?
- How have these changes helped your team or department operate more effectively?

- What factors in the workplace have helped you apply your new knowledge and skill (for example, supervisor's support, team culture, attitudes to innovation, incentives)?
- What factors in the workplace have made it difficult for you to apply your new knowledge and skill?
- Has applying your new knowledge and skill had any unexpected consequences? If so, give some examples of these.

## Questions for supervisors:

- How has attending the [name of programme] changed what [reporting person's name or other identifier] does?
- What examples can you provide of them applying their new knowledge and skill?
- How has this benefited them?
- How have these changes helped your team or department operate more effectively?
- What factors in the workplace have helped them apply their new knowledge and skill (for example, your support as supervisor, team culture, attitudes to innovation, incentives)?
- What factors in the workplace have made it difficult for them to apply their new knowledge and skill?
- Has applying their new knowledge and skill had any unexpected consequences? If so, give some examples of these.

Questions for peers would be similar to those for the supervisor, apart from references to supervisory aspects.

### *Analysis processes within a summative evaluation*

Having looked at how to approach data collection in a summative evaluation, we next need to look at how the data can be analysed. In Chapter 8 we explained how, once the needs analysis process has identified the different interventions which would be appropriate, it is useful to create a logic model which shows what the theory of change for the overall programme of interventions is. As well as helping the original analysts create an implementation plan, the theory of change also can serve as a framework for structuring the evaluation. The process described for carrying out a needs analysis followed systemic principles in order to identify a coherent and interconnected set of activities which will (it is hoped) lead to a desired outcome. The theory of change should capture this, so what the evaluation needs to do is consider each intervention and its relationship with others in order to work towards an assessment of how well the overall theory of change has worked and whether the desired outcome has been achieved.

This method of carrying out an evaluation is often described as *theory-based evaluation* (also sometimes known as theory-driven evaluation). Theory-based evaluation is a way of carrying out evaluations which has been used since the 1930s but came to prominence in the 1980s through the work of Huey-tsyh Chen.[14] The process has been defined as "any evaluation strategy or approach that explicitly integrates and uses stakeholder, social science, some combination of, or other types of theories in conceptualizing, designing, conducting, interpreting, and applying an evaluation".[15]

It is an attractive evaluation methodology to integrate within a systems-based approach to learning evaluation because of its obvious connections with the principles of systems thinking in general and similarity to some systems thinking methodologies. For example, the more modern conceptions of theory-based evaluation place a great deal of importance on developing "contextualised, comprehensive, ecological program theory models".[16] Theory-of-change logic models can sometimes be developed using the principles of causal flow diagrams, as utilised within System Dynamics. Also, the process we have just described, of using theory-based evaluation and then contribution analysis to draw conclusions, is very similar in practice to the use of Soft Systems Methodology. In SSM we generate a conceptual model based on drawing a rich picture and formulating a root definition: here we make use of an existing logic model (which may have relied on SSM to be designed) or develop a new one. In SSM we compare our conceptual model against reality: here we use our logic model as a framework for questioning what has happened in practice. So while the techniques may come from different philosophical backgrounds, the practice is very similar.

Apart from the parallels with systems thinking approaches, there are other reasons a theory-based evaluation process has benefits for the evaluation of learning interventions. If we have carried out a thorough needs analysis, we will already have developed a theory of change, even though it may not have been articulated clearly as such in a needs analysis report.[17] While there may be clearly expressed desired outcomes for a formal learning intervention in terms of the achievement of defined learning objectives, stakeholders may recognise that there are less tangible outcomes emerging from the intervention (and, as discussed earlier, traditional approaches for training evaluation usually fail to give these any consideration).[18] Another reason may be that the evaluator has also played a role in designing or delivering the intervention and sees the evaluation as being an essential part of ongoing programme development. The structure of the theory-of-change logic model also provides a framework around which the evaluation is publicly structured, making it easier to avoid letting confirmation bias shape the conclusions of the evaluation.[19]

Nevertheless, various criticisms have been made about theory-based evaluation, and it is important to consider these, as they can help us use the approach more effectively. It has been described as being more time consuming and therefore being resource intensive.[20] A more fundamental criticism is that evaluators should only really be interested in the overall effectiveness of an intervention, not in how it works (the 'black box' argument).[21] While this may be true in some instances, in the case of evaluating a formal learning intervention we are certainly interested in what happens inside the black box: is it the acquisition of knowledge and skills which improves performance or some other factor? It has also been argued that evaluations based around a theory of change are actually an evaluation of the theory of change rather than of the situation of interest.[22] This can be countered by the evaluator always remembering that the theory of change is a social construct and is not a fixed, reified object. It may well have weaknesses and limitations, and the process of evaluation should not be constrained by the limitations of the logic model: if questioning reveals other drivers which have not been incorporated within the model, these should be investigated and not ignored as irrelevant.

Overall, theory-based evaluation can work very well in evaluating formal learning interventions, but perhaps because of the predominance of Kirkpatrick and his ilk, use of the technique has largely been confined to the medical and social care sectors.[23]

At this point it is important to consider the question, "What do we do if we do not have a theory of change?" The reality is that given the relatively small percentage of formal learning interventions which are designed on the basis of a thorough needs analysis,[24] there may well be no explicit theory of change. If that is the case, it is important to try and construct the logic model before starting. That may seem daunting, but as will become apparent as we work through this chapter, the techniques we use for a systemic evaluation are very similar to those used for needs analysis, and it will be possible to construct a theory of change as the evaluation proceeds. Remember that we are not evaluating the theory of change itself but are using it as a guide to structure our evaluation, so while it will require some effort in order to construct a theory, an initial absence is not a showstopper.

Having established that the underlying philosophy of our evaluation is that it is based around the theory of change, we need next to think about the practicalities: what data we will collect and how we will try to make some sense of it. If our evaluation is to be useful and offer meaningful observations about how effective formal learning interventions have been in terms of achieving the desired objectives, we have to be able to draw some conclusions about causality. This is not easy to do, particularly as taking a systems perspective seems to constantly stress the complexity of human behaviour systems, of non-linear responses and of the constant interaction of wicked problems.

Once we have gathered some data and spent time reflecting on it, we may have some 'gut reactions' about what it means (following similar principles to 'grounded theory',[25] where theory is developed from qualitative data), but it is important to use some systematic process which enables us to draw some defensible conclusions. One way to do this is by using *contribution analysis*, a systematic way of making sense of data coming out of a theory-based evaluation process.[26]

The starting point for contribution analysis is to define what is an acceptable criterion for causality. Kirkpatrick pointed out that finding absolute proof that training improves performance is impossible: all we can hope for is evidence to show that it does beyond a reasonable doubt: "be satisfied with

*Table 10.1* Attribution and contribution questions

| Attribution questions | Contribution questions |
|---|---|
| Has the programme caused the outcome? | Has the programme made a difference? That is, has the programme made an important contribution to the observed result? |
| To what extent has the programme caused the outcome? | Has the programme influenced the observed result? |
| How much of the outcome is caused by the programme? | How much of a difference has the programme made? How much of a contribution?' |

evidence, because proof is usually impossible to get".[27] John Mayne[28] suggests that the following logic chain needs to be followed in order to be able to infer causality:

1    There needs to be a plausible and informed theory of change, supported by stakeholders, which has driven the intervention (which, if we have carried out a thorough needs analysis, will be the case).
2    The activities were implemented as defined within the theory of change.
3    What the theory of change said would happen did happen, and assumptions were proved valid.
4    External factors, such as environmental issues and alternative explanations, which could influence the intervention are assessed and their contributions are recognised or shown to be insignificant.

It is also important to distinguish between the words 'attributed to' and 'contributed to'. Within the contribution analysis lexicon, 'attributed' is a much harder assertion of causality, whereas 'contributed' is used in order to suggest that a particular input 'played a part' in the development of the output. This is well illustrated by comparing the statements in Table 10.1.[29]

Essentially, contribution analysis is about finding *likely influences.*[30]

Contribution analysis is a relatively new approach to sense making, and there are, as of yet, few practical tools available for applying it, although one was developed to evaluate the effectiveness of training delivered to teaching support assistants in Denmark.[31] John Mayne has suggested a six-step approach (illustrated in Figure 10.4) to carrying out a contribution analysis, acknowledging that different contexts may call for the application of different analytical tools.[32] It should be noted that this suggested approach is very similar to that used for the needs analysis process in Chapter 8.

### Step 1: Define the situation of interest

Define the scope of the causal situation being considered (in our terminology, defining the boundary conditions for the delivery of a formal learning intervention). If a thorough needs analysis was carried out and is available, much of this data will already be to hand, but if not, a first step will need to be a quick analysis of why the learning intervention was implemented.

*Figure 10.4* Steps in contribution analysis

### Step 2: Develop the theory of change

This may or may not, of course, be available. If it is not, then one will need to be created by carrying out a brief needs analysis process. Along with a logic model, there will need to be a list of risks and assumptions made, what other factors might influence the chain of causality and what challenges there might be to the reliability of the model.

### Step 3: Gather initial evidence

In this step the data collection process starts in order to make some initial assessments about operation of the theory of change. Data needs to be gathered on what results have been seen, how links in the chain are working in practice, other factors influencing the outcomes and any other explanations as to why outcomes other than from our initial theory of change have been achieved.

### Step 4: Put together an initial contribution story

The initial data, such as from a desk review of quantitative or qualitative reports or interviews with evaluation commissioners, is reviewed and assessed critically. Gaps and inconsistencies in the data are identified, and plans are made to investigate these.

### Step 5: Seek out additional evidence

It may become necessary to review the theory of change or to examine certain parts more closely. Triangulating data may become more important.

### Step 6: Revise and strengthen the contribution story

The additional evidence is used to strengthen the story we are creating about the operation of the logic model.

Although a simple, essentially linear six-step model helps explain the basic principles of the contribution analysis process, in practice Steps 3, 4, 5 and 6 are something of an ongoing, iterative process in which data gathered is analysed, gaps are identified, further data gathering takes place, a contribution story slowly emerges and so on.

We can next look at how to apply contribution analysis within a theory-based evaluation by returning to the ATPA case study, which we used in Chapter 6.

Although we are following this theory-based evaluation approach, the overall framework for the evaluation is the same B–P–R structure as we have used before (Figure 10.5):

- Consider boundaries, what is in and what is out.
- Take account of different perspectives.
- Think about what relationships within the situation of interest mean.

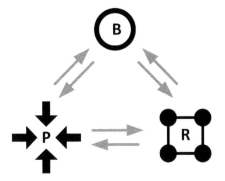

*Figure 10.5* The B–P–R framework

## An evaluation case study: what happened at ATPA?

In Chapter 8 we looked at how to carry out a systemically based needs analysis by looking at the case study of the Advanced Technology Procurement Agency (ATPA). We saw how it was changing its operational model from being an agency which procured technology on behalf of clients to one which was helping its clients carry out the procurement themselves. This required a major change in its operational ethos and in the day-to-day activities of its supply chain teams.

We now need to imagine that a year or so has passed and that the director has asked that an evaluation of the training delivered to the supply chain teams be carried out. So in this chapter we will work through how a systems thinking approach to this evaluation project would be carried out.

### Step 1: Define the situation of interest

The aim in this first stage is to define the boundaries for the evaluation, which will include what the expectations of the evaluation are (what is in or out), who needs to be involved or consulted, and practical issues such as timescales. This should all be defined within a terms-of-reference agreement for the evaluation project. After some initial discussions, it is decided that the aim of the evaluation will be to look at all three possible levels of learning: whether people have learnt from the content of the training programmes, if the learning provided covered the right topics and if formal learning was the most appropriate concept for the intervention.

Boundaries also define what stakeholders want to learn from the evaluation and the confidence they will expect. At this stage it is useful to explain to stakeholders that contribution analysis provides likely, probable conclusions, not definite ones! Also use the boundary analysis to find out what other factors may influence the outcome and assess the plausibility of the proposed intervention.

Note that in this case study the theory of change and the associated logic model have already been developed (shown later in Figure 10.6), in which case it would be a good idea to use this to help define the scope of the project. However, in many evaluation projects an initial needs analysis may not have been carried out, or there may be no adequate theory of change, in which case it will have to be developed from scratch, which is covered in Step 2.

As we saw in Chapter 6, Critical Systems Heuristics (CSH) is a very useful tool to use when trying to decide who or what is in or out of whatever situation of interest we are considering. This applies to both needs analysis and evaluation.

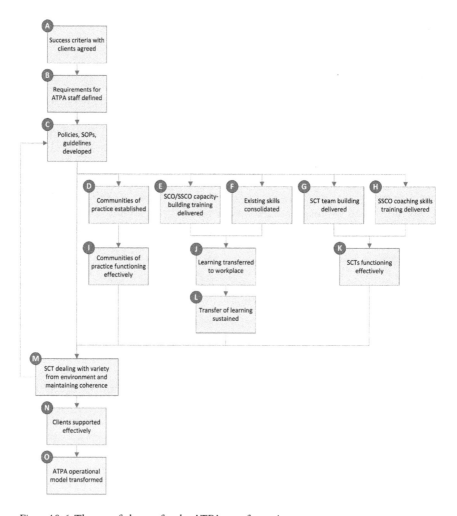

*Figure 10.6* Theory of change for the ATPA transformation

When working through the CSH questions, we have in mind a particular system or situation of interest. In this particular case the system we are considering is what we might call the 'ATPA training system', which consists of the human resources function and the trainers contracted to deliver certain training.

There are a number of boundary issues we want to explore at this stage. Broadly speaking, these include:

- Who has played a role in the design and delivery of the training programme?
- Who was not involved but perhaps should have been?
- What was included within the design for the training and what was not included?
- How was the design and delivery of the programme managed, and what could have been done more effectively?

When we have the answers to these questions we will have a much better idea about who can usefully be consulted during the course of the evaluation so that we have different perspectives on various aspects of the situation rather than just those of the core stakeholders (trainers and participants).

Questions to put to key stakeholders during the process of agreeing terms of reference and defining the scope of the evaluation are shown in Table 10.2.[33] However, as noted previously, formal explanations of Critical Systems Heuristics use language which is not very accessible to non-systems academics. So as we did in Chapter 8, we will edit the key 12 questions in order to make them relevant to our specific purpose, in this case evaluation.

If we were to ask these questions about the ATPA project, the sort of issues we might find coming up include:

- The criteria determined for the training courses are not necessarily commensurate with those that are really needed in order to help supply chain teams contribute towards achieving overall needs of the organisational change programme (Q.1).
- The objectives for the training are not clear or are not obviously in line with the overall criteria for the organisational transformation (Q.3).
- Not all of the activities covered within the training programme are relevant to the organisational transformation (Q.7).
- The content for the training was suggested by an external consultant, and there may not have been adequate consultation with stakeholders before delivery (Q.8).
- No representatives from the technology end users in the client countries were consulted about any aspect of the training design (Q.11).
- End users have different ideas about how the relationship between ATPA and client government procurement functions should be changed in order to improve the service to them (Q.12).

Table 10.2 CSH questions for evaluating a formal learning intervention

| CSH question | Questions to ask in the field |
|---|---|
| 1 What is/ought to be the purpose of what people in the situation of interest are doing? | What did the overall programme of learning-related and organisational interventions seek to achieve? With hindsight, how relevant was this intention? What should the overall intention have been? How do training objectives relate to the overall criteria set for the change programme? |
| 2 Who is/ought to be the intended beneficiary of what the people are doing? | Who took part in the training? Who indirectly benefited from the training? Is there anyone who did not take part in the training but who perhaps should have? |
| 3 What is/ought to be the measure of success of what people are doing? | What are the programme's learning objectives? Are these objectives stated in observable, behavioural terms? How do these objectives relate to the overall criteria set for the change programme? What has been done to see if participants have achieved these criteria? Are there any other ways in which the training programme could be seen as having beneficial (unintended) consequences? Are there any ways in which the process of seeing if participants have achieved the criteria could be improved? |
| 4 What conditions of success are/ought to be under the control of the people involved? | What resources have been needed for implementing the training programme (time, equipment, accommodation etc.)? How well has managing these resources been done? What could have been done better? |
| 5 Who is/ought to be in control of the conditions of success of what people are doing? | How has the training programme been designed, managed and implemented? What role have the stakeholders (managers, team members, trainers) played in making decisions about implementing the training programme? Have there been any problems or difficulties in the implementation? If so, what have these been and why have they arisen? |
| 6 What conditions of success are/ought to be outside the control of who makes decisions about what people are doing? | How were the learning objectives for the training programme identified? What role did anybody else play in identifying or agreeing these objectives? What factors influenced the implementation of the training? How were these determined? What role should anyone else have played? |
| 7 What are/ought to be relevant knowledge and skills for what people are doing? | What was included within the training programme? Was there anything not included within the training programme that should have been? |

| CSH question | Questions to ask in the field |
|---|---|
| 8 Who is/ought to be providing knowledge and skills related to what people are doing? | Who decided what the content for the training programme would be?<br>Was there anyone with relevant knowledge who was not involved in the design process? |
| 9 What are/ought to be regarded as assurances that what people are doing is successful? | What criteria were used to select the trainer who designed and delivered the training programme?<br>How well suited for delivering the programme did they turn out to be?<br>What could have been done better about procuring this particular skill? |
| 10 What are/ought to be the opportunities for the interests of those negatively affected by what people are doing? | What opportunities have there been for people affected by the training (client government counterparts, end users) to provide feedback on the training programme?<br>What opportunities should there have been? |
| 11 Who is/ought to be representing the interests of those negatively affected by but not involved with what people are doing? | Which people (if any) from the group affected by the training have been consulted in any way about the design or delivery?<br>Which people should have been consulted? |
| 12 What space is/ought to be available for reconciling differing worldviews regarding what people are doing among those involved and affected? | What opportunities have been provided for consulting with the people affected by the training on its design and delivery?<br>What opportunities should have been provided? |

These issues coming out of the boundary analysis illustrate a number of issues which need to be examined further, as they may be factors which could influence the effectiveness of the logic model in enabling the overall outcomes to be achieved. For example, it would be useful to try and engage with representatives from the end user group to see if they feel that the service to them from the client government counterparts has benefited from ATPA's transformation. This may not be easy to do: boundary decisions often relate to sensitive political issues, and getting honest answers or even getting access to ask the questions may be difficult. Nevertheless, exploring these alternative perspectives can have a profound impact on conclusions about the effectiveness of a formal learning intervention.

When we have answers to as many of these questions as is possible, it will be easier to decide on the way forward who to talk to and what to talk about. At this stage it is often useful to prepare an inception report, which describes progress so far and provides a plan of what is proposed for the subsequent data collection and analysis stages.

### Step 2: Develop the theory of change

With the terms of reference for the evaluation agreed, the first step is to look at the theory of change (which, for convenience, is repeated here as Figure 10.6, but with each activity labelled to make it easier to refer to each one later in the process). If there had been no theory of change, at this stage it would be necessary to develop one. How to do this is covered in Chapter 8.

Following on from the boundary definition, it is important to gather different perspectives on this logic model to see what agreement or disagreement there is. This can help us identify potential threats to the implementation of the model which could have an impact on how well it is able to achieve its desired outcomes.

### Step 3: Gather initial evidence

We now use the individual activities within the logic model (Figure 10.6) and the connections between them to develop a framework of questions that we use in the evaluation process. Table 10.3 shows an initial development of questions based on the activities within Figure 10.6.

*Table 10.3* Evaluation questions based on the logic model

| Activity | Questions suggested |
| --- | --- |
| A | What were the success criteria agreed? |
| | Were there any timescales associated with these? |
| | Does ATPA have its own success criteria? |
| | Do the customers (client government procurement agencies or end users) have their own success criteria? |
| N | How is the support offered to clients being monitored or evaluated? |
| | How would we decide if this support is effective? |
| A–N | How does the assessment of how well clients have been supported compare with the initial criteria? |
| B | How were the requirements defined? |
| | What are the requirements? |
| | Who was involved in the requirements definition process? |
| C | Have all necessary guidelines and policies been developed and made available? |
| | Have there been any comments regarding such things as usability of these references? |
| C–M | Are people using the guidelines and procedures? |
| | What observations do people have about how useful these are? |
| D | Have any informal learning networks or communities of practice been established? |
| | How are these being supported by the organisation? |

| Activity | Questions suggested |
|---|---|
| I | What is the level of activity within the networks? |
| | What perceptions of adding value are there about these networks? |
| D–I | What support systems (human resources, technical infrastructure) have been created in order to support informal learning networks and communities of practice? |
| | What activities are being implemented in order to sustain the communities of practice? |
| E, F, G, H | These are formal learning events, and if ATPA has a learning evaluation policy similar to the one described earlier, data should be available in the form of completed event surveys and records of individual learning. Questions to ask here include: |
| | • How useful has the formal learning been seen to be? |
| | • Has the design of each intervention taken into consideration potential obstacles to learning transfer? |
| | • Has the content of each intervention been appropriate? |
| | • Was the way in which the intervention was delivered effective and cost efficient? |
| | • Have there been any other, unexpected, benefits arising from the intervention? |
| J | What evidence has there been that learning has been transferred? |
| | What obstacles and enablers have been identified as influencing learning transfer? |
| K | How well are the teams functioning? |
| | How is this being assessed? |
| | What else has changed in the way the teams function since the delivery of the training programme started? |
| | How much do team members think that activities G and H contributed to improving the effectiveness of the teams? |
| L | Has the transfer of learning been shown to be sustainable? |
| M | What evidence is there that teams are dealing effectively with operational variety? |
| | What challenges have there been which teams have not been able to deal with on their own? |
| | How much do teams think that individual training interventions contributed to their ability to deal with variety? |
| | What do teams think might have happened had any of the training interventions not been delivered? |
| N | How effectively are clients being supported? |
| | How is this being measured? |
| | What feedback has been received from clients? |
| | What gaps in knowledge and skill has this feedback uncovered? |
| | What organisational policies or guidelines have been shown to be in adequate in some way? |
| O | To what extent does the current operational practice agree with the model originally defined? |
| | What differences are there? |
| | What might account for these differences? |
| | What differences are there in the overall operational context between now and the start of the change process? |

Note that there are some overlaps here with questions which may have been asked in the boundary-setting stage. Of course, there is no need to ask questions repeatedly unless there is a need to triangulate data.

How to gather this initial data will vary from one project to another. A desk review of existing information, such as data from formative evaluations, in particular responses to the reflection survey, will be important after this initial stage. Surveys and interviews can also contribute to this. Depending on the nature of the task under consideration, it may be possible to collect quantitative data which provides some indication about levels of performance. In Table 10.3 this initial evidence gathering would probably provide answers to activities A to H, so that we could move on to Step 4. To gather further data about changes of behaviour and impact (roughly corresponding to activities I to O in the logic model) will almost certainly require some primary research in the form of surveys and interviews, which would encompass Step 5.

### Step 4: Put together an initial contribution story

Answers to the questions asked in Step 3 will have generated a significant amount of data. The next step is to interrogate the data in order to start to put together a picture of what is working well and what could be improved. John Mayne suggests a number of useful questions to ask:[34]

- Which links in the logic model seem to be strong (good evidence available, strong logic, low risk and/or wide acceptance)?
- Which links seem to be weak (little evidence available, weak logic, high risk and/or little agreement among stakeholders)?
- How credible is the overall story within the logic model?
- Does the pattern of results and links validate the logic model?
- Do stakeholders agree with the story? Based on the evidence gathered, do they agree that the programme has made an important contribution (or not) to the observed results?
- Where are the main weaknesses in the story? Weaknesses might include:
  - clarity about which results have been achieved
  - lack of validation of key assumptions within the logic model
  - clarity of understanding about other factors influencing outcomes
  - gaps in the data

To help explore the contribution story of the formal training programme as it relates to organisational impact, it can be useful at this stage to use the Viable System Model. As we are at this stage looking at the behaviour of individuals who have completed the training programme, our initial system-in-focus is at the team level, which is represented by the ATPA recursion level 2 diagram (Figure 10.7).

As before in Chapter 8, there are various questions we can ask to develop our understanding about how this system is working. Table 10.4 summarises what questions may be useful for doing this.[35]

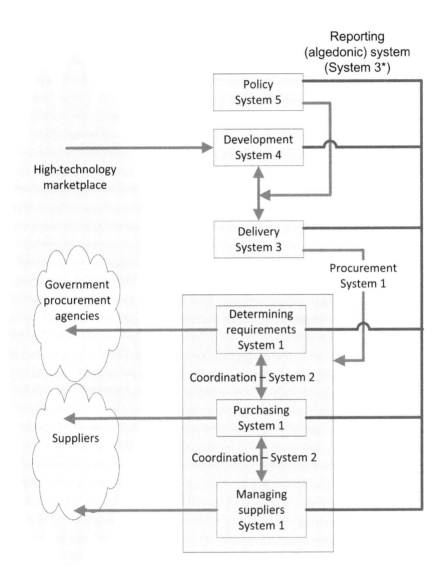

*Figure 10.7* ATPA recursion level 2

Having used VSM to reflect on impact at the team level, it may next be useful to move up one level of recursion to explore impact at the organisational level (Figure 10.8).

Because of the recursive nature of VSM, we can use the same questions to explore viability this level. This may uncover different issues, for example:

- Under the old model it made operational sense for government procurement counterparts to work with separate experts within ATPA

*Table 10.4* Information for the level 2 recursion

| System | Information to be found |
|---|---|
| 1 | How are the government procurement agencies changing? |
| | To what degree has the training enabled System 1 to deal with changes in the operational environment? |
| | How has the SSCO training and team building contributed to effective management of each System 1 activity? |
| | How have new policies and guidelines affected the accountability of each System 1 activity? |
| 2 | How has the training contributed to the effectiveness with which the different System 1 functions work with each other? |
| | Have processes for coordinating the different System 1 activities changed as a result of new policies or training activities? |
| | How are new processes viewed? |
| 3 | What components are there for monitoring and controlling the System 1 activities? |
| | How has this changed as a result of changes in the operational model? |
| | Has training dealt with issues about System 3's control of System 1s? |
| 3* | How does System 3 monitor what is happening in the System 1s in the new operational model? |
| | Has training dealt with reporting procedures? |
| 4 | Has training dealt with situational awareness within the operational environment? |
| | How well do people monitor and adapt to their environment? |
| | What are the attitudes to innovation in the new operational model? |
| | Have training and operational changes introduced any kind of 'operations room' where information is brought together for decision-making activities? |
| | Has training helped people use information from the environment to inform System 5? |
| 5 | Has the training helped people understand how the vision of the supply chain team will have changed as a result of the overall operational changes? |
| | How effectively has training communicated a new vision through the team? |

(a procurement specialist, a logistics specialist and so on). However, because within the new model there is more emphasis on relationships rather than technical skills, System 4 may identify a frustration within the government procurement departments that they are still dealing with three separate people. They would prefer to have one person providing support on procurement, logistics and market intelligence.

• Because of the greater variety of needs that counterparts have, each supply chain team feels that it needs more autonomy than is allowed by the existing System 3.

Each of these issues is an example of an unexpected property emerging from the new operational model and raises a potential training need. This shows how using VSM at multiple levels can help us reflect on the delivery of the programme from a perspective other than the original logic model so that we can

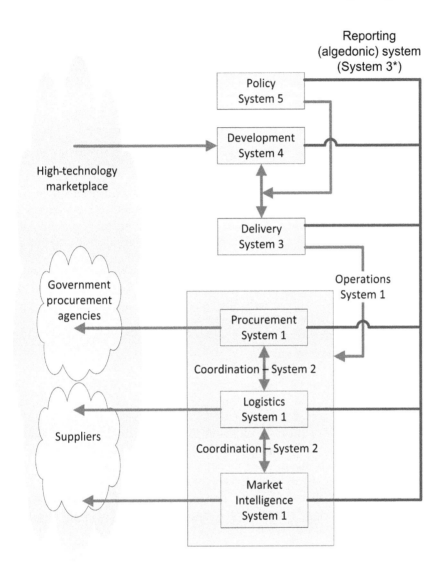

*Figure 10.8* ATPA recursion level 1

identify and reflect on unexpected factors which can be affecting the achievement of the desired outcomes.

### Steps 5 and 6: Work iteratively to final conclusions

As discussed, Mayne's six-step approach to contribution analysis works well as an explanatory model, but in practice data gathering and analysis go on continuously so that we iteratively move towards a set of conclusions.

The conclusions made should draw on the web of evidence collected in order to be able to explain the likely influence that the learning intervention had on achieving the outcomes. These should be based on Mayne's criteria for causality:

- A plausible and informed theory of change.
- Activities implemented as defined within the theory of change.
- What the theory of change said would happen did happen, and assumptions were proved valid.
- External factors are recognised or shown to be insignificant.

A report should also describe unintended consequences of the intervention, both positive and negative. Positive consequences, of course, are always welcome, as they are evidence of added value that the intervention has brought. They also contribute to organisational learning in that they further understanding of the complex dynamics of performance improvement initiatives.

Recommendations for action are essential, covering those things which can remedy identified weaknesses in the intervention and actions which can strengthen what has worked well. Such recommendations should cover three levels of learning, content and concept:

- Is the content being learnt?
- Is the content the right content?
- Is the concept for the learning intervention right?

We will now have completed a systemically based evaluation of a formal learning intervention. The methodology aims to address many of the weaknesses inherent in more familiar approaches, such as the complications of human behaviour systems being wicked problems, problems in assessing causality and taking the dynamic nature of performance into consideration.

The techniques described in this chapter make it possible for the evaluation to take different perspectives into consideration, to move up levels within the organisational setting and consider both external factors which may have had a bearing on the effectiveness of the intervention and what unintended consequences the intervention itself has had. Finally, they can give us a better understanding of the ongoing dynamics of what the learning intervention has stimulated and how the situation may unfold as time goes by.

## Summary

Here are the key points from this chapter.

**Addressing weaknesses in traditional approaches.** Systemic approaches to training evaluation can help deal with some of the weaknesses of traditional approaches, such as a reluctance to deal with complex patterns of causality and limited ways for judging the value of learning interventions.

**Learning–content–concept.** A systemic approach to evaluating training aims to provide answers to the three questions: is content being learnt, is it the right content and is the concept for the training the right one?

**Learning evaluation strategies.** Developing a formal policy for evaluating formal learning is essential in order to help with a focus on priorities, help the organisation buy in to the importance of evaluation and establish standard procedures for both formative and summative evaluations.

**Formative evaluations.** Formative evaluations examine the process of delivering formal learning and can help identify what works well and what needs to be improved. They should focus on gathering information about the utility of the learning provided and what obstacles there may be in transferring this learning to the workplace.

**Summative evaluations using theory-based evaluation.** Structuring an evaluation around change provides a systemic way of exploring the many potential causal linkages which can contribute to a change in performance.

**Defining boundaries.** It is important at the start of the evaluation process to identify who and what should be included within the evaluation activity and who and what can be left out.

**Contribution analysis.** An iterative approach to gathering and analysing data order to develop a contribution story is an effective way to assess the contribution that a formal learning intervention is likely to have made to the eventual outcome.

## Notes

1 Mayne, J., 2008. Contribution Analysis: An Approach to Exploring Cause and Effect. *ILAC Brief Number*, 16, pp. 1–4.

2 Kraiger, K., Ford, J.K. & Salas, E., 1993. Application of Cognitive, Skill-Based and Affective Theories of Learning Outcomes to New Methods of Training Evaluation. *Journal of Applied Psychology*, 78(2), p. 311.

3 Bateson, G., 1972. *Steps to an Ecology of Mind*, Ballantine, New York.

4 Goldstein, I.L. & Ford, J.K., 2001. *Training in Organizations (4th Edition)*, Cengage Learning, Boston, MA.

5 Derven, M., 2012. Building a Strategic Approach to Learning Evaluation. *T+ D*, 54, pp. 54–57.

6 Torres, R.T. & Preskill, H., 2001. Evaluation and Organizational Learning: Past, Present and Future. *The American Journal of Evaluation*, 22(3), pp. 387–395.

7 Alliger, G.M. & Janak, E.A., 1989. Kirkpatrick's Levels of Training Criteria: Thirty Years Later. *Personnel Psychology*, 42(2), p. 337.

8 Alliger, G.M., Tannenbaum, S.I., Bennett, W., Traver, H. & Shotland, A., 1997. A Meta-Analysis of the Relations Among Training Criteria. *Personnel Psychology*, 50(2), pp. 341–358.

9 Derived from the Learning Transfer System Inventory (for more information, see Chapter 9).

10 Kraiger, Ford & Salas, 1993, op. cit.

11 Kraiger, Ford & Salas, 1993, op. cit.

12 Gegenfurtner, A., 2011. Motivation and Transfer in Professional Training: A Meta-Analysis of the Moderating Effects of Knowledge Type, Instruction, and Assessment Conditions. *Educational Research Review*, 6(3), pp. 153–168.

13  Hummelbrunner, R., 2015. Learning, Systems Concepts and Values in Evaluation: Proposal for an Exploratory Framework to Improve Coherence. *IDS Bulletin*, 46(1), pp. 17–29.

14  Chen, H., 1990. *Theory-Driven Evaluations*, Sage, New York.

15  Coryn, C.L., Noakes, L.A., Westine, C.D. & Schröter, D.C., 2011. A Systematic Review of Theory-Driven Evaluation Practice from 1990 to 2009. *American Journal of Evaluation*, 32(2), p. 201.

16  Coryn, C.L. et al., 2011, op. cit., p. 202.

17  Fitz-Gibbon, C.T. & Morris, L.L., 1996. Theory-based Evaluation. *Evaluation Practice*, 17(2), pp. 177–184.

18  Fitz-Gibbon & Morris, 1996, op. cit.

19  Rogers, P.J. & Weiss, C.H., 2007. Theory-based Evaluation: Reflections Ten Years On. *New Directions For Evaluation*, 2007(114), pp. 63–81.

20  Gorman, D., 1993. A Theory-Driven Approach to the Evaluation of Professional Training in Alcohol Abuse. *Addiction*, 88(2), pp. 229–236.

21  Scriven, M., 1994. The Fine Line Between Evaluation and Explanation. *Evaluation Practice*, 15, pp. 75–77.

22  Scriven, 1994, op. cit.

23  Gorman, 1993, op. cit.; Umble, K.E., Cervero, R.M., Yang, B. & Atkinson, W.L., 2000. Effects of Traditional Classroom and Distance Continuing Education: A Theory-Driven Evaluation of a Vaccine-Preventable Diseases Course. *American Journal of Public Health*, 90(8), p. 1218.

24  Arthur Jr., W., Bennett Jr, W., Edens, P.S. & Bell, S.T., 2003. Effectiveness of Training in Organizations: A Meta-Analysis of Design and Evaluation Features. *Journal of Applied Psychology*, 88(2), p. 234.

25  For more information, see: https:// en.wikipedia.org/wiki/Grounded_theory, accessed 14 April 2016.

26  Mayne, J., 2012. Contribution Analysis: Coming of Age? *Evaluation*, 18(3), pp. 270–280.

27  Kirkpatrick, D.L., 1994. *Evaluating Training Programs*, Berrett-Koehler, San Francisco, p. 70.

28  Mayne, 2012, op. cit., pp. 272–273.

29  Patton, M.Q., 2012. A Utilization-Focused Approach to Contribution Analysis. *Evaluation*, 18(3), pp. 364–377.

30  Patton, 2012, op. cit., p. 367.

31  Lemire, S.T., Nielsen, S.B. & Dybdal, L., 2012. Making Contribution Analysis Work: A Practical Framework for Handling Influencing Factors and Alternative Explanations. *Evaluation*, 18(3), pp. 294–309.

32  Mayne, 2012, op. cit.

33  Adapted from Reynolds, M. & Holwell, S., 2010. *Systems Approaches to Managing Change: A Practical Guide*, Springer, London.

34  Mayne, 2008, op. cit.

35  Based on the VSM template provided in Flood, R. & Jackson, M.C., 1991. *Creative Problem Solving: Total Systems Intervention*, Wiley, New York.

# 11 Bringing it all together

I first came across systems thinking as a small part of a management module which I was studying with the Open University in about 1995. It seemed an interesting approach, but I struggled to see how it could a play part in what I did as a training consultant. Nevertheless, I persisted and as the years went by parts of it started to make more sense, and I could see where they could be helpful. Eventually I committed myself to a much more rigorous course of study into the subject, and it was then that I started to fully appreciate what possibilities it offered.

Nowadays, every time I look at a training project I see systemic aspects, whether it is in developing a learning strategy, designing the programme itself or evaluating a programme which has been run. Embracing systems thinking meant spending more time in reflective practice and thinking about how I learn, and I realised that writing things down is a very powerful learning tool for me. And so the idea for the book came.

The aim of the book has been to provide a practical guide to using systems thinking methodologies to carry out training needs analysis and training programme evaluation. What we have seen by working through the use of systems tools to carry out these two different activities is that we can use the same methodologies throughout. Which perhaps should not be a surprise: needs analysis and evaluation are essentially the same activities but set within different contexts. A needs analysis is a review of a situation of interest within an organisation carried out in order to identify things which can be done in order to improve performance, while an evaluation is a review of a programme which has been implemented within a situation of interest designed to improve performance. The only difference is in the boundaries.

Although the book has looked at many different concepts and tools associated with systems thinking, what it has hopefully shown is that there is a thread running through the whole process of needs analysis, design and evaluation. That thread is held together by the B–P–R model: investigate the boundaries of the situation of interest, explore different perspectives held by stakeholders and see what the relationships are among elements of the situation.

While there is no prescriptive way to use the different methodologies described, what we have seen is that Critical Systems Heuristics provides a solid foundation for identifying the boundaries of the situation: what is in or out and, most importantly, whether the decisions about being in or out are valid. Other techniques such as the Viable System Model and Soft Systems Methodology provide alternative yet complementary ways of making sense of data as we collect it. Other techniques such as System Dynamics and Social Network Analysis may also prove to be useful. These can all look quite challenging to use, but with practice they become second nature, and ways to do things quickly and efficiently become more obvious. SSM in particular can be a laborious methodology to use, but by recognising that we can use it in the so-called Mode 2, where we just use bits which are relevant, we can still make useful progress.

We have also looked at key ideas such as emergence, viability and requisite variety, concepts which complexity theory bundles together in such a way that we can start to appreciate the importance of integrating formal and informal learning, making it possible for people to deal with the constantly changing challenges which working lives throw at them.

Mathematicians sometimes talk about the 'elegance' of a mathematical proof. For me, systems thinking provides a very elegant way to look at the more challenging aspects of enabling learning within an organisation: working out what needs to be done and seeing if what has been done has worked. The elegance comes from the similarity between the needs analysis and evaluation stages. While the situations are different, how we deal with them is the same.

It also makes it possible to propose a unified systemic approach to needs analysis and evaluation, as shown in Figure 11.1.

This shows us that we can systematically follow a systemic model for the whole needs analysis and evaluation process. The needs analysis process explains the internal dynamics of the workplace situation of interest and how it relates to its environment. This allows us to define a theory of change for implementing learning and non-learning interventions, which then become the basis for the subsequent evaluation. By working forwards all the time we can start to develop a much clearer idea about the real relationships between our interventions and subsequent changes in behaviour and organisational performance.

The systemic process helps us reconceptualise 'training' as being just a part of a much more powerful *learning system*, which brings together the advantages of formal learning activities with the flexibility and environmental awareness of informal learning. The needs analysis process sets the success criteria for this system, as well as identifying what is needed within it and how it should be implemented.

The learning system then plays out. We examine what happens in the formal learning interventions and find out if people learn and ask the learners if they think they can transfer the learning. We look to see if there are any changes in behaviour in the workplace and if this has the desired (or any unexpected) impact on what gets achieved. We can then compare what we have found with what we hoped to find and draw the appropriate conclusions about the performance of our learning system.

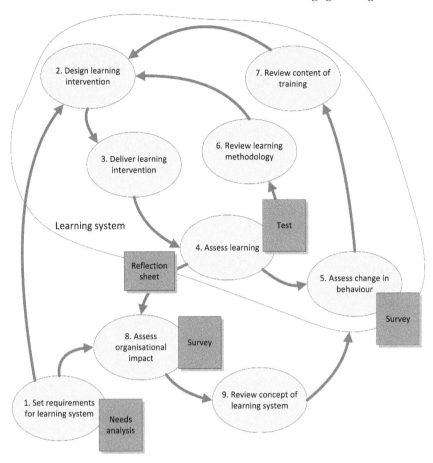

*Figure 11.1* An overall systemic approach to needs analysis and evaluation

The elegance of this model is just one reason systems thinking has the potential to have a powerful impact in improving the quality of formal learning interventions. It has the power to make performance improvement solutions much more holistic, with these integrated solutions coming automatically out of the analysis process.

Organisations may be a complicated tangle of wicked problems, but with systems thinking approaches we can find our way through to identify solutions which will make things better.

That must be worth it.

# Index

For Product Safety Concerns and Information please contact our EU
representative GPSR@taylorandfrancis.com
Taylor & Francis Verlag GmbH, Kaufingerstraße 24, 80331 München, Germany

www.ingramcontent.com/pod-product-compliance
Ingram Content Group UK Ltd.
Pitfield, Milton Keynes, MK11 3LW, UK
UKHW021841240425
457818UK00007B/257